CELLULOID
SAN FRANCISCO
THE FILM LOVER'S GUIDE TO BAY AREA MOVIE LOCATIONS

JIM VAN BUSKIRK AND WILL SHANK

CHICAGO
REVIEW
PRESS

Library of Congress Cataloging-in-Publication Data

Van Buskirk, Jim.
  Celluloid San Francisco : the film lover's guide to Bay Area movie
  locations / Jim Van Buskirk and Will Shank.— 1st ed.
      p. cm.
  Includes bibliographical references and index.
  ISBN 1-55652-592-3
      1. Motion picture locations—California—San Francisco—
  Guidebooks.   2. Motion picture locations—California—San Fran-
  cisco Bay Area—Guidebooks.   3. San Francisco (Calif.)—In motion
  pictures.   I. Shank, Will, 1951–   II. Title.
  PN1995.67.S36 2006
  384'.8'097946—dc22

                                                        2006020297

Cover design: Emily Brackett, Visible Logic
Interior design: Pamela Juárez
All photographs not otherwise credited are by Will Shank.

© 2006 by Jim Van Buskirk and Will Shank
All rights reserved
First edition
Published by Chicago Review Press, Incorporated
814 North Franklin Street
Chicago, Illinois 60610
ISBN-13: 978-1-55652-592-6
ISBN-10: 1-55652-592-3
Printed in the United States of America
5 4 3 2 1

For the many moviemakers who have filmed
in the San Francisco Bay Area

For the enjoyment of movie lovers everywhere and

For Stassa

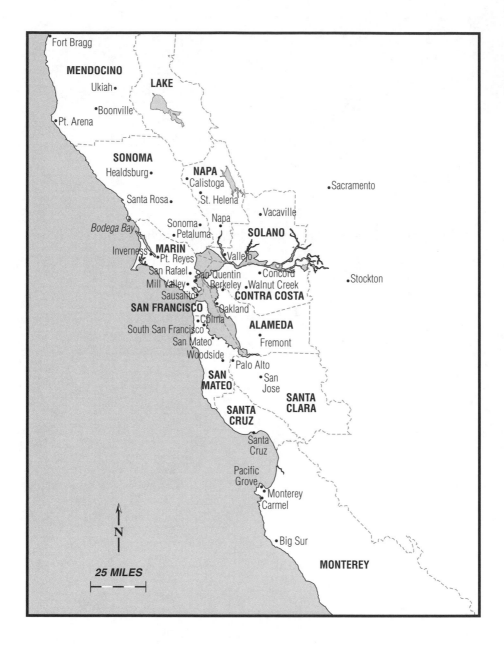

Contents

Acknowledgments   vii

The Magic of Movie Locations: An Introduction   ix

City and County of San Francisco 1

    Civic Center and Tenderloin   5

    The Mission District, Potrero Hill, the Waterfront
    South of the Bay Bridge, and SOMA (South of Market)   27

    Downtown, the Financial District, Chinatown, and
    Nob Hill   49

    Russian Hill, North Beach, and Telegraph Hill   105

    Western San Francisco   153

Northward 209

    Marin, Sonoma, Napa, and Mendocino Counties   211

Eastward 249

    Alcatraz, Angel, Treasure, and Mare Islands and Alameda
    and Contra Costa Counties   251

Southward **293**

San Mateo, Santa Cruz, and Monterey Counties   295

Resources   317

Index   321

Acknowledgments

A book is seldom completed in isolation, and this one is no exception. We have many people to thank for their assistance and support along the way:

Michael Colby for suggesting the alliterative title so many years ago;

Jim Reiter for his ongoing support, from potential coauthor to still-photograph scout;

Judith Ogus for her masterful maps;

Valerie Wolcott and Ira Kleinberg for their assistance setting up the original database;

Tom Harding for his assiduous editing;

Bob Grimes for his comprehensive list of films set in and/or shot in San Francisco;

Scott Trimble for allowing us to use much of the detailed information on NorCalMovies.com;

Hank Donat for similarly allowing access to his wonderfully idiosyncratic MisterSF.com;

Alfonso Felder of the San Francisco Neighborhood Theater Foundation;

Miguel Pendas and Hilary Hart of the San Francisco Film Society;

Ami Zins and Janet Austin of the Oakland Film Commission for their enthusiastic assistance;

the supportive staff at the Pacific Film Archive: Nancy Goldman, Susan Wester, Jason Sanders, and particularly Stephanie Boris;

Jim's colleagues at the San Francisco Public Library, especially Susan Goldstein, Pat Akre, Mike Levy, Adam Markosian,

Jason Baxter, Cher DelaMere, Joan Haskell, Gardner Haskell, and Michael Sherrod-Flores.

Additional advice, encouragement, and information was provided by Ted Loewenberg, Mark Page, Jenni Olson, Rick Gerharter, Bill Hayes, Lawrence Helman, Susan Stryker, Joe Long, Alice Carey and Paul Fisher, Gerry Crowley, Eleanor Bertino, Bill Lanese, John Gullotto, Jan Wahl, Peter Crimmins, Cathy Chase, Pete Collins, Stacey Pulverente, Jason Fain, Aaron Peskin and Nancy Shanahan, and any others whose names might have fallen off our list in the rush to completion.

Much appreciation to Yuval Taylor, designer Pamela Juárez, our meticulous editor Lisa Rosenthal, and the rest of the team at Chicago Review Press who helped shape this book into its present form.

And finally, to our beloved partners whose patience and support throughout the entire project enabled us to finish it without being institutionalized. Jim thanks Allen Sawyer, and Will thanks U. B. Morgan.

The Magic of Movie Locations: An Introduction

Jim Van Buskirk

In 1962, on a trip from the suburbs of Los Angeles to visit my grandparents in Idaho, my family and I stopped in San Francisco. For weeks, my parents had regaled my brother and me with descriptions of what we would see during our stay there: the fancy Top of the Mark bar at the Mark Hopkins Hotel, the swank Cliff House Restaurant, the vast Emporium department store. San Francisco sounded exciting; I couldn't wait.

As we drove through Chinatown, I suddenly spotted a familiar park. "Look," I exclaimed, "that's where *Flower Drum Song* was filmed!" No one seemed nearly as interested as I was to have recognized the very spot in Portsmouth Plaza where Mei Li sings "One Hundred Million Miracles." My father finally found a place to park (no mean feat even in those days), and we walked down Grant Avenue.

"Grant Avenue, San Francisco, California, USA . . ." I knew the song lyrics by heart, because the motion picture soundtrack to *Flower Drum Song* was the very first LP I'd bought with my own money. (Vinyl albums were the only way to reexperience the movie at that time, before the introduction of videocassettes and DVDs.) I listened over and over to Nancy Kwan sing "I Enjoy Being a Girl" and James Shigeta croon "You Are Beautiful" as I scrutinized their images on the back of the record jacket.

Now I was really there, right where they made the movie. It was indeed "the most exciting thoroughfare I know." I danced and sang with glee while my family trudged on. I was overjoyed when I noticed black-and-white stills from the movie in several shop windows. My parents were right: San Francisco was a wonderful place. I no longer cared if we saw any of those other attractions—they all paled in comparison because now I had stood in the very spot that was in a movie.

Growing up 45 minutes from Hollywood, I was always fascinated with movies and moviemaking. But this was the first time I had been at the actual site of a film. That early thrill never abated. San Francisco continued to play a major role in my imagination through the movies. Watching *Vertigo* (1958), *Bullitt* (1968), *Birdman of Alcatraz* (1962), *What's Up, Doc?* (1972), and *Point Blank* (1967), I fantasized about living in San Francisco someday. I scrutinized episodes of television programs like *Love on a Rooftop* (1966–67) and the *Doris Day Show* (1968–73) to further feed my appetite for this city. My dream came true when I moved to San Francisco in 1972. As I explored my new hometown, I was particularly fascinated when I happened upon the sites where movies were filmed. I collected magazine and newspaper articles, maps, and anecdotes while I pursued my growing passion.

Years later at San Francisco's opulent Castro Theater, I attended a screening of *Flower Drum Song* (1962) as part of the Asian American Film Festival. As the Panavision movie began on the big screen, the familiar first few notes of the opening fanfare brought tears to my eyes. I could never have imagined that all these years later I would be reexperiencing, in San Francisco, this memorable movie of my childhood. In the audience of mostly Asian Americans, I was rapt as Nancy Kwan, James Shigeta, and Robin Shimatsu (who played the little girl) came onstage in person. They explained that *Flower Drum Song* had been the first major motion picture to portray the lives of contemporary Asian Americans. Never mind that some of the Chinese characters were portrayed by Japanese or Korean actors. "To Hollywood we all looked alike," the actors laughed. The stars joked ruefully about how *Flower Drum Song* failed to inspire the expected succession of films accurately representing the Asian American experience.

Watching the film on the big screen, I was surprised to see that the scene at Portsmouth Plaza as well as those along Grant Avenue appeared to have been filmed on sets. How could it be? All these years I had remembered it so clearly. This was not in San Francisco's Chinatown at all. It was only a re-creation of it. I was incredulous. I had been duped by a Hollywood set. If the filmmakers didn't care whether their cast members were Chinese, why would I assume they'd strive for authenticity in location?

When I met Will Shank, he turned out to be a kindred spirit who shared my dual passions for San Francisco and films. When we first discussed this project, two things impressed us the most: the important role that San Francisco has played in motion pictures, and that no one

Nancy Kwan on a Hollywood set of Grant Avenue. *Courtesy of Photofest*

has documented this rich history. The more we traded stories about our favorite San Francisco films, the more we realized that our interests and expertise were complementary. We lamented the fact that, despite the various magazine and newspaper articles we'd collected, we'd never found a book with all the information we sought. We quickly realized we wanted to write it: a classic case of writing the book one wants to read. I tentatively suggested a collaboration. Will, a photographer, would shoot the contemporary locations, while I, a librarian, would undertake much of the research. We sketched out the book proposal, growing increasingly excited about the elements we would include.

As we told people about the book, we found that many had their own personal list of favorite films shot locally. In our initial book proposal we claimed, "San Francisco has been the locale for more than 400 classic (and some not-so-classic) films." Imagine our surprise when in the course of our research we amassed a list of over 1,500 films and television series set in and/or shot in the San Francisco Bay Area. As industrious and motivated as we were, we immediately realized that we could not document all of them. But that did not deter us from creating this much needed resource, so we developed some criteria to select films to include: We focus on popular feature films currently available on VHS or DVD, excluding the many unavailable documentaries, experimental films, and shorts shot here, and we include none of the many porno films made by the Mitchell Brothers, Falcon, or other local studios. We do, however, make an exception for television shows, despite the fact that many of them are not readily available for viewing. (This is our tip-of-the-hat to Philo T. Farnsworth, who invented television technology in San Francisco in 1927.) The city by the bay became world renowned as the setting for such series as *Full House* (1987–95), *McMillan and Wife* (1971–76), *Party of Five* (1994–2000), *Nash Bridges* (1996–2001), and—perhaps most famously—*The Streets of San Francisco* (1972–77).

The first five chapters focus on the city and county of San Francisco and are organized by neighborhood to facilitate touring. Because one neighborhood segues into another, we have sometimes made seemingly arbitrary distinctions in an effort to delineate territories. The sites are indicated on the maps in a sequence to minimize driving and maxi-mize sightseeing. In the chapters "Civic Center and Tenderloin," "Down-town, the Financial District, and Chinatown," and "Russian Hill, North Beach, and Telegraph Hill," sites are close enough together (and parking so challenging) that we advise walking. For sites outside the city, a car will definitely be necessary. Many of these places welcome visitors, others are private property. (Remember: be discreet as you look; be sure not to trespass or disturb residents. Stay well aware of your surround-ings, especially after dark and in neighborhoods like the Tenderloin.) For armchair travelers, the index will facilitate looking up various sites associated with a favorite film, actor, or director.

When a friend of mine, a native San Franciscan who grew up in China-town, heard about this project, she shared with me her family's brush with the movies. Her brother, a member of Boy Scout Troup #3 in 1962, had participated in the filming of *Flower Drum Song* on Grant Avenue. He hadn't seen Nancy Kwan, but he did remember parading up and down the thoroughfare in front of the cameras. This information sent me back to the movie yet again. Repeatedly pressing the "replay" and "pause" buttons, I still could not distinguish between studio sets and real San Francisco. Ultimately, I became enthralled by the filmmaker's ability to simultaneously capture and re-create the city by the bay. As San Francisco continues to fascinate filmmakers and filmgoers, we hope this book will inspire its readers. Who knows, maybe we'll catch you singing and dancing down Grant Avenue as I did more than 40 years ago.

A Brief History of Filmmaking in San Francisco

The Bay Area's prominent place in moviemaking history traces its beginnings to 1878 in Palo Alto, when industrialist Leland Stanford hired photographer Eadweard Muybridge to help settle a bet that at full stride a horse's four hooves leave the ground at the same time. (They do.) Since that historic occasion, hundreds of movies have been made wholly or partially in, or about, San Francisco.

Clint Eastwood as *Dirty Harry* and police plan their strategy to find the Scorpio killer terrorizing San Francisco. In *A Siegel Film: An Autobiography*, Don Siegel recounts how he and screenplay writer Dean Reisner went to San Francisco to scout locations. "Of course in one of the most beautiful cities in the world, no matter where the camera is placed, the set-up looks fantastic." *Courtesy of Art, Music, and Recreation Center, San Francisco Public Library*

In 1912, before Hollywood became the world center of filmmaking, Gilbert M. Anderson, of the Chicago-based Essanay Film Manufacturing Company, made a series of silents in locations throughout northern California, later building a major movie studio in the small town of Niles, halfway between Oakland and San Jose. Essanay went on to produce more than 400 consecutive film dramas, delighting nickelodeon audiences with their adventures of Bronco Billy (Gilbert M. Anderson) and the Little Tramp (Charlie Chaplin as his most famous character).

From these beginnings, San Francisco's connection to movie lore was solidified. The city became infamous as the site where movie stars came to let off steam away from the fans and publicity of Hollywood. Sometimes they got carried away. For example, Fatty Arbuckle's career was ruined even after he was acquitted of the rape and murder of Virginia Rappe during a drunken weekend in a suite at the St. Francis Hotel. Polk Street was the original location of Frank Norris's famous novel *McTeague*, but because the postearthquake neighborhood was deemed too modern, Eric von Stroheim used the intersection at Laguna and Hayes Streets to film his ill-fated epic adaptation titled *Greed* (1924).

The San Francisco Bay Area has been called "Hollywood North" because it is home to many creative enterprises, including George Lucas Films and Industrial Light & Magic in Marin County, Saul Zaentz's Fantasy Films in Berkeley, Francis Ford Coppola's American Zoetrope in San Francisco, and more recently, Pixar and Chris Columbus's 1492 Productions. Many writers, actors, and directors reside in the Bay Area, including screenwriters Joe Eszterhas (*Basic Instinct* [1992]), and Diane Johnson (*The Shining* [1980]), film historian David Thomson, and actors Danny Glover, Whoopi Goldberg, Robin Williams, and Kathleen Quinlan. Celebrities born and raised in the Bay Area include Clint Eastwood, Lee Merriweather, Carol Channing, Natalie Wood, Janet Gaynor (who worked as an usher at the Castro Theater), Katherine Ross (an alum of Del Valle High School in Walnut Creek), and Tom Hanks (an alum of Skyline High School in Oakland).

Because the city is constantly changing, feature films shot on location also become inadvertent historical documents of how the city looked at particular times. For example, Don Siegel shot *The Lineup* (1958) just as the elevated highway of the Embarcadero was being completed, and he incorporated that feature into the plot. After being severely damaged in

George Lucas oversees location filming of his first film, *American Graffiti* (1973).
Courtesy Pacific Film Archive, University of California, Berkeley

the 1989 Loma Prieta earthquake, the highway was demolished, but it is permanently preserved in this 1958 film.

Similarly, Ashley Judd and James Caviezel filmed *High Crimes* in Union Square in 2000 immediately before it was closed for a year and a half, reopening with a completely different look. Long gone are such cinematic landmarks as Kezar Stadium, Playland-at-the-Beach, and the old Hall of Justice.

Sometimes filmmaking leaves a physical mark, like Alta Plaza Park's cracked steps from *What's Up, Doc?* (1972). Other times the effect is economic, like the many welcome jobs that are created for local cast and crew during production. And there is the ephemeral thrill of knowing, for instance, that a star such as Julie Andrews paraded on the pavement in the little-known neighborhood of the Excelsior while filming *The Princess Diaries* (2001). Sometimes people choose a particular restaurant or hotel just because it was used as a location in one of their favorite movies.

In *The Lineup*, Eli Wallach, Richard Jaeckel, and Robert Keith hold Dorothy Bradshaw and Cheryl Callaway hostage atop the newly constructed Embarcadero freeway. Don Siegel had directed the pilot of the CBS television series *The Lineup* (1954–60). When Columbia asked him to direct the film feature, he felt it would be a mistake to use the same title, preferring *The Chase*. Siegel writes, "The shot in which the car comes to a sudden stop at the edge of the unfinished highway was no trick shot. There was a five-story sheer drop. We were photographing the action from the fifth-story window of the city's YMCA." *Courtesy Pacific Film Archive, University of California, Berkeley*

The San Francisco Bay Area has also stood in for other places: Cape Cod in *The Russians Are Coming, The Russians Are Coming* (1966); the Midwest in *Skidoo* (1968) and *Tucker* (1988); Baltimore in *The Assassination of Richard Nixon* (2004); and Florida, Houston, Washington, D.C., and New York in *The Right Stuff* (1983). San Francisco is so iconic that there are movies named for (though not necessarily filmed in) many Bay Area towns (*Sausalito* [1948]) and neighborhoods (*North Beach* [2000], *Nob Hill* [1945], *Pacific Heights* [1990], *Presidio* [1988], *The Mission* [2000], and *The House on Telegraph Hill* [1951]).

Somewhat surprisingly, many of the most famous San Francisco movies were filmed on Hollywood soundstages, perhaps using a bit of stock or

In the original *Dirty Harry* (1971), Clint Eastwood pulls his navy blue sedan into a red zone on Pine Street and parks. He has just bitten into a hot dog from Burger Den when he encounters a bank holdup in progress. It is here that Eastwood taunts Albert Popwell as the wounded robber with his now classic: "Ah, I know what you're thinking, punk. You're thinkin', 'Did he fire six shots or only five?' Now, to tell the truth, I've forgotten myself in all this excitement. But being as this is the .44 Magnum, the most powerful handgun in the world, and will blow your head clean off, you've got to ask yourself a question: 'Do I feel lucky?' Well, do ya, punk?" The shoot-out and car crash were reportedly shot on a Hollywood back lot, the only nonlocation set in the film. *Courtesy Pacific Film Archives, University of California, Berkeley*

second-unit footage. This category includes favorites such as *The Maltese Falcon* (1941), *Barbary Coast* (1935), *Gentleman Jim* (1942), and *San Francisco* (1936). Sometimes a brief aerial shot of the skyline or the Golden Gate Bridge under the opening credits and the clang of an off-screen cable car are enough to establish the feeling of being in San Francisco.

Some filmmakers respect the integrity of the cityscape more than others, shooting interiors in the same building used for exteriors or establishing enough time for characters to realistically get across town. Philip Kaufman's *Invasion of the Body Snatchers* (1978) and Blake Edwards's

Experiment in Terror (1962) are apt examples. Other directors indiscriminately sprinkle a few colorful locations throughout their films, causing locals to laugh when a character turns a corner into another neighborhood that is actually miles away, as in *Towering Inferno* (1974), *EDtv* (1999), and *So I Married an Axe Murderer* (1993).

You'll find these and many other films described in *Celluloid San Francisco*, whether you use it as a guidebook during your visit to this fabulous city or as an armchair guide to special moments in moviemaking history. Whether you're a longtime resident or a brief visitor, a cinephile or a casual moviegoer, we hope you enjoy reading *Celluloid San Francisco* as much as we enjoyed compiling it.

—Jim Van Buskirk
January 2006

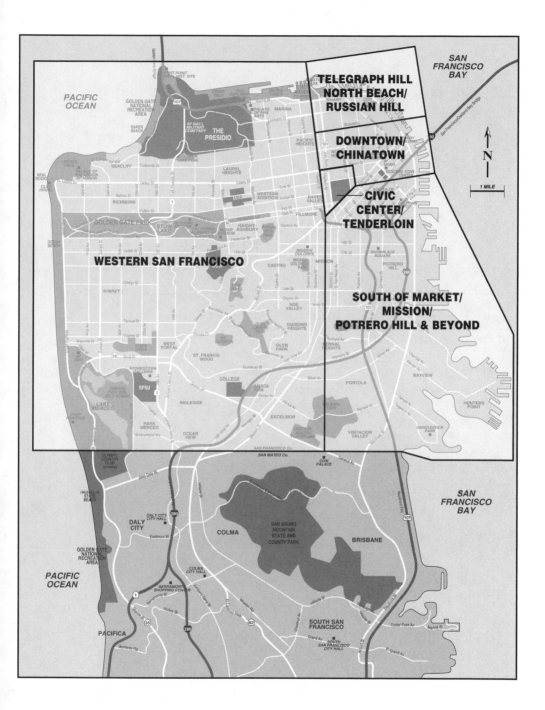

Civic Center and Tenderloin

Gene Hackman as Jedediah Tucker Ward opposes Mary Elizabeth Mastrantonio as his estranged daughter Maggie in *Class Action* (1991), filmed in the San Francisco Board of Supervisors' chambers at City Hall. *Courtesy of Pacific Film Archive, University of California, Berkeley*

This tour, which is best accomplished on foot, begins at City Hall, one of the city's most treasured and photogenic landmarks. It circles around the Civic Center area before veering off into the Tenderloin neighborhood, and ends back at California Hall, a few blocks from its point of origin.

Civic Center

Civic Center is one of America's great architectural complexes, and one of the most recognizable features of San Francisco's cityscape. The grand

collection of municipal buildings was begun in 1913 under the leadership of Mayor James Rolph. It is California's most clear-cut example of the influence of the City Beautiful movement of the late 19th century, which sought to improve the urban environment through beautification. Located within the Civic Center Historic District, it is where politicians gather; patrons of the arts flock to operas or concerts; bibliophiles congregate; and political demonstrations frequently take place. It has long been a favored site for filmmakers, too. For example, the vibrant Heart of the City farmer's market, held in United Nations Plaza on Sundays and Wednesdays, was used as the background for *Sausalito* (2000).

A number of cities in the United States have "tenderloin" districts. According to urban legend, these rough-and-ready inner-city neighborhoods get their nicknames from the police who patrolled them: police received hazard pay (or bigger bribes—stories vary) for working these areas and were therefore able to regularly dine on steak. The 'Loin is remarkably close to the Union Square tourist and shopping areas, as well as the Civic Center area. So many Vietnamese immigrants have opened shops and restaurants in the area in the past 25 years that banners now refer to the neighborhood as "Little Saigon." The residents also include drug dealers, addicts, the homeless and mentally unstable, and sex workers. This diverse mix creates a lot of contrasts, such as the sight of a strung-out junkie passed out in front of a $300-a-night hotel.

1. San Francisco City Hall
1 Carlton B. Goodlett Place

San Francisco City Hall, referred to as "The Crown Jewel" of the city, is one of the finest examples of beaux arts architecture in America. The architect was Arthur Brown Jr., who also designed the Opera House, Veterans Building, Temple Emanuel, Coit Tower, and 50 United Nations Plaza. Opened in 1915 and now designated as a national landmark, City Hall has appeared in many, many films.

It was the first building constructed in the Civic Center, replacing the 1870s City Hall, which was destroyed in the 1906 earthquake. It encompasses over 500,000 square feet and is spread over two full city blocks. Its dome rises 308 feet, 16 feet higher than the U.S. Capitol dome. The mayor's office, the Board of Supervisors' chambers, and other city offices are located there.

After the 1989 Loma Prieta earthquake damaged City Hall, along with many other buildings, a base isolation system was installed, using

rubber bearings to help protect the building against future damage. The work, begun in March 1995 and completed in 1999, included seismic construction and historic preservation. The grand public light courts, elegant marble walls and floors, skylights, and the breathtaking marble staircase under the rotunda make this an obvious attraction for film-makers. In January 1999, San Francisco mayor Willie Brown led a ceremony to officially change the address of City Hall to 1 Dr. Carlton B. Goodlett Place to honor one of San Francisco's most influential liberal voices for nearly half a century. Carlton Benjamin Goodlett (1914–97) was an African American teacher, physician, and publisher of the *Sun-Reporter*, San Francisco's oldest weekly black newspaper.

In June 1999, shortly after the seismic reinforcement and restoration, a nightclub scene for *Bicentennial Man* was staged in City Hall's grand interior. Local jazz favorite Paula West portrayed a big band singer in the Chris Columbus film starring Robin Williams. One night the sprinkler system malfunctioned, pouring 300 gallons of water into the beautiful historic space, delaying filming but causing no permanent damage.

In 1978, for the Colin Higgins comedy *Foul Play* starring Goldie Hawn and Chevy Chase, the exterior steps and glorious rotunda staircase were draped with a red carpet. Awaiting the arrival of the Pope (played by San Francisco philanthropist and bon vivant Cyril Magnin), extras swarmed what was supposed to be the Opera House. The fourth floor was used as the U.S. Capitol in *The Right Stuff* (1983).

Several films of the *Dirty Harry* series used City Hall locations. Shot in the actual mayor's offices over Memorial Day weekend, one pivotal scene in *Dirty Harry* (1971) portrays Clint Eastwood as San Francisco police inspector Harry Callahan, frustrated with the bureaucracy of law and order. It is here that the mayor (John Vernon) reads the Scorpio killer's handwritten note to the chief of police (John Larch) before Harry mouths off to them.

The following year's *Magnum Force* (1973) saw "Dirty" Harry Callahan and his new partner, Early Smith, temporarily reassigned from homicide to stakeout duty. The opening scene of the film depicts report-

ers trying to get a statement about the acquittal on a technicality of Carmine Ricca for the murder of a family. The defendants are followed outside where demonstrators surround their limousine. In *The Enforcer* (1976), immediately prior to a photo op with the mayor awarding him a letter of commendation, Harry tells his supervisor, McKay, that they made a big mistake. When McKay suspends Harry and asks for his badge, Harry tells him to "stick it up your ass." In the second and final season of the CBS television series *Phyllis*, which ran from 1975 to '77, Phyllis Lindstrom (Cloris Leachman) worked in City Hall as administrative assistant to supervisor Dan Valenti (Carmine Caridi).

In *The Wedding Planner*, the 2001 romantic comedy, wedding planner Jennifer Lopez falls for pediatrician Matthew McConaughey. He, unbeknownst to her, is about to become one of her bridegrooms. The interior of McConaughey's doctor's office was filmed in City Hall. In another scene, Lopez enters City Hall and walks from a ladies' room down a long hallway before her impending marriage to Mister Wrong, Massimo (played by the "Italian" Justin Chambers). The plot twists and turns before Lopez and McConaughey find that they were meant for each other.

City Hall is often depicted as the city's courthouse, which it is not. (San Francisco's Civil Court is housed across the street at 400 McAllister, and the criminal court is at 850 Bryant.) City Hall exteriors and hallways were used in *Jagged Edge* (1985) when it became the Superior Court for the County of San Francisco. Here, against the wily Peter Coyote, Glenn Close defended Jeff Bridges, charged with murdering his rich wife. Jeff Bridges was back in City Hall when it became a Chicago courthouse in *Tucker: The Man and His Dream* (1988). City Hall was again a courthouse in *Class Action* (1990). The mother of Gene Hackman's wife, Mary Elizabeth Mastrantonio, dies of a heart attack as she descends the stately stairs. It was yet again a courthouse in 1995 for *Murder in the First*. When Brendan Fraser comes to in *Bedazzled* (2000), he is looking up at the rich carving of the rotunda and wonders "Is this heaven?" "God, no," says Elizabeth Hurley as the devil. "It's the courthouse." When Fraser realizes that his deal with the devil is broken, he races around the marble floors, ecstatically yelling, "I get to keep my soul!"

One of the most dramatic uses of this municipal building was in *A View to a Kill* (1985). While interiors and exteriors were used as the "State Office Building," many of the interiors and an office (#306) were shot on sets in England. So were the elevator scenes depicting a trapped Roger Moore (as James Bond) and Tanya Roberts. When Christopher Walken's evil character sets City Hall ablaze, the special effects crew used 50 30-pound tanks of propane, which could be turned on and off, and giant flares. Mayor Dianne Feinstein approved the burning of City Hall, and in appreciation of the city's cooperation, the film's world premiere was held May 22, 1985, at the Palace of Fine Arts as a benefit for the Mayor's Youth Fund.

In Phil Jouanou's neo-noir thriller *Final Analysis* (1992), San Francisco shrink Isaac Baar (Richard Gere) tries to aid his patient Uma Thurman and her sister Kim Basinger, but he finds himself professionally compromised by his attraction to Basinger, the femme fatale. The trial chamber scenes are a mix-up of several locations, but in one scene Gere awaits the outcome of a murder trial on an upper floor of City Hall, overlooking the central rotunda. Gere also arrives here in an exterior shot when Basinger is booked into "jail," which does not exist in reality at City Hall.

In the real world, City Hall is where, on January 14, 1953, Marilyn Monroe married Joe DiMaggio. It is also where, on November 27, 1978, Dan White, who had recently stepped down as supervisor, shot the liberal mayor George Moscone and Harvey Milk, San Francisco's first openly gay supervisor. During the trial in 1979, a psychiatrist testified that White had been depressed at the time of the crime, citing White's uncharacteristic consumption of Twinkies and Coca-Cola as evidence, and suggesting that this may have worsened his depression. The eventual manslaughter verdict sparked the White Night riots and gave rise to the interpretation that White's lawyers had used the "Twinkie Defense" to claim that the depression was *caused by* Twinkies. The devastating double homicide and the events surrounding it were vividly depicted in the moving documentary *The Times of Harvey Milk* (1984), by San Francisco's Rob Epstein and Richard Schmiechen, which won the 1985 Oscar for best feature documentary.

2. Veterans' War Memorial Building
401 Van Ness Avenue

In the 1987 made-for-television thriller *Love Among Thieves*, Audrey Hepburn portrayed Baroness Caroline DuLac, a renowned concert pianist with a secret. After a concert in the Green Room on the sec-

ond floor, the elegant Hepburn sneaks downstairs to steal three priceless Fabergé eggs with which she will bargain for her abducted fiancé's life. Posters advertising the baroness's concert were displayed around the area during filming, which was done over several days.

In *Twisted* (2004), Ashley Judd is Jessica Shepard, a female police officer investigating a series of murders, who finds herself in the center of her own investigation when former lovers start dying around her at a furious pace. This psychological thriller was shot entirely on location in fall 2002. "I'd been wanting to make a film noir in San Francisco for many years," said director Philip Kaufman. Hallways in this building were used to represent corridors of the police headquarters.

Getting Even with Dad (1993) opens with Ted Danson and his gang (Saul Rubinek and Gailard Sartain) staking out the fictional offices of Professional Coin Grading Services located in the War Memorial Building. The San Francisco Museum of Modern Art had vacated the building to move to 151 Third Street, and the filmmakers took advantage of the rehabilitation in progress by having Danson and gang make their escape during the heist scene by sliding down a chute set up for construction debris.

3. War Memorial Opera House
301 Van Ness Avenue at Grove Street

This building, designed by Arthur Brown Jr. in the French Renaissance style, opened to the public on October 15, 1932. It was on this stage on June 26, 1945, that President Harry Truman signed the United Nations charter. The world-renowned San Francisco Opera and San Francisco Ballet present their annual seasons here.

Don Siegel's *The Lineup* (1958), the expanded version of the CBS television series (1954–60), opens with San Francisco Opera Company executive Philip Dressler (Raymond Bailey) arriving on a ship from the Orient. A porter steals Dressler's bag and tosses it into a taxi, which careens into a truck, veers away, killing a policeman, and finally runs into a ditch, killing the taxi driver. When it is discovered that the dapper Dressler's suitcase contained a figurine with enough heroin in it "to supply every addict in San Francisco for two weeks," detectives Quine (Emile Meyer) and Guthrie (Warner Anderson) go to the Opera House to interview him.

Memorial Court between the Opera House and the War Memorial building.

The interior of the Opera House (but not the exterior) was used for the dramatic denouement of *Foul Play* (1978), with Goldie Hawn and Chevy Chase. During the staging of *The Mikado*, the camera surveys the opulent auditorium, reminiscent of the end of Alfred Hitchcock's *The Man Who Knew Too Much* (1956).

The memorial court between the Opera House and the Veteran's War Memorial Building, with City Hall in the background, was used by Francis Ford Coppola as the exterior of the Chicago Court House in *Tucker: The Man and His Dream* (1988). The Detroit automobile makers and their Washington political connections get the Securities and Exchange Commission to investigate Tucker's business operations. Jeff Bridges as Preston Tucker is tried on charges of taking millions of dollars from prospective car dealers under false pretenses. Bridges is standing outside the Opera House when he sees the headline "Tucker Loses

Chicago Plant" and the completed Tucker cars start circling the entire block, which leads him to remark, "50 or 50 million—what's the difference? It's the idea that counts—and the dream."

The gold elements of the iron fences and gates are still visible, thanks to Coppola's willingness to pay for them to be regilded.

In *Pretty Woman* (1990), set in Los Angeles, Richard Gere invites Julia Roberts to opening night at the San Francisco Opera. One brief establishing shot of San Francisco's illuminated downtown is the only footage actually filmed in San Francisco. Plans to shoot the opera scene in San Francisco were thwarted by the Loma Prieta earthquake of October 17, 1989. The entrance to the San Francisco Opera House was actually Los Angeles' Museum of Natural History.

4. Department of Public Health
101 Grove Street at Polk

In *By Hook or by Crook* (2001), a low-budget independent film by local filmmakers Harry (aka Harriet) Dodge and Silas Howard, Shy (Howard) is a handsome small-town loner who heads to the big city to

immerse herself in a life of crime. On her journey, she meets her match in Valentine (Dodge), a wiseacre adoptee who is searching for her birth mother. The two lonely grifters join forces and embark on a journey through the skid-row streets of San Francisco as they steal and swindle their way toward understanding themselves and the world around them. At one point Val goes to the Department of Public Health to find records of her birth.

Philip Kaufman's 1978 remake of Don Siegel's 1956 science fiction classic *Invasion of the Body Snatchers* moves the setting from a small town to San Francisco. Donald Sutherland notices friends complaining that their close relatives have changed in some way. When questioned later the friends themselves seem changed as they deny everything or make lame excuses. Witnessing an attempted "replacement," Sutherland realizes that he and his friends must escape or suffer the same fate. The office where Brooke Adams and Sutherland work was filmed at the Department of Public Health (room #320). Kaufman has commented on how much easier it is to use the same building for interiors and exteriors. From this site he could film the characters' watching people being replaced by pods adjacent to City Hall.

5. Civic Center Plaza
Bounded by Polk, McAllister, Larkin, and Grove Streets

Roger Spottiswoode's 1993 *And the Band Played On*, based on the book by *San Francisco Chronicle* journalist Randy Shilts, boasted an all-star cast including Matthew Modine, Alan Alda, Ian McKellen, B. D. Wong, Lily Tomlin, Swoosie Kurtz, and Richard Gere, among many others. The made-for-television movie dramatizes the story of the discovery of the AIDS virus, from the early days in 1978 when numerous San Francisco gay men began dying from unknown causes, to the identification of the HIV virus. Although much of the action takes place in San Francisco, little was actually filmed there. Shots of the candlelight vigil for November 1985 used footage of an actual AIDS vigil at Civic Center Plaza as well as shots moving down Market Street. The movie's 1981 Halloween parade used footage of a gay pride parade (there is no Halloween parade in San Francisco) down Market Street as well.

In *The Enforcer* (1976), the third installment of the *Dirty Harry* series, Harry and his new partner, Inspector Kate Moore (Tyne Daly), must track down the People's Revolutionary Strike Force (based on the

Symbionese Liberation Army) who have kidnapped the mayor and are demanding $2 million ransom. Harry and Kate learn that the mayor is being held on Alcatraz Island and plan to rescue him. After Harry has been suspended from the force, Kate chases after Harry out of City Hall to offer her assistance. As they cross the plaza, he finally relents, "come on, take a walk." Immediately they are at Coit Tower. In 2002, lawyer Ashley Judd sits on a bench (when there were benches) in front of City Hall to converse with FBI agent Tom Bower in *High Crimes*.

The famous final scene of *Invasion of the Body Snatchers* depicts Donald Sutherland wandering throughout the Civic Center. The scene during which he is confronted by Veronica Cartwright was shot in the plaza with rows of the oddly gnarled sycamore trees and City Hall in the background.

6.   San Francisco Public Library
100 Larkin Street at Grove

Designed by James Ingo Freed and Cathy Simon, the main library opened in April 1996. Shortly thereafter, the library's operation was interrupted with several days of shooting for *City of Angels* (1998), standing in for the Los Angeles Public Library, which apparently didn't

San Francisco Public Library.

have the right look. This Americanization of Wim Wender's *Wings of Desire* (1988) depicts an angel (Nicolas Cage) longing to know more about human beings. Finding himself attracted to a hardworking doctor (Meg Ryan), he decides to sacrifice his heavenly status and fall to earth to experience love. Coincidentally, the building's architects appropriated some design features from the Staatsbibliothek, Berlin's vast public library, which was featured in the Wim Wenders original. The CBS series *Nash Bridges* (1996–2001), starring Don Johnson and Cheech Marin, used the San Francisco Public Library frequently when it was shot in San Francisco.

7. Asian Art Museum
200 Larkin Street between McAllister and Fulton

Previously situated in Golden Gate Park, this venerable museum now inhabits the building that formerly housed the San Francisco Public Library, which was completely reconfigured by Italian architect Gae Aulenti. In *Maxie*, Paul Aron's 1985 comedy, Jan (Glenn Close) and Nick (Mandy Patinkin) live in a Victorian house on Alamo Square. He works for Valerie Curtin as a reference librarian in the San Francisco History Room on the third floor of the old Main Library. A few interior shots also show the card catalog on the second floor.

In Colin Higgins's 1978 comedy, *Foul Play*, Goldie Hawn portrays a librarian, but none of her scenes in a library were shot at San Francisco Public Library. *The Streets of San Francisco* (1972–77) used the side door in the middle of the Fulton Street facade as the main entrance of the San Francisco Police Department.

The offices of Glenne Headley and police lieutenant Hector Elizando are housed in the old main library in *Getting Even with Dad*. The 1994 film ends with Headley, Ted Danson, and Macaulay Culkin leaving down the center staircase, exiting out the front doors, and crossing Larkin Street to say their good-byes in front of the Civic Center Plaza reflecting pool and fountain, which have since been removed.

8. Fox Theater Site
1350 Market Street at Polk

The Fox Theatre in San Francisco opened in 1929 as one of the grandest theaters ever built for the showing of motion pictures. Designed by Thomas W. Lamb for William Fox in style that has been described as a combination of baroque and French Renaissance, the Fox was meant to be a part of a large office complex, which was never finished. The Fox was similar to, but grander in detail than, two other theaters designed by Lamb: the Midland in Kansas City, Missouri, and the Loews Jersey in Jersey City. The Fox was apparently copied in 1932 by S. Charles Lee for the smaller scale Los Angeles Theatre.

Saturday, February 16, 1963, was a sad day in San Francisco when, due to a decline in attendance, the 4,651-seat Fox was demolished and replaced by a modern apartment building and shopping center. The interior furnishings and decorations were auctioned off and still occasionally surface from time to time around the Bay Area. A few artifacts are housed at the Oakland Museum, and the main curtain is in use in the main auditorium at the Grand Lake Theatre in Oakland. The magnificent Wurlitzer organ is now located in the El Capitan Theatre in Hollywood.

"Farewell to the Fox," February 16, 1963. *Courtesy of San Francisco History Center, San Francisco Public Library*

Tenderloin

9. Flatiron Building
1020 Market Street at Taylor and Golden Gate

Neil Jordan's 1994 adaptation of Anne Rice's bestselling novel *Interview with the Vampire: The Vampire Chronicles* begins in contemporary San Francisco. The film opens by panning over the Golden Gate Bridge, the Ferry Building, the illuminated buildings of Embarcadero Center, and down Market Street, stopping at this site. On the top floor of a seedy hotel in the Tenderloin, reporter Daniel Malloy (Christian Slater) interviews the vampire Louis de Pointe du Lac (Brad Pitt). Both exteriors and the triangular interior were used. After recounting his 200-year existence as a vampire, at the end of the film Brad Pitt runs out of the building, into a car, and drives across the Golden Gate Bridge.

10. Hamlin Hotel
385 Eddy Street at Leavenworth

Don Siegel's original *Invasion of the Body Snatchers* (1956) ended with Kevin McCarthy running down the street trying to warn people about the alien invasion. In Philip Kaufman's 1978 remake, McCarthy has a cameo in which he's still running frantically down the street yelling, "They're here! They're here!" before being hit by a car and killed. Phoning the police from the Hamlin Hotel, Donald Sutherland mistakenly places it at "Leavenworth and Turk."

The Hamlin Hotel played a major role in Jenny Bowen's 1981 comedy *Street Music*, appearing as the Victory Hotel, where much of the action is centered. Elizabeth Daily (aka E. G. Daily) plays Sadie, an ambitious singer, and Larry Breeding (who died before the film was released) is Eddie, her slacker boyfriend. Together they join the elderly residents of the dilapidated hotel, who are threatened with eviction. As a Falcon tour bus driver, Eddie relays mischievous misinformation about Fisherman's Wharf, the Japanese Tea Garden, and Alcatraz ("once one of the Hawaiian Islands"). Sadie sings in Huntington Park and on the street in front of the Little Fox Theatre (home for many years to the play version of *One Flew Over the Cuckoo's Nest* and later Francis Ford Coppola's American Zoetrope Studio). When she finally gets booked into a club, it is Mr. Hyde's (formerly Chez Jacques) on the corner of California and Hyde. Actor

Ned Glass is quoted as saying the two films he's proudest of making are *West Side Story* and *Street Music*. (Did he forget *Charade*?)

11. York Hotel

> 940 Sutter Street at Leavenworth

In Alfred Hitchcock's classic San Francisco film *Vertigo* (1958), Jimmy Stewart as Scottie follows Kim Novak as Judy to her apartment house, the Empire Hotel (now the York). Her front apartment corresponds to rooms #501 and #502. Scottie insists on making her over in the image of Madeleine, and only discovers who Judy actually is when, in this room, she recklessly puts on the necklace that had belonged to Madeleine.

12. Regency Building
1290 Sutter Street at Van Ness

Swing (2004), Martin Guiggui's independent feature, was shot in various locations in San Francisco and Oakland. Caught between his dream of being a full-time musician and the conventional life of his security-minded father, Anthony Verdi (Innis Casey) in an otherworldly 1940s nightclub meets a beautiful older woman (Jacqueline Bisset) who teaches him to swing dance. From her, he learns that only if he follows his heart and starts being who he truly is can he find real happiness. Tom Skerritt, Jonathan Winters, and Barry Bostwick also appear in what was to be Nell Carter's final film. The Regency Center, formerly part of an Eagle's Lodge, is a beautiful gem hidden inside the Regency Theater space. With its rich wood paneling, leaded glass windows, and old-fashioned stage, it is a perfect setting for the mysterious swing club. In addition, below this small theater is a larger ballroom, formerly Avalon Ballroom, later the Regency I Theater.

13. Cathedral Hill Hotel
1101 Van Ness Avenue at Geary

In Francis Ford Coppola's gripping psychological drama *The Conversation* (1974), Gene Hackman plays Harry Caul, a nationally known

expert on surveillance, who has been hired to record the conversations of two of "the Director's" employees (Frederic Forrest and Cindy Williams). Some years earlier, Harry's work directly led to the murder of three people, and now he has reason to fear that it will happen again. In 1974 this hotel was the Jack Tarr Hotel, the location where the overheard plan is "to meet at 3:00, next Sunday, in room #773." After having finally figured this out, Hackman installs himself in the adjacent room to "witness" what happens. The nefarious doings are not exactly what he had imagined.

14. Marquee Lofts
1000 Van Ness Avenue at Alice B. Toklas Place

In Pat O'Connor's *Sweet November* (2001), a remake of the 1968 Sandy Dennis/Anthony Newley vehicle, wacky, miscast Charlize Theron takes a new lover every month, only to fall in love with Mr. November, Nelson Moss (Keanu Reeves). The interiors of his apartment were shot here. This historic landmark building, completed in 1921, was originally built for Don Lee's Cadillac dealership. The architecture, a combination of decorative motifs and traditional building materials, was considered a symbol of the emerging commercial style in the 1920s and signified the beginning of America's automobile revolution. The lobby has been preserved as the lobby to a multiplex movie theater.

15. Star's Café
555 Golden Gate Avenue at Van Ness

In *Nine Months* (1995), Chris Columbus's remake of Patrick Braoude's 1994 *Neuf Mois*, Samuel Faulkner (Hugh Grant) panics when he learns that his girlfriend of five years, Rebecca Taylor (Julianne Moore), is pregnant. Samuel, a child psychiatrist frustrated by children, doesn't want the baby, but Rebecca wants to settle down, even if she has to be a single mother. Both the exterior and the interior of Jeremiah Tower's popular restaurant were used in the scene where Hugh and Julianne go to dinner and the hostess turns out to be the girl whom Hugh dated during the breakup. The flamboyant Tower and his food empire have since moved on to other venues.

16. California Hall
625 Polk Street at Turk

California Hall, built in 1912 as "Das Deutsches Haus," was home to the Rathskeller, a favorite police hangout, and scene of a real-life scandal. It has also been a live-concert venue, and it currently houses the California Culinary Academy.

California Hall.

Dirty Harry, directed by Don Siegel in 1971, was loosely based on the true episode of the Zodiac serial killer, who terrorized San Francisco in the late 1960s (and who was never caught). The character of Dirty Harry appeared in four sequels: *Magnum Force* (1973), *The Enforcer* (1976), *Sudden Impact* (1983), and *The Dead Pool* (1988). In one early scene, Eastwood responds to a radio call of an "804 in progress" at this location and rushes to stop a suicide attempt by being lifted by a crane to the top of the building. He feigns brutal indifference, and when the man, an Elvis impersonator, tries to take Harry down with him, Harry knocks him out and brings him down safely. Across the street the sign of the Embassy Restaurant and Lounge is visible. "Now you know why they call me 'Dirty Harry,'" he tells his new colleague, Chico Gonzales, played by Reni Santoni. "[I get] every dirty job that comes along."

The Mission District, Potrero Hill, the Waterfront South of the Bay Bridge, and SOMA (South of Market)

Whoopi Goldberg in *Burglar* (1987) gives Bob Goldthwait a ride on a stolen police motorcycle on Potrero Hill, a favorite neighborhood with filmmakers for its hilly terrain and views of downtown. *Courtesy of Pacific Film Archive, University of California, Berkeley*

This tour, for which a car is advised, begins just south of Market Street, a few blocks south from the end of the previous tour. After traversing the heart of the Mission District, we explore Potrero Hill, with its photogenic views of downtown, then continue along the bayfront. The tour circles from Pac Bell Park through the South of Market area, then ends with sites southward in Bernal Heights, Hunter's Point, and Candlestick Park.

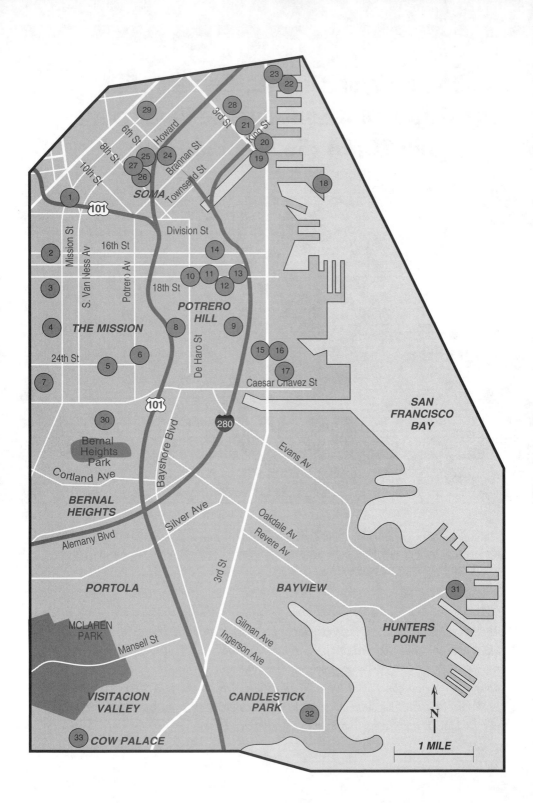

The Mission District

The Mission is one of the city's low-rent districts, but, in expensive San Francisco, "low-rent" is a relative term. During the dot-com boom of the 1990s, the tension between nouveau riches and the longtime, mostly Latino, population was keenly felt, especially in the Mission. But it is not the "skid row" that Midge (Barbara Bel Geddes) calls it in *Vertigo* (1958), when she mistakenly decides that Gavin Elster is looking for a handout because his address is in "the Mission." (It turns out to be his fancy office at a shipyard in Mission Bay.) The Mission has attracted filmmakers since at least 1915, when Charlie Chaplin filmed a scene from *A Jitney Elopement* at a bicycle shop that was located at 20th and Folsom streets.

A 2000 independent film called *The Mission* (also known as *City of Bars*), directed by Loren Marsh, was shot in Mission District residences, locales, and businesses, including Dolores Park and the 500 Club. The film features a local architectural beacon on its posters and Web site: the deco blade sign of the New Mission Theatre at Mission between 21st and 22nd streets. Although closed to the public as a movie palace since 1993, the New Mission was saved from demolition by neighborhood activists and listed on the National Register of Historic Places. It is also a San Francisco Landmark, as the 2,800-seat *grande dame* of a string of movie houses along Mission Street and the design of blue chip architects the Reid Brothers (who also designed the Fairmont Hotel), with a renovation by art deco architect Timothy Pflueger in the 1930s. (He also built the Castro Theatre and Oakland's Paramount.) Although its future use remains unclear, locals are determined that it will not meet the fate of the lost and lamented spectacular Fox Theater (see Civic Center).

1. **Mel's Drive-In**
   120 South Van Ness Avenue at Mission Street
   This Mel's Drive-In, one of many locations that stand in for 1962 Modesto in George Lucas's *American Graffiti*, was closed and demolished shortly after filming ended in 1973. The story of the adventures of Dewey High School graduates cruising the strip one summer night before two of the gang leave town for college was also filmed in Petaluma and at the Mel's that survives at 3355 Geary Street. The license plate on John Milner's (Paul Le Mat's) car reads "THX 1138," a sly reference to Lucas's early (1971) sci-fi thriller of the same name. After a

Actors await direction from George Lucas on the outdoor set of his first film, *American Graffiti* **(1973).** *Courtesy of Pacific Film Archive, University of California, Berkeley*

series of minor roles in forgettable movies, Harrison Ford was working as a self-taught carpenter when he was asked to audition for Lucas's low-budget coming-of-age movie. In this surprise commercial success, Ford played a secondary role alongside stars Ron Howard and Richard Dreyfuss, but the most important aspect of the film was that it marked Ford's first collaboration with Lucas. Ford was asked to get a crewcut for the film, but refused, stating that his role was too brief, and offered to wear a hat instead. Lucas reluctantly agreed, and Ford appears hatted. Ford was still making his living as a carpenter in 1977 when he landed his first major role as the renegade starship captain Han Solo in Lucas's intergalactic adventure movie, *Star Wars*.

2. **Royan Hotel**
   405 Valencia Street at 15th Street

   In *By Hook or by Crook* (2001), Shy, a handsome small-town loner (Silas Howard), heads to the big city to immerse herself in a life of crime. On her journey, she meets her match in Valentine (Harry aka Harriet Dodge), a wiseacre adoptee who is searching for her birth mother. The two lonely grifters join forces and embark on a journey through the skid-row streets of San Francisco as they steal and swindle their way toward understanding themselves and the world around them. Shy gets a room in this seedy hotel, where she rehearses her fantasy of robbing local stores. The two butch stars, Dodge and Howard, cowrote, costarred, and codirected this award-winning indie.

3. **Elbo Room**
   647 Valencia Street

   One of several locations in the Mission District used in *Dream for an Insomniac* (1998), Café Blue Eyes, the café owned by Seymour Cassell's character, was supposedly at 1040 Pine Street, putting it between Taylor and Jones. In one scene Ione Skye and Mackenzie Astin add to the many painted murals in nearby Clarion Alley. Tiffanie De Bartolo's romantic comedy also stars Michael Landes, as the closeted gay nephew, and local actor Sean San Jose Blackman.

4. **The Lexington Club**
   3464 19th Street at Lexington

   In *By Hook or by Crook* (see site #2), after Shy rescues Valentine from getting beat up near the piers, they decide to head to the Lexington Club, a lesbian bar. Once there, Shy steals Valentine's wallet and leaves.

5. **24th Street between Mission Street and Potrero Avenue**

   Louis Malle filmed *Crackers* (1984)—short for "safecrackers"—along 24th Street, a commercial strip in the Mission. A remake of the Mario Monicelli 1958 classic *Big Deal on Madonna Street* with Marcello Mastroianni, it is about a gang of incompetent burglars that includes Donald Sutherland, Jack Warden, Wallace Shawn, and Sean Penn. Although a lot of the storefront businesses have changed since 1984, many of the location shots made on this stretch of 24th, such as La Palma Delicatessen, China Books, and the York (now Brava) Theater, are still identifiable. One interior scene was filmed at La Rondalla, a Mexican restaurant at Valencia and 20th streets, which is decorated for Christmas year-round.

6.   San Francisco General Hospital
1001 Potrero Avenue at 23rd Street

This is where state's witness Johnny Ross (Pat Renella) and cop Carl Stanton (Carl Reindel) are taken after they are shot in *Bullitt* (1968), the ultimate San Francisco chase movie. Scenes shot at San Francisco General used real doctors and nurses for verisimilitude.

After Max Klein (Jeff Bridges) crashes his car into a wall to make a point about inertia to Carla Rodrigo (Rosie Perez), who is in the backseat holding a heavy toolbox, both driver and passenger end up at San Francisco General in Peter Weir's *Fearless* (1993). (The toolbox goes through the windshield.) Perez lives nearby, with husband Manny (Benicio del Toro), in the vicinity of Shotwell and 20th Streets in the Mission. She and Telegraph Hill resident Bridges form a difficult-to-understand bond after they are both in a plane crash in Bakersfield. Their relationship creates a conflict in Bridges's marriage to Isabella Rossellini.

7.   387 Fair Oaks at 25th Street

After too many martinis, Zoe (Robin Tunney), in the 2002 flick *Cherish*, has a fateful encounter with a man who enters her car, steps on the accelerator, mows down a cop, and then flees on foot. Tunney is arrested for drunken vehicular homicide and several other crimes and is sentenced to confinement in her walk-up apartment (the rooftop views suggest a Potrero Hill location), wearing an ankle bracelet that sounds an alarm if she tries to leave. Meanwhile, she's trying to prove her innocence by tracking down, via the

Internet, the real culprit, who is stalking her. She manages to escape her apartment and finally finds him at this address. Ultimately, she is able to alert the police, who apprehend him and clear her name.

Potrero Hill

Potrero has the charming architecture and dramatic vistas of classic San Francisco living without the crowding, hubbub, and difficult parking of the downtown neighborhoods.

8.   20th Street

Natives know better when Frank Bullitt's (Steve McQueen's) car turns off 20th and Kansas Streets on Potrero Hill and is immediately on Russian Hill—these areas are several miles away from each other in reality. (Another impossibility and a bit of fun trivia: during the course of the classic *Bullitt* chase scene, the villain's car lost a total of five hubcaps.)

768 De Haro Street.

The hillside house 768 De Haro at 20th is the Potrero Hill location where Mike Stone (Karl Malden) lives with his coed daughter (Darleen Carr) in the TV series *The Streets of San Francisco*. The show, based on characters from the book *Poor, Poor Ophelia* by Caroline Weston, ran from 1972 to 1977 and was filmed entirely on location.

9.   1243 19th Street at Texas

The corner residence stands in for *Pacific Heights* (1990), when Patty Palmer and Drake Goodman (Melanie Griffith and Matthew Modine) buy their dream house, only to have it trashed by psychopathic tenant Carter Hayes (Michael Keaton). The house atop Potrero Hill is across town from Pacific Heights. It was distressed for the filming to conform to the plot line of first-time homeowners improving a fixer-upper, and then repainted for its new owners.

Locals never understood why John Schlesinger filmed *Pacific Heights* (1990), starring Melanie Griffith and Matthew Modine, on Potrero Hill. *Courtesy of Pacific Film Archive, University of California, Berkeley*

10. 18th Street between Missouri and Texas

Blooms Saloon, and Farley's Café across the street from it, are both featured in *Sweet November* (2001). Inside Blooms Saloon, Nelson Moss (Keanu Reeves) performs a karaoke serenade to woo Sara Deever (Charlize Theron). The deck of the saloon was also used as the deck of Sara's home. The romantic drama tells the story of serial romancer Theron, who hooks up with a new guy every month for a very private reason. Reeves is Mr. November.

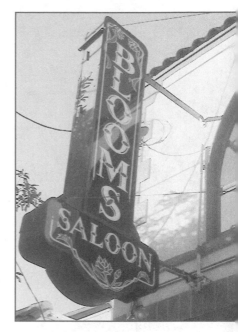

11. Farley's Café
1315 18th Street near Missouri

The lead characters in *Sweet November* (2001) meet and eat in this Potrero Hill neighborhood café. An obnoxious couple comes in and the foursome endures an awkward scene in which each couple can't quite believe the other couple's relationship.

12. Intersection of Missouri and 18th Streets

This intersection is the location of the apartment (1400 18th Street) where Bernie (Whoopi Goldberg) lives over a corner shop in *Burglar* (1987). When she looks down and sees that cops are on their way up to investigate, she calmly makes herself a sandwich and takes it into her secret annex while the police burn through her metal front door. The shop is now Christopher's Books, where Keanu Reeves works in *Sweet November* (2001). The bookstore owner recalls that whenever Reeves came in, he was usually followed by a gaggle of girls. During the cold October filming, Charlize Theron stood in doorways smoking, but never came into the bookstore. Theron's character Sara lives at this intersection, but interiors were shot on a Treasure Island soundstage.

13. Pennsylvania Street

A renegade cop in *Magnum Force* (1973) orders a limousine to pull off the 280 freeway at Pennsylvania and Mariposa Streets for crossing the double line. Then the cop assassinates the four men in the car. Other scenes on Potrero Hill include a chase scene down the twists of Vermont Street. The law offices of Morgan Freeman are located at 391 Pennsylvania at 19th Street in *High Crimes*, the 2002 Ashley Judd vehicle that costars Freeman as unconventional lawyer C. W. Grimes.

14. The Galleria
101 Henry Adams Street at Alameda

In the one-of-a-kind musical *Can't Stop the Music* (1980), a pseudobiography of the Village People directed by Nancy Walker, Bruce Jenner's mother (Barbara Rush) books the Village People to perform at her charity auction here. The San Francisco finale, which also features the Ritchie Family, was designed by Jules Fisher Enterprises and John Tedesco. Tammy Grimes, who portrays Sydney Channing in the film, memorably said of the city, "I love San Francisco; my favorite ex-husband lives there."

The Waterfront South of Bay Bridge

15. San Francisco Drydock

A variety of films have used this site. In *The Dead Pool* (1988), the fifth and final film in the *Dirty Harry* series, 20th and Illinois is the set where Liam Neeson, as Peter Swan, is filming the fictitious movie *Hotel Satan,* and also where the final sequences are shot. Members of the rock group Guns n' Roses have cameos in this film at this location. Also, in *Magnum Force* (1973), several of the wharf scenes involving the vigilante motorcycle cops were shot at the San Francisco drydock. Off camera, at the end of the scene where the cops threaten Dirty Harry, and then tear away, they all ran into each other.

Gavin Elster's (Tom Helmore's) offices in *Vertigo* overlook the docks at 20th and Illinois, called "Bethlehem Shipyards" in *Footsteps in the Fog*, the Hitchcock site location study. In the 1978 remake of *Invasion of the Body Snatchers*, 3rd Street at 22nd is "Pod Central," the warehouse where the pods are cultivated before being transported throughout the city. Matthew Bennell (Donald Sutherland) ultimately destroys the facility. Nearby is the spot where Elizabeth Driscoll (Brooke Adams) falls asleep and is "replaced" in this film. This was one of the few sets used in *Body Snatchers*.

16. American Can Company
Between Illinois and Kentucky, 20th, and 22nd Streets

In *The Right Stuff* (1983), Philip Kaufman used this building to stand in for Cape Canaveral, Florida. This was one of many Bay Area sites used during the 12 weeks of local shooting. The Tom Wolfe screenplay, based on his book, tells the story of the marketing of the original seven Mercury astronauts, played by a cast who were about to become big stars, including Ed Harris, Dennis Quaid, and Fred Ward.

17. 435 23rd Street at Illinois

Groove, the 2000 indie feature by Greg Harrison, features daytime and nighttime scenes of exteriors of the warehouse where all-night dance parties called "raves" take place.

18. Pier 50 (Mission Rock)

Alfred Hitchcock's *Marnie* (1964) was filmed on board the SS *President Cleveland*, which was docked at the American President Lines in February that year for a one-day location shoot with Tippi Hedren and Sean Connery. In this psychological thriller, Mark (Connery) and Marnie (Hedren) marry although he has well-founded doubts about the sanity of his bride, whose only close relationship is with her horse. Their honeymoon cruise leaves from here for Honolulu and Fiji.

In the teen romance *Susan Slade* (1961) the SS *Grover Cleveland* arrives here from Santiago, Chile, with teenage ingenue Connie Stevens and her parents on board after an overseas mission for Papa (Lloyd Noland). Stevens does not yet know she is pregnant with the baby of her shipboard lover, who is about to meet an untimely end. In true 1960s fashion, the humiliated unwed mother-to-be hides away on the Monterey peninsula, and Mama (Dorothy McGuire) claims the baby is her own, thus saving face for the entire family, in this Delmer Daves soaper.

19. Lefty O'Doul 3rd Street Bridge
3rd Street at China Basin

The members of the People's Revolutionary Strike Force arrange for the bridge to be raised just as the mayor is being driven from Candlestick Park along 3rd Street, in 1976's *The Enforcer,* with Clint Eastwood and Tyne Daly. At the corner of 3rd and China Basin, the mayor's limousine is ambushed, and he is kidnapped by members of the group (based on the Symbionese Liberation Army, who were making big news in the late 1970s).

In the 1985 James Bond adventure *View to a Kill,* the sequences of the police chasing the fire truck commandeered by Roger Moore (in his last Bond role) and Stacey Sutton (Tanya Roberts) were shot at night over four weeks. Included were Market Street at Battery, Potrero at 17th (where the Chevron Station's sign was knocked off), and this bridge, where the truck zooms across but the cop cars get stuck. The bridge was named for the popular native San Francisco baseball star after his death in 1969.

20. SBC Park (formerly Pac Bell Park)

In Philip Kaufman's thriller *Twisted*, Jessica Shepard (Ashley Judd), a police officer investigating a series of murders, finds herself at the center when her former lovers start dying around her. This psychological thriller was shot entirely on location in fall 2002. "I'd been wanting to make a film noir in San Francisco for many years," says director Philip Kaufman. Another scene features a found body (with a crab scuttling across it). This was shot near Pier 48, with Pac Bell Park in the background, during the two hours of an actual Giants game. The filming continued through the night. Another body is found floating near Piers 30–32. The set for Judd's apartment was built on a soundstage in the Presidio. Others were built on Treasure Island. Other locations include Red's Java Hut, Hills Brothers Building, Crissy Field, Sea Lions at Pier 39, and City Hall.

21. 701 3rd Street at Townsend

Harry Callahan (Clint Eastwood) pronounces his most famous line, "Go ahead . . . make my day!" at, or near, the McDonald's at 695 3rd Street at Townsend, in the shadow of Pac Bell Park. It was a Burger Island when the third *Dirty Harry* movie, *Sudden Impact*, was filmed here in 1983. Alternatively, the classic scene with his most famous line where Dirty Harry taunts a black gunman holding a waitress hostage may have happened at the Acorn Cafe. (The line, "Go ahead, scumbag, make my day," was originally uttered by Gary Swanson in the 1982 film *Vice Squad*.) There is considerable disagreement over the site of the establishment. Hank Donat disputes the commonly accepted address of Burger Island at 695 3rd Street, saying, "The McDonald's at 701 3rd Street was also Tiger's Burger Joint. Before that, 701 3rd was Doggie Diner No. 29. Some movie guides incorrectly give the McDonald's address as 695 3rd Street and state that the location was a Burger Island restaurant at the time Eastwood filmed there. However, Burger Island was alive and well at 695 3rd Street in January 2003. Burger Island occupied #701 from 1991 to 1996. Between Tiger's and Burger Island #701 was Fats Burger and Fat Cat Burgers." The controversy may continue, but the intersection still resounds with Dirty Harry's most famous line.

22. Hills Brothers Plaza
The Embarcadero at Harrison Street

In *Sneakers* (1992) this waterfront complex, formerly a coffee manufacturing plant, is the site of the handoff where Martin Bishop (Robert Redford) narrowly escapes disaster when Donald Crease (Sidney Poitier) calls him back to the car to take a call from his "mother." The maroon Volkswagen Karmann Ghia convertible driven by Redford (in the handoff scene) is the same vehicle driven by Mike Myers in *So I Married an Axe Murderer*—also filmed in San Francisco—the following year. In *A Smile Like Yours* (1997), Danny and Jennifer Robertson (Greg Kinnear and Lauren Holly), desperately trying to have a baby, make repeated trips to the fertility clinic located there. On several occasions Marianne Muellerleile as Nurse Wheeler intimidates Kinnear on his way to the masturbatorium. In one scene, as the couple exits the facility, they are confronted with kids everywhere. A girl on a bike runs into Kinnear and her mother lashes out at him.

Philip Kaufman also filmed a scene from *Twisted* with Ashley Judd at the Hills Brothers Building in 2004.

23. Kennedy Hotel
226 Embarcadero at Howard Street

Called "Hotel Daniels" in *Bullitt* (1968), this is where Johnny Ross and Carl Stanton are shot by two hit men in room #634. The elevated Embarcadero freeway ran outside the hotel's west side, but both highway and hotel were victims of the 1989 Loma Prieta earthquake. The corporate headquarters for The Gap, Inc. stands in the hotel's place today.

SOMA (South of Market)

24. Hall of Justice
850 Bryant at 7th Street

In the 1967 pilot for Raymond Burr's *Ironside* television series, both the old Hall of Justice near Kearny and Washington, and the new Hall of Justice here, were used for filming. The old one was torn down in 1969 and replaced with the Chinatown Holiday Inn. In the first of the

Dirty Harry flicks, this building appears in the opening sequence with bells tolling to a stone memorial, "in tribute to the police officers of San Francisco who gave their lives in the line of duty," echoing director Don Siegel's similar tribute at the beginning of *The Lineup* (1958).

25. The End Up
401 6th Street at Harrison

Barhoppers line up on the sidewalk to get into the End Up after the rave in *Groove* (2000).

26. San Francisco Studios
375 7th Street at Harrison

Gala parties in the summer of 1985 celebrated San Francisco Studios' new facilities featuring three soundstages with a total of 30,000 square feet. San Francisco Studios was headed by Roberta Smith Riley, a former location scout for *The Streets of San Francisco* (1972–77) and for films, and funded in the amount of $2 million by two dozen investors. Only one film, *Telephone* (1987), was shot completely at San Francisco Studios before it declared bankruptcy in 1990.

27. 7th Street and Folsom

In *Boys and Girls* (2000), the interior of "Brainwash," a combination laundromat and café at 1122 Folsom, is where Jennifer (Claire Forlani) jumps up and starts asking the clientele about "Mr. Right," posing such existential questions as "What if there is no such thing as love?"

Controversy over the San Francisco filming of *Basic Instinct* (1992) centered on its stereotypical depiction of an ice pick–wielding lesbian played by Sharon Stone. When *Sentinel* gay newspaper publisher and bar owner Ray Chalker rented his Rawhide II, a well-known gay country-western bar located at 280 7th Street, to the production company Carolco to shoot a short scene, demonstrators passed out flyers saying "Greed is Ray Chalker's Basic Instinct." Just 10 years later, Stone was an international superstar (and San Franciscan), Hollywood's portrayal of sexual minorities had improved, a sequel to *Basic Instinct* had fallen apart in development, and Chalker was out of business.

28. South Park

Between 2nd and 3rd Streets, Brannan and Bryant Streets

Once a highly desirable residential neighborhood, before cable cars climbed to the hilltop mansions halfway to the stars in the late 19th century, the elliptical South Park hit the skids in the 20th century until the dot-com boom. It found itself at the center of the new high tech industry in the 1990s, only to fall again with the dot-com bust. Indie film *Dopamine* chronicles the exploits of some latecomer South Park computer geeks in 2003. Named for the natural pleasure drug that human beings produce when in love, *Dopamine* explores the ups and downs of Rand (John Livingston), the creator of a computer-animated bird ("Koi-koi"), and his romancing of a teacher, Sarah (Sabrina Lloyd), who lets her students use the software on a trial run. The action centers on the offices at 7 South Park and Caffé Centro, a coffee shop at the intersection of Jack London (Center) Street and South Park.

29. *San Francisco Chronicle*

901 Mission Street at 5th

Mike Myers as Charlie Mackenzie goes here to the offices of the fictional *San Francisco Globe* to investigate the story of the killer on the loose in *So I Married an Axe Murderer* (1993).

American beauty Lizzy (Candice Bergen) works here in Lina Wertmüller's first English-language film, *A Night Full of Rain* (1978), and her Italian paramour Paolo (Giancarlo Giannini) is seen waiting for her outside the building in a long shot.

30. 180 Manchester Street
Bernal Heights

Bernal Heights is a quiet hillside village south of city center that is perhaps best remembered as the neighborhood where Patty Hearst, kidnapped by the Symbionese Liberation Army, was finally found in 1975. Wayne Wang used it when he filmed Amy Tan's bestselling novel, *The Joy Luck Club,* about Chinese American mothers and daughters in 1993. This residence is the cool modern home of the chic, successful Waverly Jong as played by Tamlyn Tamita.

31. Hunters Point

In *It Came from Beneath the Sea*, scientists track the movement of a giant octopus threatening San Francisco from this southern vantage point, now plagued by remnants of nuclear waste. In the classic 1955 black-and-white B-movie, the creature looms in the waters near San Francisco amidst a love triangle of scientists who try to solve the mystery.

32. Candlestick Park
Candlestick Point, Bay View

The Giants officially named their new stadium Candlestick Park on March 3, 1959. In Blake Edwards's *Experiment in Terror* (1962), Kelly Sherwood (Lee Remick) is given a ticket to the S.F. Giants playing Los Angeles on Friday, August 18, 1961, in the upper stands. (It cost $2.50). After the game, she is accosted in the crowded corridors by a hooded creep, Red Lynch (Ross Martin). After a shoot-out with the police he runs onto the field and is shot down on the pitcher's mound. The end is a series of retreating shots of the stadium. *The Fan* (1996) starring Wesley Snipes and Robert DeNiro was filmed by Tony Scott at Candlestick Park. DeNiro is in *The King of Comedy* mode as crazed hanger-on Gil Renard, who is obsessed with most valuable player Bobby Rayburn (Snipes).

Candlestick Park, circa 1960s. *Courtesy of San Francisco History Center, San Francisco Public Library*

33. Cow Palace
2600 Geneva Avenue and Santos Street

When the 1915 Pan-Pacific International Exposition's huge livestock display proved to be one of its most popular attractions, local business leaders resolved to build a permanent structure in San Francisco to house a great animal livestock exposition. In 1925 the San Francisco

Exposition Company was formed to finance the project, and the land was purchased in the Marina District, the site of the 1915 fair. As the economy worsened during the 1930s depression, resistance developed to using public funds for construction of a livestock pavilion. Benny Horne, in the *San Francisco News*, asked, "Why, when people are starving, should money be spent on a 'palace for cows'?" The phrase was turned around, and the now world-famous name was born. In 1935, after relocating from the original site, ground was broken, and through the WPA Program, the construction of the Cow Palace employed thousands of previously unemployed workers.

Since opening in April 1941 with the Western Classic Holstein Show, the Cow Palace has welcomed more than 50 million visitors. During World War II the huge structure, rented by the federal government for $1 per year, was filled with troops embarking for the war zone. As the war progressed, the pavilion was converted into a huge repair garage. In 1948, the Ringling Bros. and Barnum & Bailey Circus started its tenure as the Cow Palace's oldest continuous renter, and the following year legislation was passed officially opening the facility to general public use. A wide variety of events were held in the arena, including boxing, Disney on Ice, political conventions, roller derby, Golden Gate Kennel Club Dog Show, tennis, wrestling, professional basketball, and ice hockey. The Palace has hosted appearances by the Royal Canadian Mounted Police, Liberace, the Billy Graham Crusade, John F. Kennedy, Evel Knievel, the Beatles, the Rolling Stones, Elvis Presley, the Grateful Dead, Santana, ZZ Top, Yes, Paul McCartney & Wings, Neil Diamond, Elton John, U2, and Prince.

The Right Stuff (1983), Philip Kaufman's adaptation of Tom Wolfe's bestselling book, recounts the history of the U.S. space program from Chuck Yeager breaking the sound barrier to the Mercury 7 astronauts. The indoor barbecue party set on July 4, 1962, in the Houston Astrodome was shot here over a period of three days. The scene featured 3,000 extras in period costumes, including 100 members of the Mountain View High School Marching Band, cheerleaders, and flag team.

Downtown, the Financial District, Chinatown, and Nob Hill

In *Swingin' Along*, inept delivery boy Tommy Noonan rides up Powell Street. Unsuccessful at a variety of creative projects until his motorcycle is destroyed, he decides to give songwriting a shot and, under the gaze of con man Peter Marshall, enters a tune in a contest. Barbara Eden, Ray Charles, Roger Williams, and Bobby Vee appear in this 1962 musical, which was also screened under the title *Double Trouble*. Courtesy of San Francisco History Center, San Francisco Public Library

This tour begins with the Hilton Hotel and weaves through the downtown area, circling around Union Square before heading into the Financial District. From there, it goes into Chinatown and ends up in Nob Hill. Because the locations are relatively close to one another and parking is challenging, we recommend searching for these sites on foot.

Downtown and the Financial District

This chapter includes the distinct but adjoining neighborhoods of Nob Hill, Union Square, and the Financial District. Nob Hill is the site of tony hotels and residences on the hill overlooking the bay. Union Square is the central plaza surrounded by an internationally renowned shopping district. The Financial District is the place where many major financial and investment institutions are located. Filmmakers have used all these areas as sites in movies from *Experiment in Terror* (1962) to *Vertigo* (1958) to *Nina Takes a Lover* (1994). Television shows such as *Midnight Caller* (1988–91), *The Streets of San Francisco* (1972–77), and *Nash Bridges* (1996–2001) also did extensive shooting in these neighborhoods.

1. **Hilton Hotel**
    333 O'Farrell Street at Mason
    "Hotel Bristol," at "888" O'Farrell Street, was the scene of much of the mayhem in *What's Up, Doc?* Peter Bogdanovich's 1972 screwball comedy pays homage to 1930s comedies like Howard Hawks's *Bringing Up Baby* (1938) by having Barbra Streisand's free-spirited character wreak

havoc on Ryan O'Neal's life as a stuffy, spacey musicologist. Four guests check into the hotel on the same day, with identical red plaid overnight bags. The first bag contains diamonds, the second underwear, the third prehistoric rocks, and the fourth top-secret papers. The bags are continually stolen, switched, and mistaken by various characters in the film, played by Madeline Kahn, Kenneth Mars, and Austin Pendleton, among others. Many of the high jinks take place at the hotel: at a formal banquet, everybody winds up under the table; in a hotel corridor, people pop in and out of doors as the elevator opens; a staid reception turns into a pie fight. Hotel rooms are broken into, curtains are set aflame, and people are trapped out on ledges without their clothes. The Hilton will never be the same.

2. Curran Theater
445 Geary Street at Mason

We all know there is no Shubert Theatre in San Francisco. This piece of trivia becomes all-important in *All About Eve* (1950), the classic look at the backstage theater life of aging actress Margo Channing (Bette Davis) and Eve Harrington (Anne Baxter), the young woman who insinuates herself into Channing's life. Here, for two week's beginning, on April 11, 1950, the cast of *All About Eve* filmed interiors of *Aged in Wood*, the play written for Channing by Gary Merrill's character. During filming, writer and director Joseph L. Mankiewicz and the cast stayed at the Fairmont Hotel. Theater exteriors were filmed at the John Golden Theater on New York's West 46th Street.

3. Coffee Dan's
O'Farrell Street at Powell

The Jazz Singer, the legendary first talkie ("Wait a minute, wait a minute, you ain't heard nothing yet") is actually a silent film with several musical and talking sequences. Directed by Alan Crosland and starring Al Jolson, it revolutionized the motion picture industry when it was released in 1927. After Cantor Rabinowitz's son Jakie tells his heartbroken mother that he is going to be on the stage, he runs away. Years later, in San Francisco, Jakie has become a singer performing at Coffee Dan's restaurant. When he sings the poignant song "Dirty Hands, Dirty Face," followed by the jazz tune "Toot, Toot, Tootsie," vaudeville dancer Mary Dale, who is in the audience, is intrigued.

4. "Drayton Gallery"
Sutter Street between Powell and Mason

In 1967 Stanley Kramer made *Guess Who's Coming to Dinner* starring Katharine Hepburn and Spencer Tracy as Christina and Matt Drayton. Their daughter Katharine Houghton meets handsome doctor Sidney Poitier on vacation in Hawaii, and after 10 days they decide to marry. When she brings him home to meet her parents they are less broadminded about the issue of his being "Negro" than she had anticipated. Set in San Francisco, the film used only a few actual locations. When Poitier and Houghton stop at Hepburn's art gallery, the assistant is unsettled by the idea of the two young people in love. The fictional gallery is obvi-

Al Jolson as *The Jazz Singer* (1927) performs in San Francisco at Coffee Dan's. *Courtesy of Pacific Film Archive, University of California, Berkeley*

ously intended to be one of Sutter Street's tonier galleries. In the exterior shots, one can see the Cartwright Hotel at 524 across the street.

5.   The St. Francis Hotel
335 Powell Street at Geary

At the turn of the century, plans were announced to make San Francisco the "Paris of the West" by building the finest hotel on the Pacific Coast. After the original St. Francis Hotel, requiring two years of construction and costing $2.5 million, opened on March 21, 1904, it immediately became the center of the city's social, literary, and artistic life by hosting high society and presenting musical entertainments and art exhibits.

When the 1906 earthquake struck at just after five in the morning on April 18, the multi-storied St. Francis withstood the quake, unlike most of its neighbors. (Legend has it that after a night on the town, the young actor John Barrymore went upstairs to his room and slept until the final alarm sounded.) The subsequent fires that broke out and rolled through neighborhoods reached Union Square, filled with homeless quake victims, early the next day. Novelist Jack London reported that the St. Francis was the last building there to catch fire. Though its interior was partially destroyed, the superstructure withstood the flames. The hotel's rehabilitation took on significance, symbolizing San Francisco's recovery from disaster. It reopened November 30, 1907. The Magneta clock, the first master clock brought to the West, was installed in the hotel's Powell Street lobby; "meet me at the clock" continues to be a popular way to arrange a rendezvous.

San Francisco became a favored getaway for much-scrutinized stars to blow off steam away from reporters eager for a scandalous story. In 1921 Fatty Arbuckle, the second most popular screen comedian—

after Charlie Chaplin—hosted a party in his suite of rooms (1219, 1220, and 1221). Hollywood starlet Virginia Rappe claimed the portly actor had ravaged her, and she died a few days later of a ruptured bladder. The tabloids had a field day, and despite the fact that Arbuckle was acquitted after three trials, his career never recovered.

In her memoir, *Being and Becoming*, Myrna Loy recounts how she went to San Francisco to shoot exteriors for *After the Thin Man* (1936). She traveled by train with William Powell and Jean Harlow, who were engaged. The management had reserved the Fleishhacker Suite for Powell and Loy, assuming they were married ("Already they considered us a couple after only five pictures together!"). Loy continues, "We couldn't be obvious about the situation with the press on our heels."

Conventioneers had taken every other room, except a little hall bedroom downstairs. Harlow suggested putting Powell downstairs and she and Loy shared the suite. "The mix-up brought me one of my most cherished friendships," Loy enthuses. "We worked terribly hard on that San Francisco location. We shot all over town, with about sixty principals and crew and hundreds of local extras; but [*Thin Man* director] Woody Van Dyke always liked a festive company, so there were lots of parties."

In Rudolph Maté's 1950 classic film noir *D.O.A.*, Frank Bigelow (Edmond O'Brien) comes to town for a vacation from his job as a CPA in Banning, California, and stays in room 618 at the St. Francis Hotel. O'Brien has inadvertently arrived for the last night of "Market Week" so the hotel is filled with traveling salesmen entertaining female buyers, who invite him to join them on the town. The next morning, feeling ill, he leaves the hotel and hops on a cable car heading downhill toward Market Street. In the next scene he is seen heading uphill toward the top of Nob Hill. He undergoes a medical examination and is horrified to learn he has suffered radiation poisoning and has only a short time to live.

In the opening scene of *The Candidate* (1972), a candidate offers his concession speech in one of the hotel's luxurious ballrooms. Then the political machine prepares to move to California. (Apparently they were supposed to be on the East Coast.) Once in California, Bill McKay (Robert Redford), a lawyer with charisma and integrity, is noticed by the Democratic Party and persuaded to run for the Senate against an apparently unassailable incumbent. He is assured he has nothing to lose, but eventually gets caught up in the political machine, sells out, and wins the election.

6. Union Square
Post, Geary, Powell, and Stockton Streets

In the opening scene of Francis Ford Coppola's *The Conversation* (1974), Cindy Williams and Frederic Forrest are walking around Union Square, unaware that their conversation is being recorded. Popular mime Robert Shields adds verisimilitude to the mix of musicians, shoppers, and others who frequent the downtown plaza. Gene Hackman plays Harry Caul, a nationally known expert on surveillance, hired by "the Director" to record the conversations of two of his employees. Some years previously, Harry's work directly led to three murders, and now he has reason to fear that it will happen again.

Famed San Francisco mime Robert Shields, who regularly performed in Union Square, appears with star Gene Hackman in Francis Ford Coppola's *The Conversation*. *Courtesy of Pacific Film Archive, University of California, Berkeley*

In *High Crimes* (2002), Ashley Judd and hubby James Caviezel go into San Francisco from their house, supposedly in Marin, but filmed in Calabasas, in Southern California. The entire Union Square sequence, shot on two nights, December 17 and 18, 2000, had originally been planned for December 11 and 12, but after arriving that Monday evening, the entire shoot was canceled when Judd became ill. The FBI takedown was shot on Maiden Lane adjacent Union Square.

In *Getting Even with Dad* (1993), while Glenne Headley, Ted Danson, and Macaulay Culkin are shopping (and hiding stolen coins) at Neiman Marcus, Saul Rubinek and Gailard Sartain are searching for the coins on Maiden Lane. The arched brickwork behind Rubinek when he tries to measure a young boy's "giant steps" is the former V. C. Morris Gift Shop at 140 Maiden Lane, designed by Frank Lloyd Wright in 1948.

Union Square circa 1960. *High Crimes* (2002) was the last movie ever filmed at *this* Union Square. A week after shooting, the park was closed for almost two years for a major redesign and renovation. The new Union Square opened on Thursday, July 25, 2002. One of the few retained elements is the central column. *Courtesy San Francisco History Center, San Francisco Public Library*

7. Neiman Marcus
150 Stockton Street at Geary

The site of City of Paris, more an institution than a department store, was rooted in old San Francisco's City of Paris Dry Goods Company. In the 1970s the beaux arts building that housed it was deemed obsolete and incompatible with the requirements of a contemporary department store. After much debate between developers and preservationists, the building was demolished and replaced in 1980 with a design by prominent architects Phillip Johnson and John Burgee, who moved the elegant City of Paris leaded glass skylight from its original location, incorporating it into the modern structure.

The opening aerial shot of Union Square in *The Conversation* was taken from atop the City of Paris department store. Brendan Fraser as *George of the Jungle* (1997) refers to Neiman Marcus as a "big shiny cave" when Ursula Stanhope (Leslie Mann) takes him shopping there for clothes. Because they have just come to town from the jungles of Africa, he has no suitable attire. Mann has temporarily lent him a dress and hat, and when Fraser wanders through Union Square cross-dressed, no one bats an eye.

8. "Davidson's Pet Shop"
Powell Street at Geary

In the opening scene of Hitchcock's classic *The Birds* (1963), Tippi Hedren walks west on Geary, turning south on Powell to enter Davidson's Pet Store, a fictitious location on the southwest corner, where a Casual Corner, purveyor of women's clothing, now stands. It is here that Hitchcock makes his cameo appearance, walking out of the shop with his two Sealyham terriers. The shop's interiors were re-created in Hollywood, based on an actual San Francisco shop, Robison's House of Pets, located on nearby Maiden Lane.

9. Hotel Bijou
111 Mason Street at Eddy

Inspired by San Francisco's rich cinematic history, the Hotel Bijou is adorned with movie palace stylings, dramatic Hollywood portraits, and a mini–movie theater in the lobby. Each guest room is named for a motion picture shot in San Francisco, with original movie stills as decorative room accents. A double feature of San Francisco–based films is screened each evening in the Petit Theatre Bijou.

10. Marriott Hotel
55 4th Street at Market

This Anthony Lumsden–designed building has been controversial since it opened in 1989. Generally criticized by architects for its ersatz art deco addition to the skyline, it has been variously likened to a Wurlitzer jukebox, a ziggurat, and a CD player.

In *How Stella Got Her Groove Back*, Kevin Rodney Sullivan's 1998 adaptation of Terry McMillan's best-selling novel, Angela Bassett plays a highly successful, 40-something San Francisco stockbroker. This is the office building where she works. Little of the film was shot in the Bay Area except for a brief establishing shot showing Bassett returning to her Marin County home. Even the San Francisco International Airport is actually the Los Angeles International Airport.

11. 856 Market Street between Powell and Stockton

Nine to Five, Colin Higgins's 1980 office comedy, stars Jane Fonda, Lily Tomlin, Dabney Coleman, Sterling Hayden, and Dolly Parton in her screen debut. Tomlin is the efficient office manager, Fonda is the newcomer, trying out her first job after a divorce, and Parton is the secretary, whom everybody in the office thinks is having an affair with her boss. These three female employees of a "sexist, egotistical, lying, hypocritical bigot" inadvertently find their chance to take revenge. Some of the morning rush hour scenes in the main title sequence during Parton's peppy title song were filmed in downtown San Francisco. Recognizable only to locals are the Albert S. Samuels clock, built in 1915, the MUNI buses, and the backs of the famous Brown twins, Vivian and Marion, in matching handbags, wigs, and leopard coats. The action immediately shifts to Fonda in Los Angeles.

12. Emporium
835–865 Market Street at 5th Street

The Emporium building was built in 1896 and rebuilt in 1908. It was San Francisco's oldest department store when, in 1996, it followed the fate of the city's other famous department stores, I. Magnin, City of Paris, and the White House, and permanently closed its doors. The vacant building is part of a $500 million redevelopment project that includes a Bloomingdale's store, office space, and a luxury hotel.

In *Woman on the Run* (1950), Ross Elliott as Frank Johnson innocently witnesses a murder before going on the lam. He works here, at the fictitious Hart & Winston, as a window dresser. His wife, Ann Sheridan as Eleanor Johnson, spends the entire film noir searching San Francisco sites for him.

13. Burritt Alley
Off Bush Street between Powell and Stockton

A plaque informs passersby that "On Approximately This Spot, Miles Archer, Partner of Sam Spade, Was Done in by Brigid O'Shaughnessy." It fails to mention that the crime occurred in Dashiell Hammett's classic American detective novel *The Maltese Falcon*, the basis for John Huston's directorial debut in 1941. In the quintessentially San Francisco story, Sam Spade's (Humphrey Bogart) investigation of his partner's murder leads to encounters with a host of strange characters all after one thing, a statue of a falcon reputed to contain priceless jewels.

Burritt Street remains little changed from the days when Hammett himself was skulking around the neighborhood, except for an apartment house that went up at the end of the alley in the 1930s. "Spade & Archer's Detective Agency" was reportedly located at 111 Sutter Street near Montgomery.

While this novel epitomizes San Francisco's unique character as a location, the film, which stars Humphrey Bogart, Mary Astor, Gladys George, Peter Lorre, and Sydney Greenstreet and used the working title *The Gent from Frisco*, was filmed exclusively in Hollywood.

Jerome Cowan as Miles Archer and Humphrey Bogart as Sam Spade confer on a Hollywood set in *The Maltese Falcon* (1941). *Courtesy of Pacific Film Archive, University of California, Berkeley*

14. Stockton "Quiet Thru" Tunnel
Stockton Street at Sutter

At noon on December 29, 1914, Mayor James Rolph opened the Stockton Tunnel, making the downtown shopping district accessible to the 40,000 residents of North Beach. The tile-lined tunnel goes under Nob Hill from Sutter to Sacramento Street.

In 1974's *Freebie and the Bean*, directed by Richard Rush, James Caan and Alan Arkin are police detectives protecting a bad guy from worse guys. Wonderful San Francisco locations abound, though they're not represented realistically. For example, a car goes into the Broadway Tunnel and comes out of the Stockton Tunnel.

Geographical realism is again compromised in Ron Underwood's 1993 film, *Heart and Souls*. Robert Downey Jr. plays a man attached to four spirit guides, all San Franciscans who died with unfinished business when the bus they were riding careened over the top of the north portal of the Stockton Tunnel. In reality, buses run *through* the tunnel, not on the street above. The "Quiet Thru" sign is to discourage motorists from honking their horns while driving through the tunnel.

Chris O'Donnell is chased through the Stockton Tunnel by a thousand hopeful brides in the 1999 film *The Bachelor*.

In *The Game*, the Van Orten brothers (Michael Douglas and Sean Penn) get a flat tire on Stockton Street, just above the tunnel. Paranoid Penn flees down the tunnel steps and runs off toward Union Square while Douglas stays behind and receives a mysterious call from a pay phone in the laudromat on the southwest corner of Bush and Stockton. From there he grabs a car for a wild ride that continues on Harrison Street and ends up in the bay.

15. Sutter-Stockton Garage
330 Sutter Street at Stockton

Gary Sinyor's 1999 comedy *The Bachelor* was based on the 1925 Buster Keaton movie *Seven Chances*. Jimmie Shannon (Chris O'Donnell) watches his single friends get married one by one. He isn't too worried until his girlfriend Anne (Renee Zellweger) catches the bouquet at a friend's wedding. He finally decides to propose to her, but botches it. Later, dressed in a tuxedo, with a priest waiting in a limousine, O'Donnell looks for her, to try again. He tracks her down, just as she's boarding a

helicopter to the airport for a flight to Athens, but Zellweger senses that his heart still isn't in it, and again declines. The "heliport" is actually the roof of this convenient and economical parking garage. After Zellweger leaves town, Jimmie finds out that his recently deceased grandfather's will stipulates that he gets his $100 million fortune only if he's married by 6:05 P.M. on his 30th birthday—27 hours hence. Unable to find Anne, Jimmie begins tracking down his past girlfriends to find a wife.

16. Claude Lane at Bush Street

First Kim Novak as Madeleine, then Jimmy Stewart as Scottie, park their cars on Claude Lane and pass through a brick door (now a window) that stands in for the back entrance of Podesta Baldocchi flower shop. At the time Baldocchi, San Francisco's premier florist, was actually located at 224 Grant Street between Sutter and Post, where its interiors were filmed by Hitchcock for *Vertigo* in 1958. Podesta Baldocchi ultimately relocated to Fourth and Brannan streets, South of Market, and its former space was occupied by North Beach Leather.

17. Lotta's Fountain
Market, Kearny, and Third Streets

The lighthouse-inspired fountain was cast in Philadelphia, shipped to San Francisco via Cape Horn, and donated to the people of San Francisco in 1875 by Charlotte Mignon (Lotta) Crabtree.

Crabtree began her career as a young girl performing for miners in gold country and went on to become one of America's most popular stage performers. After the 1906 earthquake, the fountain, one of the few remaining structures on Market Street, became a central meeting place for San Franciscans and a message center where people could find information about survivors and which buildings were still standing. The oldest surviving monument in San Francisco, and a National Historical Landmark, it was lovingly restored to its original glory in 1999. Survivors of the 1906 earthquake return to the site at 5:13 A.M. every April 18 to stand in witness to San Franciscan resiliency.

W. S. Van Dyke's *San Francisco* (1936) opens with people pouring champagne into a very accurate reproduction of Lotta's fountain on New Year's Eve 1905. Jeannette MacDonald arrives at Clark Gable's Paradise gambling hall and beer garden looking for work as a singer. After embarrassing her, Gable hires her. Nob Hill socialite Jack Holt and Maestro William Ricciardi of the Tivoli Opera House hear her and offer her a chance to do opera, but Gable has her under a two-year contract, which she sorrowfully stands by. Later she does leave for the Tivoli, where she is soon the star while Gable's place is closed down. At the annual "Chicken Ball," MacDonald, out of guilt, sings a rousing "San Francisco" on behalf of Gable, her former lover and employer. When she wins the $10,000 prize, a resentful Gable refuses to accept her charity, and throws the prize money to the floor. As she storms out of the hall, the famous earthquake begins to rumble. Buildings collapse and streets split wide

open. When the city catches fire, the army dynamites whole sections of the town to prevent its spread. At the end of the movie, the citizens of San Francisco sing the "Battle Hymn of the Republic." As they look out over the ruins, the scene dissolves into a view of the contemporary (circa 1936) city from Twin Peaks.

18. Sheraton Palace Hotel
2 New Montgomery Street at Market

William Ralston commissioned an architect to study Europe's finest hotels and, in the process of financing his $5-million-dollar project, exhausted his banking empire. Weeks before the Palace's grand opening, he learned that the Bank of California would close, and the following day his body was found floating in the San Francisco Bay. His partner, Senator William Sharon, fostered his dream by finishing the project and on October 2, 1875, the Palace Hotel opened its doors. Among the new hotel's features were four hydraulic elevators known as "rising rooms," allowing guests to reach the hotel's top floors effortlessly, and rooms equipped with an electronic call button.

The Palace survived the 1906 earthquake, but was overtaken by the ensuing fires, and closed its doors for the first restoration. The famous opera tenor Enrico Caruso, a guest there during the earthquake, vowed he would never return, and didn't. Three years later the carriage entrance, now transformed into the Garden Court, was recognized as one of the world's most beautiful public spaces. With its incredible architecture, domed stained glass ceiling, and Austrian crystal chandeliers, the Garden Court became the site for some of the nation's most prestigious events. In 1919 President Woodrow Wilson hosted two luncheons there in support of the Versailles Treaty, which ended World War I. In 1945 the official banquet honoring the opening session of the United Nations was held in the Garden Court. In January 1989 the Palace closed its doors for a major restoration, reopening two years and millions of dollars later.

Herbie the Love Bug drives through the Garden Court in 1974's *Herbie Rides Again*. In *Jade* (1995), William Friedkin directed a script by Joe Eszterhas about a police investigation of the murder of a wealthy businessman. In an early scene David Caruso and Chazz Palminteri take turns dancing with Linda Fiorentino at a Black and White Ball. (The Sheraton Palace is never a venue for this real-life biannual fundraiser, one of the city's largest, benefitting the San Francisco Symphony's education programs for over 75,000 young people.) Local dance instructor Cynthia Glinka was responsible for choreographing the dancing so that there were "no holes" among the dance extras, as the camera follows the lead players around the parquet. Caruso rushes out to make a phone call and viewers get a glimpse of the famous large Pied Piper painting by Maxfield Parrish in the bar.

In a scene in *The Game* (1997), Michael Douglas is told by a hotel desk clerk in the lobby that his younger brother Sean Penn has destroyed his room and the authorities have been called. At the end of the film, Douglas tries to kill himself by jumping off the roof of the fictional "CRS" building. He crashes through the glass ceiling of the Palace's Garden Court Restaurant. To his astonishment he lands on a large pillow and finds himself at his own surprise birthday party.

19. Nina M. Designs
52 2nd Street at Jessie

The Bachelor, Gary Sinyor's 1999 romantic comedy, ends here. On the fire escape of this building (which coincidentally houses Nina M. Designs, purveyor of wedding announcements), Chris O'Donnell and Renee Zellweger are married by priest James Cromwell. Below them the entire intersection is filled with hundreds of women in wedding dresses. Filmed in mid-December, the extras were very cold and wrapped their shoulders with aluminum foil between takes. More trivia: Zellweger's bouquet changes from peach-colored roses to yellow flowers at least three times, apparently because of different takes.

20. McKesson Building
600 Market Street at Post Street

Stanley Donen's 1967 original *Bedazzled* starred Dudley Moore as Stanley Moon, a short-order cook hopelessly in love with waitress Margaret Spencer (Eleanor Bron). Hoping to win the girl with seven wishes, he sells his soul to the devil, Peter Cook. Raquel Welch appears as Lilian Lust. In Harold Ramis's 2000 remake, Brendan Fraser is in a similarly lowly job, a computer programmer, but this time the devil is a curvacious Brit, played by Elizabeth Hurley, who wreaks havoc on Fraser's wishes to woo Frances O'Connor. The "Synedyne Building" ("Synergy + Dynamics") is where lonely and nerdy computer programmer Brendan Fraser holds the door open for hundreds of incoming employees before going upstairs to his loser cubicle, where he is surrounded by colleagues who barely contain their disdain for him. Many of the downtown rush scenes were shot around Market and Montgomery.

In *The Net* (1995), computer programmer Angela Bennett (Sandra Bullock), while investigating abnormalities on the Internet, is chased in and out of an AIDS march at the corner.

21. Crocker-Anglo National Bank
1 Montgomery Street at Post

Architect Willis Polk designed this 13-story building for the First National Bank of San Francisco (in 1870, the first bank to be nation-

ally chartered in California, which consolidated with Crocker in 1926). The steel-frame building with reinforced concrete floors was completed in 1908 in a record-setting 10 months at a cost of $1,350,000, as part of the post-earthquake construction boom. It is faced with granite and Indiana sandstone. A rotunda supported by granite Doric columns marks the entrance to an opulent marble banking room in which massive fluted columns support a gold-leafed coffered ceiling, a design element taken from the Paris Opera.

In *Experiment in Terror* (1962), Blake Edwards's black-and-white psychological thriller, Lee Remick as Kelly Sherwood gets a phone call from a man with an asthmatic voice (Ross Martin) who plans to use her to steal $100,000 from the bank where she works as a teller. If she doesn't cooperate or if she tells the police, he threatens to kill her and/or her teenage sister Toby (Stephanie Powers). However, she manages to contact FBI agent John Ripley (Glenn Ford), who races around the city following leads. This is the bank, interior and exterior, where Kelly Sherwood works.

The alley street behind the bank, where Kelly uses the parking garage and lunches at the restaurant, is now part of the Crocker Galleria.

22. Flatiron Building
540–548 Market Street at Sansome and Post

Crazy Like a Fox, the CBS television series, ran from 1984 to 1986. Jack Rubenstein played Harrison K. Fox, a conservative young attorney trying to develop a successful law practice in San Francisco to support his wife, Cindy (Penny Peyser), and their young son, Josh (Robby Kiger). Fox's unconventional father, Harry, played by Jack Warden, was a lovable con artist and private eye, constantly getting involved in murder cases and complicating his son's life. The office window marked "Harrison 'Harry' Fox," seen at the start of every episode, remained on this building until 2001.

23. Citicorp Center
1 Sansome Street at Sutter

One Sansome Street at Market is a neoclassical building designed by Albert Pissis in 1910 for the London-Paris National Bank, added onto by George Kelham, and gutted to become the entrance portico to the Citicorp Center (1984) by Pereira and Associates at its rear. This is one of several examples of integrating banking institutions into modern structures. A 30-ton remnant from the facade of the Holbrooke Building, which stood on the site of the Citicorp Center, has been incorporated into the Citicourt Café on the ground floor. A wall display on the left as you enter the café chronicles the history of the site. Inside the portico on the right is a statue, the Star Figure, which is a reproduction of a parapet ornament sculpted by A. Sterling Calder for the 1915 Panama Pacific International Exposition. In *Sweet November* (2001), Keanu Reeves's character Nelson has a business lunch inside Citicorp Center.

24. Pacific Stock Exchange
301 Pine Street at Sansome

The Pacific Stock Exchange was designed in 1915 by J. Milton Dyer and remodeled in 1930 by noted San Francisco architects Miller & Pflueger under the direction of Timothy L. Pflueger. The imposing structure's facade of stately Doric columns fronts on Pine Street. The two monumental sculptures that flank its entrance are the works of sculptor Ralph Stackpole and are named "Agriculture," represented by feminine figures, and "Industry," represented by masculine figures. Believing that great art should be an integral part of great architecture, Pflueger, one of California's earliest architects to incorporate classic European modernism into his work, commissioned a number of the era's most renowned artists and craftsmen to work on the project. Especially noteworthy is a fresco by Mexican muralist Diego Rivera on an interior stairway.

Philip Kaufman's 1983 adaptation of Tom Wolfe's bestselling book *The Right Stuff* recounts the early history of the U.S. space program, from the breaking of the sound barrier by Chuck Yeager to the advances made by the Mercury 7 astronauts. The film stars Sam Shepard, Scott Glenn, Ed Harris, Dennis Quaid, Fred Ward, Barbara Hershey, Kim Stanley, Veronica Cartwright, and Jeff Goldblum, among many others. San Francisco's financial district stood in for New York during a ticker tape parade scene. The lighting in this film was carefully matched with that of the

San Francisco's financial district stands in for New York during a ticker tape parade in *The Right Stuff* (1983) starring Ed Harris as John Glenn and Mary Jo Deschanel as his wife, with Donald Moffat as Lyndon B. Johnson.
Courtesy of Pacific Film Archive, University of California, Berkeley

original archival footage also used in the film. Shooting was done on a bank holiday.

25. Transbay Terminal
Mission Street at 1st Street

Opened in 1939, this terminal served the three inter-urban railways that ran on the lower deck of the Bay Bridge. An electric train served Contra Costa County, Sacramento, and Chico (!) on the Sacramento Northern. After the trains stopped running in 1958, the building reopened as the San Francisco terminus for the East Bay's AC Transit system. Currently the site is scheduled to be rebuilt as the largest transportation hub west of New York. In 1999, Juliette Lewis and Giovanni Ribisi ride their bikes here on their first date, though they refuse to call it that, in *The Other Sister* (1999). As soon as they enter the building, however, they are in Union Station in Los Angeles.

In *Getting Even with Dad* (1993), Macaulay Culkin hides a duffle bag in the lockers here. He later has an emotional scene with his father, Ted Danson, who pulls him off a Greyhound bus and promises to be a better father.

26. Fremont Street Exit

In *Dead Pool* (1988) a macabre sports lottery is placing bets on which celebrity is going to die next and crossing names off a list as each of them meets their demise. A serial killer who preys on famous figures enters the scene, dramatically changing the odds. When Clint Eastwood and aggressive television journalist Patricia Clarkson find their names on the list, the game gets too close to home. After Harry's arrest of a gambling kingpin results in a conviction for murder, a group of four thugs follow him off the Bay Bridge and attack him on this underpass. They shoot up Harry's car and try to kill him, but he overpowers and kills them.

27. 75 California Street
At Davis Street

In *A Smile Like Yours* (1997), Lauren Holly and Joan Cusack own a small fragrance store downtown. When they introduce a new perfume, "Seventh Scent," with powerful aphrodiasic qualities, they become wildly successful, with generous offers from investors to buy their discovery.

28. Hyatt Regency
5 Embarcadero Center, bounded by California, Sacramento, Drumm, and Market Streets

The lobby interior of the "Glass Tower" in *The Towering Inferno* is the Hyatt Regency Building's soaring atrium designed by John Portman and completed in 1973. Principal photography finished on September 11, 1974. While the building's exterior was shot at the Bank of America Building, the central heating plant/air conditioning facility and water tank scenes were shot in Century City, and the Glass Tower miniature exteriors were shot in 20th Century Fox Ranch, in Malibu Creek State Park.

The 1979 science fiction adventure *Time After Time*, based on Jack Finney's novel, was filmed by director Nicholas Meyer throughout

San Francisco. H. G. Wells (Malcolm McDowell) has just invented a time machine but hasn't tried it out yet. One of Wells's friends, Jack the Ripper (David Warner), makes his escape using the time machine. McDowell follows Warner into San Francisco of the late 1970s where he meets Amy (Mary Steenburgen), a bank clerk, who teaches Wells about life in the 1970s while they pursue Jack, who is continuing his murderous activities. In its use of the futuristic Hyatt Regency, the film pays homage to William Cameron Menzies's set designs for *Things to Come*, the 1936 film based on H. G. Wells's book *The Shape of Things to Come*, Meyer later discovered that John Portman had also been inspired by Menzies's set. The expansive lobby, the elevator cabins, the rotating Equinox restaurant—all are used to great effect. The foot chase through the adjacent Embarcadero Centers with their distinctive tiles, also designed by Portman, also served as an excellent use of this San Francisco location.

Various characters in *High Anxiety* (1978) stay at this hotel during a psychiatrist convention. The vertiginous architecture adds to the psychosis of Richard Thorndike (Mel Brooks). The location was still considered "modern" at the time of filming, a few years after the hotel opened.

29. Vaillancourt Fountain
Justin Herman Plaza

When the Vaillancourt Fountain was unveiled at Justin Herman Plaza and Four Embarcadero Center in 1971, it was widely reviled. *San Francisco Chronicle* columnist Herb Caen said it looked like a pile of poop, while others were content to merely call it an eyesore. So harsh was public criticism that its embittered creator, French Canadian sculptor Armand Vaillancourt, was run out of town. Built on land cleared for the Embarcadero Freeway and BART, the fountain is built on the site of

former hotels and bars in an area once well populated by seamen. When it's working, the fountain releases thousands of gallons of water from its apertures. A series of large square stepping-stones allows visitors to walk through its roaring presence, and an upper catwalk provides alternate vistas.

In Harold Ramis's *Bedazzled* (2000), Brendan Fraser is dropped out of one of the devil-induced wishes and lands in the Vaillancourt Fountain up to his knees. When he emerges with soggy trousers he complains to the devil, played by Elizabeth Hurley. Unsympathetic, she whines that her "life is a living hell."

30. Ferry Building

From its strategic location at the foot of Market Street at the center of the city's financial, banking, and transportation district, the Ferry Building is the city's primary portal. Its dramatic clock tower has been the icon of the San Francisco waterfront for more than 100 years. Opening in 1898 on the site of the 1875 wooden Ferry House, the Ferry Building became the transportation focal point for anyone arriving by train from the East, as well as for all the East Bay and Marin residents who worked in the city. From the Gold Rush until the 1930s, arrival by

ferryboat was the way most travelers and commuters arrived in the city, as many as 50,000 people a day. The opening of the Bay Bridge in 1936 and the Golden Gate Bridge in 1937, along with mass use of the automobile, rendered the commute by ferry obsolete. By the 1950s, the Ferry Building was used very little, its large open interior filled in, and in 1957 the double-deck Embarcadero Freeway was built across its face. In 1989, the Loma Prieta earthquake caused extensive damage to the freeway, providing the impetus to tear it down in 1991. Extensive renovation of the Ferry Building is now complete, the exterior and main public hall of one of San Francisco's most cherished, cinematic landmarks restored to their original grandeur for use by ferry passengers and the public at large.

In the opening shots of *The Maltese Falcon* (1941), the Ferry Building prominently displays a sign reading "Golden Gate Bridge: Fiesta May 27." Scott Trimble suggests that this advertisement is for the opening of the bridge four years earlier, implying that old stock footage was used in the 1941 John Huston film. One additional stock cityscape looking east along Mission and Howard Streets, ending at the Embarcadero, with Treasure Island and Yerba Buena Island in the distance, firmly establishes the location.

In the classic B movie *It Came from Beneath the Sea*, a giant octopus rises from the Pacific Ocean and threatens to destroy 1955 San Francisco. Directed by Robert Gordon, this was the first film made by the special effects team of Ray Harryhausen and Charles H. Schneer. Kenneth Tobey, Faith Domergue, Ian Keith, and Donald Curtis star as the scientists, involved in a love triangle, who lose the attempt to prevent the huge octopus from strangling and partially destroying the Ferry Building.

Timothy Hutton, a tourist about to be married the next day, has lost one of his shoes in the 1999 feature *SFO*. He searches the city for his missing shoe with the help of the beautiful, and unhappily married, Maria Grazia Cucinotta. Director Alan Jacobs has been quoted as saying, "Time figures heavily in the movie, because it's set on the night that the clocks are set back. We got permission to change the time on the Ferry Building. We have a shot with two guys in harnesses, hanging outside, turning back the hands on the clock. Actually the time was being changed from inside the building. We shot that at around 4:30 in the morning." In contrast to his previous movie set in San Francisco, *Nina Takes a Lover* (1994), Jacobs maintains that *SFO* is "a celebration of San Francisco in the way that Woody Allen's *Manhattan* is a celebration of Manhattan."

Serial (1980), based on Cyra McFadden's novel and directed by Bill Persky, satirizes the mythological inhabitants of Marin County. Commuters Martin Mull and Bill Macy come and go on the "Harbor Emperor" of the Red and White Fleet. Mull spots his kidnapped daughter among purple-clad cultists giving out flowers to Sausalito commuters on the pier behind Ferry Building and attempts to rescue her.

In *Sudden Impact* (1983), the fourth of the *Dirty Harry* series, the only one directed by Clint Eastwood, a serial killer is on the loose in San Francisco, and the police trace a link to a small town farther down the coast. Harry Callahan upsets the press and the mayor and is shipped south, to San Paulo, to investigate. When Eastwood is ambushed at the Ferry Plaza by four hit men, he manages to shoot three, then is chased by more men around the Ferry terminal. He outfoxes and shoots them all.

As *Dr. Dolittle*, Eddie Murphy lunches alfresco at Gabbiano's in 1998. The restaurant behind the Ferry Building has since been renovated.

31. Embarcadero One
Battery Street, between Clay and Sacramento

In 1974 Francis Ford Coppola filmed *The Conversation* entirely on location in San Francisco. Chiefly a character study of wiretapper Harry Caul, this thriller deals with paranoia, invasion of privacy, bugging, and the importance of one's conscience. Gene Hackman is joined by cast members John Cazale, Frederic Forrest, Cindy Williams, Teri Garr, Harrison Ford, and Robert Shields. Hackman's character, a nationally known expert on surveillance, has been hired to record the conversations of two of "the Director's" employees. This is the location of the offices of the Director (a cameo by Robert Duvall), who has apparently hired Gene Hackman to undertake the surveillance. A very young Harrison Ford is the Director's assistant. The adjacent One Maritime Plaza over Front Street between Washington and Clay is also used. The buildings under construction might be the Golden Gateway.

32. Transamerica Building
600 Montgomery Street at Clay

Director Philip Kaufman, in his 1978 remake of Don Siegel's 1956 classic science fiction thriller *Invasion of the Body Snatchers*, moves the setting from a small town to the city of San Francisco. Donald Sutherland starts noticing that people are complaining that their close relatives are acting odd or are different in some strange way. Witnessing an attempted "replacement," Sutherland realizes that he and his friends must escape or suffer the same fate.

Kaufman points out that images of the 48-story Transamerica Pyramid, jokingly referred to by the filmmakers as "pod central," lurk throughout the film. The building, designed by William Pereira, caused a ruckus when it was built in 1972 as the headquarters of Transamerica Corporation, then the parent company of United Artists, which produced the film. Its distinctive silhouette, which diversifies the skyline, has since become a beloved icon.

33. "Barbary Coast"
Pacific Avenue, Jackson, Montgomery, and Sansome Streets

A century or so ago, the eastern flank of the Financial District formed part of the Barbary Coast, where wood from ships, abandoned by prospectors rushing to stake their claim in the Gold Rush, built hotels, bars, stores, and, eventually, the landfill on which the neighborhood of Jackson Square stands today. While other districts attracted more legitimate enterprises, the Barbary Coast became the center of sex, violence, hard drinking, and gambling by rough-and-tumble seamen and would-be prospectors hoping to cash in by other-than-legal means. The Barbary Coast was the home of "Killer's Corner" (Jackson and Kearny), "Deadman's Alley," and "Murder Point," all aptly named for the debauchery that pervaded the neighborhood. Many ships from the Barbary Coast era are still buried under the Financial District.

The term "Barbary Coast," which comes from the pirate coast of North Africa, appears in many film titles: *Flame of Barbary Coast* (1945), *Barbary-Coast Bunny* (1956), *Barbary Coast Gent* (1944), *Midnight on the Barbary Coast* (1929), *Law of the Barbary Coast* (1949), *Last Night of the*

Barbary Coast (1915), and *Camille of the Barbary Coast* (1925) as well as the 1975–76 ABC television series *Barbary Coast.*

In Howard Hawks's 1935 cinematic *Barbary Coast*, Miriam Hopkins plays new arrival Mary Rutledge who, finding her fiancé dead, takes a job with bad guy Edward G. Robinson at the Bella Donna casino. Mayhem ensues. Harry Carey, Walter Brennan, and Joel McCrea also star.

The opening of *Alexander's Ragtime Band* (1938) shows the San Francisco Bay and then a plaque for the Fairmont Hotel, where Tyrone Power is in the midst of playing a violin concert. He excuses himself to go work at the Excelsior Bakery, but really goes to perform in Alexander's Ragtime Band at "Dirty Eddie's, the Pride of the [Barbary] Coast." There he meets Alice Faye and they go on to perform at the Ship Café and then the Sunset Inn.

Gentleman Jim is Raoul Walsh's 1942 adaptation of *The Roar of the Crowd*, the 1925 autobiography of famed boxer James J. "Gentleman Jim" Corbett. The story of the colorful Irish American fighter is set largely in San Francisco's 1890s Barbary Coast.

Richard Fleischer's 1954 version of the Jules Verne classic *20,000 Leagues Under the Sea*, for Walt Disney, depicts Kirk Douglas, Peter Lorre, and the rest of the crew leaving a fictional location on the San Francisco waterfront (that looks like a set from *Bonanza*) before going out to sea to encounter James Mason as Captain Nemo in a submarine and battling the giant squid. Two years later, in another film adaptation of a Jules Verne novel, *Around the World in Eighty Days*, David Niven and Cantinflas encounter Marlene Dietrich and Frank Sinatra performing in a saloon on the Barbary Coast. (Interesting bit of trivia: The term "cameo," referring to a small part played by a famous person, was coined for this film.)

34. Foote, Cone & Belding
733 Front Street at Pacific Avenue

Claiming to be the largest West Coast Advertising agency, Foote, Cone & Belding temporarily became the fictional "Jabe & Dunne Advertising Agency" in the 2001 remake of *Sweet November*. The original 1968 version, set in Greenwich Village, starred Sandy Dennis as the kooky but kind girl who takes a different man under her wing every month hoping to help them, and Anthony Newley as Mr. November. In the remake,

Charlize Theron befriends Keanu Reeves, who worked for this firm until they fired him.

35. Vallejo Street at Sansome

The Hulk topples a cable car reportedly at this intersection, which in reality is blocks away from the rail. Several other scenes were shot from the same intersection. The cast of Ang Lee's 2003 science fiction film includes Eric Bana, Jennifer Connelly, Nick Nolte, Sam Elliott, Josh Lucas, Paul Kersey, Cara Buono, Todd Tesen, Lou Ferrigno, Stan Lee, and Daniel Dae Kim. In most cases movie scenes involving cable cars are shot a block or two away from actual tracks so commuter service isn't disrupted. After the Golden Gate bridge, San Francisco's second most-recognized symbols are the cable cars, especially when they're out of control or they crash, as in *The Rock* (1996).

36. Bank of America Building
555 California Street at Kearny

One in a string of disaster movies, *The Towering Inferno* (1974) was among the highest-grossing box office hits of the mid-1970s. Two novels inspired by the construction of the World Trade Center and public concern over what might happen if a fire occurred in one of the tow-

ers were published at the same time. After the success of *The Poseidon Adventure* in 1972, Warner Brothers bought the rights to *The Tower* by Richard Martin Stern for $390,000. Eight weeks later Irwin Allen of 20th Century Fox discovered *The Glass Inferno* by Thomas N. Scortia and (San Franciscan) Frank M. Robinson and bought the rights for $400,000. To avoid having two similar films competing at the box office the two studios joined forces and pooled their resources, each paying half the production costs, the first-ever joint production by two major studios. In return, 20th Century Fox got the U.S. box office receipts and Warner got the receipts from the rest of the world. Scriptwriter Stirling Silliphant took seven main figures from each novel and incorporated them into the screenplay, as well as the major climax of each novel: the lifeline rescue to an adjacent rooftop from *The Tower*, and the exploding water tanks from *The Glass Inferno*. The three words that make up the titles of the two novels were combined to give the name of the film, and the name of the building that is on fire (the Glass Tower).

The film's plot focuses on the 138-story skyscraper in the heart of San Francisco, which is just finishing completion. A huge celebratory gala, complete with VIP guests, is planned to celebrate the dedication of what is promoted as the world's tallest building. A fire breaks out due to shoddy wiring installed by the contractors, which is not the heavy-duty wiring the architect specified. Various safety features short circuit, and the Glass Tower becomes a huge towering inferno trapping nearly 300 guests on the building's 135th floor. The fire chief devises a daring plan to rescue the panicked guests, but his efforts quickly become a battle against time.

Newman and McQueen were each paid $1 million and 7.5 percent of box office receipts, and their names are staggered in the opening credits, closing credits, and on the posters, so that depending on which way you read it (top to bottom or left to right) both appear to get top billing. Principal photography for *The Towering Inferno* finished on September 11, 1974. The ground-level exterior of the Glass Tower is the 52-story

Bank of America building, built in 1969. The central heating plant/air conditioning facility and water tank scenes were shot in Century City, and the Glass Tower miniature exteriors were shot in 20th Century Fox Ranch, in Malibu Creek State Park. The gala opening of the hotel with various dignitaries attending looked more like an Academy Awards ceremony starring Steve McQueen, Paul Newman, William Holden, Faye Dunaway, Fred Astaire, Susan Blakely, Richard Chamberlain, Jennifer Jones, O. J. Simpson, Robert Vaughn, Robert Wagner, and Dabney Coleman.

Dirty Harry (1971), based on an unpublished story by Harry Julian and R. M. Fink, was loosely based on the true episode of the Zodiac serial killer. Zodiac, who was never caught, terrorized San Francisco in the late 1960s. *Dirty Harry* marked Clint Eastwood's segue from "spaghetti Westerns" to portray a hardboiled cop who ultimately takes private revenge on the crafty sniper. Eastwood went on to appear in four sequels: *Magnum Force* (1973), *The Enforcer* (1976), *Sudden Impact*

Early in *Dirty Harry*, Andy Robinson as the Scorpio killer is shown on top of the Bank of America building training his rifle on an unsuspecting target. *Courtesy Art, Music and Recreation Center, San Francisco Public Library*

(1983), and *The Dead Pool* (1988). In the opening sequence of *Dirty Harry*, a baby-faced killer trains his high-powered rifle with a telescopic lens on an unsuspecting woman wearing a yellow swimsuit in a pool on the rooftop of the Chinese Cultural Center Holiday Inn. He pulls the trigger, fatally wounding her, as the water in the pool is clouded crimson. Later, Harry locates the sniper's position atop the Bank of America Building and discovers a spent shell, which he places in a used envelope addressed to himself at Homicide Department with a return address of Provo, Utah. This begins the search for "the Scorpio Killer."

In *High Crimes* (2002), Ashley Judd's law firm, Franklin, Dade, Heller, & Associates, is said to be located at Union Towers, 60800 Union Street. That address does not exist. The exterior is the Bank of America at 555 California Street, while interiors were filmed at Chase H & Q, 1 Bush Street, at Sansome.

A view of the Bank of America building is featured prominently in *Fearless* (1993) when Jeff Bridges perches on the rooftop of nearby 400 Montgomery Street in a death-defying balancing act.

37. "Man Loh's Oriental Roof Garden"
772 Commercial Street at Kearny

After artist Frank Johnson (Ross Elliott) innocently witnesses a murder, he fears that he will be killed as well, in *Woman on the Run*, Norman Foster's 1950 film noir. Johnson's wife, Eleanor (Ann Sheridan), asked by the police to help them find where her husband is hiding, is initially reluctant to admit their marriage was shaky, but eventually agrees to help Inspector Ferris (Robert Keith). Assisted by reporter Danny Leggett (Dennis O'Keefe), who seems attracted to her, Eleanor later learns that Leggett is the murderer, and is using her to lead him to her husband. Victim #2 is pushed from the balcony of "Man Loh's Oriental Roof Garden," 772 Commercial Street. Another film site, among many San Francisco locations, is "Sullivan's Grotto" just up the street at 785 Commercial Street.

38. First Bank
550 Montgomery Street at Commercial

Sam Weisman's 1997 live action film *George of the Jungle* is based on Jay Ward's classic cartoon characters with a story by Dana Olsen. Heiress Ursula Stanhope (Leslie Mann) treks off to Africa for adventure, and to get away from fiancé Lyle Vandergroot (Thomas Haden Church), who follows her anyway. Ursula is rescued from a lion attack by George (Brendan Fraser), who whisks her to his jungle tree house where they are smitten by each other. Returning with her to San Francisco, it is George's turn to be bewildered by the urban jungle. This is the location used for "Stanhope Bank," Ursula's family's bank, where she bursts in on her father (John Bennett Perry), prepared to break the news about Lyle, George, and everything.

39. Chartered Bank of London
465 California Street at Montgomery

In 1979, Nicholas Meyer made his debut as a director filming Jack Finney's novel *Time After Time*. Herbert G. Wells has just invented a time machine but hasn't tried it out yet. When one of his friends is found to be Jack the Ripper, Jack makes his escape using the time machine. Herbert follows Jack into San Francisco in the late 1970s where he meets Amy, a bank clerk, who teaches Herbert about life in the 1970s while they pursue Jack, who is continuing his murderous activities.

This is the location where Mary Steenburgen works as Amy, the bank clerk, and first sees Malcolm McDowell as Herbert. Steenburgen and McDowell met on the set of the film, and McDowell says in the DVD that they tell their two children if you want to watch them fall in love, rent this movie. Later McDowell is quoted as saying, in an oblique reference to his battle with alcoholism and drug abuse that ultimately cost him his marriage, "My career was set, hers was just starting and she wasn't going to work in England. But then it all went south." Steenburgen went on to marry Ted Danson.

Chinatown

Roughly defined by Broadway, California, Kearny, and Powell streets, San Francisco's Chinatown claims to be the largest outside of Asia. Following China's defeat by Britain and a series of natural catastrophes resulting in famine, peasant uprisings, and rebellions, many Chinese in the mid-19th century sought their fortune in "Gum San" (Golden Mountain— the Chinese name for America). Initially praised for their work ethic, the Chinese labor force became a threat to the mainstream. Racial discrimi-

nation and repressive legislation drove the Chinese from the gold mines to the sanctuary of the neighborhood that became known as Chinatown. The only ethnic group in the history of the United States to be specifically denied entrance into the country, the Chinese were prohibited by law to testify in court, to own property, to vote, to have family members join them, to marry non-Chinese, and to work in government and other institutional agencies. While many Chinese families have moved to the more suburban Richmond District, there remains a vibrant Chinese cultural experience not far off the tourist path. The main thoroughfare in Chinatown is Grant Avenue, formerly known as Dupont Guy, and made famous by a song in Rodgers & Hammerstein's *Flower Drum Song* (1962). Chinatown is the site of several cinematic chase sequences, notably in *Jade* (1995), *Presidio* (1988), and *What's Up, Doc?* (1972).

Ryan O'Neal encounters a Chinese New Year's Day Parade during the chase sequence in *What's Up, Doc*? (1972). *Courtesy of Pacific Film Archive, University of California, Berkeley*

40. Hall of Justice
750 Kearny Street at Washington

This was the site from 1910 to 1967 of the Hall of Justice. It appeared in many films including *The Lineup* (1958), *Woman on the Run* (1950), and *The Lady from Shanghai* (1948). It is probably most recognizable, however, as Ironside's office and apartment in the NBC television series *Ironside*, which ran from 1967 to 1975. Robert Ironside (Raymond Burr) had been chief of detectives for the San Francisco Police Department for many years when a would-be assassin's bullet left him paralyzed from the waist down. He convinced the police commissioner to appoint him as a special consultant. With former assistants Don Gallaway and Barbara Anderson (and, later, Elizabeth Bauer), and an ex-

Old Hall of Justice, 1962. *Courtesy of San Francisco History Center, San Francisco Public Library*

delinquent (Don Mitchell) who became his aide and bodyguard, Ironside used a specially equipped police van and a wheelchair to conduct investigations. Though Burr was better known for his Perry Mason role, Ironside became a memorable San Francisco character. This building was demolished in 1967, but the series used exterior shots of it through 1975. The new Hall of Justice at 7th and Bryant Streets was also used in the popular series. The Chinatown/Financial District Holiday Inn, now on this site, was featured in the opening sequence of *Dirty Harry* (1971). The hotel's rooftop swimming pool is where the Scorpio sniper kills a young woman.

Directly across Kearny Street is Portsmouth Square. Known as the "Heart of Chinatown" because Chinatown started along one side of the square and now extends around and beyond it, Portsmouth Square is rich with history. It was named for the USS *Portsmouth*, commanded by Captain John B. Montgomery, after whom Montgomery Street was named. It was here on the plaza that Captain Montgomery first raised the American flag near the Mexican adobe customhouse on July 9, 1846.

The opening scene in *Flower Drum Song* (1962), in which Mei Li and her father sing "A Hundred Million Miracles," was set in Portsmouth Square, but shot in Hollywood. Wayne Wang's first feature film, *Chan Is Missing* (1982), is a commentary on the complexities of the Chinese American experience. Two cab drivers, Jo (Wood May) and Steve (Marc Hayashi), search San Francisco's Chinatown for Chan Hung, a mysterious character who has disappeared with their $4,000. Their quest leads them on a journey that illuminates the many problems experienced by Chinese Americans trying to assimilate into contemporary American society. Wayne Wang lived in Los Altos, San Francisco, and Berkeley from 1967 through the 1980s. He also shot much of *Dim Sum: A Little Bit of Heart* (1986) and parts of *The Joy Luck Club* (1993) in Chinatown.

41. Li Po
916 Grant Avenue at Washington

Named for the Chinese poet Li Po (701–762) this dark bar with its cavelike entrance is one of the many Chinatown locations in *Chan*

Is Missing (1982). It appears again in *Dim Sum: A Little Bit of Heart* (1986), in which Kim Chew is an immigrant Chinese widow in San Francisco, anticipating the new year with some unhappiness. She's 62 and hopes to make a trip to China to pay last respects to her ancestors, but a fortune-teller has told her that she'll die this year, and she worries about her unmarried daughter, Lauren Chew. Her cheerful brother-in-law, Li Po's bartender, is played by Victor Wong. (Wong also appears in Wayne Wang's *Eat a Bowl of Tea* [1989] and *The Joy Luck Club* [1993].) Actual interiors of apartments in Chinatown and Richmond districts were obviously used for the characters' abodes, and shots of SFO and the Chinese cemetery in Colma were also used in this low-budget production.

42. Golden Dragon Restaurant
816 Washington Street at Grant

In *Chan Is Missing* (1982), Wayne Wang's intriguing exploration of the complexities of Chinese Americans trying to assimilate into contemporary American society, Henry, the cook, self-mockingly sings "Fry me to the Moon" in this Chinese restaurant.

43. New Asia Restaurant
772 Pacific Avenue at Grant

In *Dead Pool* (1988), the fifth and final film in the *Dirty Harry* series, gunmen shoot up this dim sum restaurant. Clint Eastwood calmly holds out a fortune cookie and reads them the fortune: "You're shit out of luck," then wastes them all.

44. Old St. Mary's Church
660 California Street at Grant

"Son, Observe the time and fly from Evil" (Ecclesiasticus 4:23): this inscription on the south face of the church clock was originally aimed at patrons of the Barbary Coast brothels operating across the way. The quote takes on new meaning in *Time After Time*, a 1979 film in

which H. G. Wells (Malcolm McDowell) travels through time to catch the infamous murderer Jack the Ripper (David Warner).

Nob Hill

45. New Russian Hill Market
1198 Pacific Avenue at Jones

In *The Rock* (1996), after getting his hair cut at the Fairmont Hotel, convict Sean Connery escapes in a stolen car and Nicolas Cage chases him through the city. Some scenes were shot in San Pedro, in Southern California, before the climax on this corner (right). "You just fucked up your Ferrari," says a motorcyclist to Cage immediately after a cable car explodes into it. (Note: Cable cars don't run on Jones, but film-makers consistently find it easier, and safer, to use motorized cable cars on alternate streets.)

46. 1153–57 Taylor Street at Clay

As Lieutenant Frank Bullitt in *Bullitt* (1968), Steve McQueen lived in this apartment building (lower right). He is seen coming and going and miraculously parking his car in this neighborhood. He buys his frozen dinners at the VJ Grocery across the street at 1199 Clay Street.

Steve McQueen as Lieutenant Frank Bullitt on the Russian Hill street corner where he lives and shops. *Courtesy Art, Music, and Recreation Center, San Francisco Public Library*

47. Pleasant Street at Taylor

Mary Fiore (Jennifer Lopez) is ambitious, hard working, extremely organized, and knows exactly what to do and say to make any wedding a spectacular event in *The Wedding Planner* (2001). But when her heel catches in a manhole cover, her busy yet uncomplicated life is turned upside down by handsome doctor Matthew McConaughey, who, unbeknownst to her, is about to become one of her bridegrooms. This is where the two leads first meet as McConaughey pushes her out of the way of a runaway garbage bin rolling down Pleasant Street, a one-block alley on Nob Hill.

48. Chambord Apartments
1298 Sacramento Street at Jones

In Rudolph Mate's film noir, *D.O.A.* (1950), Frank Bigelo, a CPA in Banning, California, leaves for a vacation in San Francisco. After enjoying a night on the town, he feels ill, and hops on a cable car. He spots a sign that reads "Medical Building" and goes inside. He has some tests taken and the results indicate a "luminous toxic matter" may have invaded his vital organs. He is doomed to die, the length of time ranging between a day or two and a week or two. Horrified to realize he's essentially been murdered, he runs out of the office. He confirms his diagnosis at another facility and then, determined to find his killers, heads to Los Angeles. The Chambord Apartments, built in 1921, is a San Francisco Historic Landmark.

49. Grace Cathedral
1100 California Street at Taylor

Following the 1906 earthquake, the Crocker family, of railroad and banking fortune, donated their ruined Nob Hill property for a diocesan cathedral, which took its name and founding congregation from

the nearby parish. Designed in French Gothic style by Lewis Hobart, it was begun in 1928 and completed in 1964 as the third largest Episcopal cathedral in the nation. The Cathedral is famed for its copy of the Lorenzo Ghiberti Florentine doors ("The Gates of Paradise"), labyrinths, varied stained glass, medieval and contemporary furnishings, as well as its carillon, organs, and choir. In 1995, the cathedral close (the cathedral and the land surrounding it) was completed, with a new front stairway, courtyard Chapter House, and Cathedral School addition.

In *The Towering Inferno*, Robert Vaughn confronts Steve McQueen's superior, Simon Oakland, here. Much has changed since the film was made in 1968: The rectory has since been removed. The Philips Union 76 gas station on the opposite corner was destroyed around 1972, when construction began on what was to have been a Hyatt Hotel. The hotel was later built as the Hyatt Embarcadero and the Gramercy Towers Condominiums were built at 1177 California at Jones.

Armistead Maupin's *More Tales of the City*, the 1998 cable miniseries based on the series of books by the San Francisco novelist, includes a particularly far-fetched plotline about cannibalism at Grace Cathedral. The nefarious goings-on in the cathedral perplex Mary Ann (Laura Linney) and Burke (Colin Ferguson), who meet in Huntington Park across the street from the cathedral. Exteriors only were shot here.

In 2001, Adam Shankman directed *The Wedding Planner* with locations around town. The romantic comedy has wedding planner Jennifer Lopez as an Italian American falling for pediatrician Matthew McConaughey. A model of Grace Cathedral appears in the opening shot with young Mary (Lopez) dreaming of being a wedding planner, and then the real cathedral appears as a wedding location.

When Joan Cusack finally gets married in *A Smile Like Yours* (1997), it is at Grace Cathedral. She and her groom ride away in a hearse emblazoned with the words "till death do us part." Glenn Close as *Maxie* (1985) worked here, and Robin Williams as the *Bicentennial Man* (1999) attended "Little Miss's" wedding here.

50. Fairmont Hotel
950 Mason Street at California

Begun in 1902, the completed but as yet unopened hotel was damaged in the earthquake and fire of April 18, 1906. To complete the restoration, the owners chose Julia Morgan, who went on to become

renowned as the country's preeminent female architect, later famous for William Randolph Heart's San Simeon and many other northern California landmarks. The luxury hotel reopened exactly a year after the earthquake. A grand reopening took place in 1947, and the Venetian Room began presenting name entertainers like Ella Fitzgerald, Nat "King" Cole, Marlene Dietrich, Joel Grey, Bobby Short, Vic Damone, James Brown, and many, many more. Ernie Hecksher and his orchestra came for a limited engagement and never left, becoming the official band for the Venetian Room. The late, lamented supper club is perhaps most famous as the place in which Tony Bennett first sang "I Left My Heart in San Francisco."

Stars often stayed here during filming. Joan Crawford was said to have required 10 boxes of facial tissues and 20 pillows, and in 1929 Helen Hayes inaugurated the hotel's new swimming pool. In a Fairmont elevator, Orson Welles unexpectedly encountered William Randolph Hearst, the model for *Citizen Kane*'s megalomaniacal character Charles Foster Kane. The cast of *All About Eve* stayed at the Fairmont Hotel during filming at the Curran Theatre in 1950. Alfred Hitchcock and his crew also stayed here while shooting *Vertigo* in 1957.

The Fairmont has starred in so many movies that, legend has it, the doorman is required to be a member of the Screen Actor's Guild. *Vertigo*'s classic San Francisco opening panoramic shot was filmed from the rooftop of the hotel. Kim Novak as Madeline later passes in front of the Fairmont on her car tour of San Francisco. No wonder—she lives across the street at the Brocklebank Apartments. In Hitchcock's last movie, *Family Plot*, filmed in 1976, Barbara Harris leaves a note with the hotel doorman for Bruce Dern.

In *Alexander's Ragtime Band*, Irving Berlin roughly chronicles his own career trajectory between 1919 and 1939. The 1938 musical portrays the professional and romantic ups and downs of society boy Tyrone Power (who prefers popular music to serious music), nice-guy pianist-composer Don Ameche, and Alice Faye, the tough-but-vulnerable singer the men both vie for. The opening of the film shows the San Francisco Bay and then a plaque depicting the Fairmont Hotel, where Power is giving a violin concert. He excuses himself to go work at the Excelsior Bakery, but really goes to perform in Alexander's Ragtime Band at "Dirty Eddie's, the Pride of the [Barbary] Coast." There he meets Alice Faye and they go on to perform at the Ship Café and then the Sunset Inn.

Richard Chamberlain waiting to film the opening scene of *Petulia* (1968) in the lobby of the Fairmont Hotel.
Courtesy of Pacific Film Archive, University of California, Berkeley

The lobby of the Fairmont appears in *Petulia*, Richard Lester's 1968 film based on the novel *Me and the Arch Kook Petulia* by John Haase. Unhappily married Petulia (Julie Christie) meets a recently divorced doctor, straitlaced George C. Scott, at the high society fundraiser that opens the film. The society types don't quite know what to make of Big Brother and the Holding Company, featuring vocalist Janis Joplin.

The ABC television series *Hotel*, based on the Arthur Hailey novel and the 1967 movie of the same name, starred the Fairmont Hotel as Hotel St. Gregory and revealed the daily behind-the-scenes life of a luxury hotel. Anne Baxter, James Brolin, Shari Belafonte-Harper, and (in the first episode) Bette Davis starred in the popular series, which ran from 1983 to 1988. Exterior scenes were used for the series's establishing shots, and a large replica of the Fairmont's plush lobby was re-created for shooting interior scenes.

In 1996 Albert Brooks and Debbie Reynolds drive by the Fairmont on their way to dinner in the city in *Mother*. Albert Brooks directed Reynolds's first film in 25 years. That same year Michael Bay directed *The Rock*, starring Ed Harris, Sean Connery, and Nicolas Cage. A group of renegade marine commandos seizes a stockpile of chemical weapons and takes over Alcatraz, with 81 tourists as hostages. The commandoes' leader, a former highly decorated U.S. general, demands $100 million ransom as restitution to families of soldiers who died in covert operations and were thereby denied compensation. He threatens to launch 15 rockets carrying deadly VX nerve gas into the San Francisco Bay area. An elite SEAL team, with support from an FBI chemical warfare expert and a former Alcatraz escapee, is assembled to penetrate the terrorists' defenses on the island. Some shots of the Fairmont Hotel's penthouse suite were used; the balcony was where the fey "stylist" cuts Sean Connery's hair. Exteriors of the hotel were mixed with footage from other locations, and most of the interiors were shot elsewhere. When Connery steals a car, he is said to be heading "west on California." He goes just about everywhere except west on California.

51. Brocklebank
1000 Mason Street at Sacramento

This luxury apartment building across the street from the Fairmont atop Nob Hill was built in 1926 by partners William Peyton Day and Charles Peter Weeks. The most famous residents of this posh address were Gavin Elster (Tom Helmore) and his wife Madeleine (Kim Novak) in *Vertigo* (1958). After Elster hires Jimmy Stewart (Scottie) to spy on Madeleine, she is seen coming and going in her Jaguar from the outdoor parking in front of the apartment house. Later, Scottie confronts a tenant here who has bought the Elsters' car.

In *Sudden Fear*, when wealthy playwright Joan Crawford realizes that her new husband is planning to kill her, she uses her writing

skills to thwart his scheme. In this 1952 noir thriller, the Brocklebank is Crawford's residence until she flees her husband and his new girlfriend, click-clacking down North Beach's cobblestone streets in stilletto heels.

In 1984 Gene Wilder, while hiding from Kelly LeBrock's husband, tottered on the ninth-story window ledge of the Brocklebank's L-shaped tower in *The Woman in Red*.

Robert Duvall, relatively unknown in 1968, drove a taxi along Mason Street past the Brocklebank in one of the first scenes of *Bullitt*.

Armistead Maupin's Tales of the City, the 1993 cable miniseries, was based on the first in the popular series of books by San Francisco novelist Maupin. Kooky characters smoke dope and savor the lotus blossoms of 1970s San Francisco under the watchful eye of Anna Madrigal of Barbary Lane. Michael "Mouse" (Marcus d'Amico) points out the *Vertigo* (1958) location to his visiting mother. In the sequel, *More Tales of the City* (1998), Deirdre Denise "DeDe" Ligon Halcyon Day (Barbara Garrick) and her husband, Beauchamp Talbot Day (Thomas Gibson), live here.

52. Mark Hopkins Hotel
"Number One Nob Hill"
999 California Street

This hotel atop Nob Hill is located on the site of the former 40-room mansion of Mark Hopkins, one of San Francisco's "Big Four," who founded what became the Southern Pacific Railroad. Hopkins, who built this grand house at the insistence of his socialite wife, Mary, died before it was finished in 1878. In the early summer of 1878, photographer Eadweard Muybridge climbed with his camera to the roof of the Mark Hopkins mansion to make 13 exposures at intervals of 15 to 30 minutes. The laborious process included coating each of his glass plates with emulsion and sensitizing them with silver nitrate, then immediately exposing and developing the photos in a portable rooftop darkroom. The result was a splendid 360° view, 16 inches high and more than 17 feet in length, which Muybridge gave in fanfold book form to members of San Francisco society.

The mansion, destroyed by the 1906 earthquake and fire, was replaced by a more modest structure built by the San Francisco Art Association (now known as the San Francisco Art Institute), which received the property from Mary Hopkins's second husband. In 1925 mining engineer and hotel investor George D. Smith bought the site, and opened the luxury hotel on December 4, 1926. The Mark Hopkins became an immediate part of San Francisco's rich and colorful history, and locals and visitors continue to visit the Top of the Mark, the 19th-floor sky lounge atop the hotel, with its panoramic views of the San Francisco Bay area—except the vertiginous Scottie Ferguson, who mentions that he'll have to drink at street level.

In *The Lineup*, Don Siegel's 1958 film based on the CBS television series, Eli Wallach and Robert Keith are searching for the three separate parcels of heroin smuggled unknowingly into San Francisco by three separate people. The final packet is concealed in a Japanese doll belonging to a little girl, Cheryl Callaway. Wallach befriends her mother, Dorothy Bradshaw, who invites the two men back to her room at the Mark

Hopkins. The little girl has found the heroin and used the "powder" on her doll's face. Wallach and Keith kidnap the mother and daughter from the hotel room.

In Peter Yates's classic *Bullitt* (1968), Johnny Ross (Pat Renella) escapes two attempts on his life and flees to San Francisco, where he is placed in protective custody by politician Walter Chalmers (Robert Vaughn), who hopes to use Ross to further his own national aspirations. At the beginning of the film Renella checks to see if there were any messages for him at the Mark Hopkins front desk. Later Steve McQueen, as inspector Frank Bullitt, enlists the aid of a Sunshine Cab driver named Weissberg (Robert Duvall) to retrace Ross's movements from the moment he arrived in San Francisco. The Mark Hopkins Hotel is their first stop.

In *Sudden Impact* (1983), the fourth of the *Dirty Harry* series and the only one directed by star Clint Eastwood, a serial killer is on the loose in San Francisco. Eastwood upsets his superiors and the press by barging uninvited into mobster Threlkis's granddaughter's wedding reception at the Mark Hopkins, and threatens to expose him with expensive prostitute "Linda Dilkert's" incriminating letters. Threlkis suffers a heart attack, and never learns there were no letters.

53. "136" Alta Linda
819 Mason Street at Pine

Apartment "4D," belonging to the *Woman on the Run* and her husband, is a hybrid location filmed here and at 1801 Laguna at Bush. This building stands in for the apartment building's rooftop. Filming, completed August 1, 1950, included many other San Francisco landmarks such as Washington Square, Union Square, and Market Street.

54. Cable Car Signal Box
California Street at Powell

The world's first cable-powered street railway was built in San Francisco by Andrew Hallidie in 1873. During the subsequent 15 years, many cities built cable railways to replace horse-powered streetcars. When electric streetcars became practical in the late 1880s, they, in turn, quickly replaced cable cars almost everywhere. Fittingly, San Francisco

is now the last city in the world to operate cable cars. San Francisco's cable cars are the only street railway in which the cars do not operate under their own power, but are propelled mechanically by "gripping" a continuously moving steel cable that runs in a conduit underneath a slot between the rails. The cable is kept in motion by an engine at the power-house, 1201 Mason at Washington, which is also a cable car museum.

San Francisco's cable cars almost became extinct in the late 1940s. But a referendum was added to the city charter—a provision that required continued operation of the cable cars. In the 1950s some routes were abandoned, leaving the current configuration. In the 1980s the system was shut down and completely overhauled, ensuring its continued operation. The crossing at Powell and California has a manned signal tower because cable cars coming uphill from the south on Powell or from the east on California cannot see cross traffic until they are almost in the intersection.

In *Woman on the Run* (1950), Ann Sheridan walks past this call booth. The building where she visits Dr. Hohler is gone, but Coast Garage where she parked her car remains.

55. Mason Street at Jackson

Ex-con and widower Ted Danson lives on the northwest corner of this intersection in *Getting Even with Dad* (1993). The building is real, though the fact that Danson always has a parking place right outside his front door is fictitious. The filmmakers use this intersection, where two cable car tracks intersect, to great advantage. In one scene, Danson's son Macaulay Culkin eludes an undercover policeman by hopping onto a cable car.

St. Elizabeth Apartment House.

56. St. Elizabeth Apartment House
901 Powell Street at Sacramento

In John Carpenter's 1992 chase caper, *Memoirs of an Invisible Man*, Chevy Chase lives in this elegant apartment house (left). He is invisible, but documentary filmmaker Daryl Hannah isn't. One scene in a taxicab is filmed outside the building at the intersection of Sacramento and Powell, and the distinctive staircase inside the St. Elizabeth is used in another scene.

57. Belgravia Apartments
795 Sutter Street at Jones

Vincent Sherman shot *Nora Prentiss* in 1947 using many San Francisco locations. Ann Sheridan as nightclub singer Nora Prentiss begins an affair with a successful San Francisco doctor who has a wife and two children. Dr. Talbot (Kent Smith) takes advantage of the sudden death of his partner, Dr. Merriam (Bruce Bennett), to fake his own death, and leave home to join Nora in New York. Drs. Talbot and Merriam have their offices in #201.

58. Cybelle's Pizza
1000 Bush Street at Jones

In Peter Bogdanovich's 1972 screwball comedy, *What's Up, Doc?*, wacky Barbra Streisand wreaks havoc with Ryan O'Neal as a stuffy, spacey musicologist in the style of Howard Hawks. As we first see Streisand, she is standing on the sidewalk watching a pizza maker throw dough into the air. When he notices her looking, the dough does not descend. The no-longer-existent Owl Drugs appears behind her. When Streisand shrugs and walks into the intersection against the light, two cars swerve to avoid her and collide. She walks on, oblivious.

This intersection appears in Thomas Carter's 1997 *Metro*. Eddie Murphy is Inspector Scott Roper, San Francisco Police Department's star hostage negotiator, and after homicidal diamond thief Michael Korda kills a friend of his, Murphy vows revenge. Korda, fleeing Murphy, leaps aboard a cable car and kills the driver. The cable car speeds down Jones out of control, crashing into dozens of cars. Murphy jumps back and forth onto the cable car from a vintage Cadillac before slowing it near the bottom of the slope. Tracks were painted on Jones Street, and the chase scene was filmed with a motorized cable car. Val Diamond, of Beach Blanket Babylon fame, appears in the film as the "Screaming Lady." This same block of Jones was decorated for Christmas (in midsummer) for a scene in *Nine Months* (1995).

59. Cala Foods
California Street and Hyde

The 24-hour Cala Foods is often the site of peculiar sightings, especially during the early hours of the morning. The oddly shaped building had recently opened when Richard Lester used it in *Petulia*. In one scene in the 1968 film, Julie Christie and George C. Scott encounter a zany night-shift check-out gal, played by actress Leigh French.

60. William's Films
1615 Polk Street at Sacramento

In June 1970, William Bushnell, a former production director for American Conservatory Theatre, sought to create the second major production company located in San Francisco, after Zoetrope. *The Fifth Horseman*, to be directed by Vic Morrow but never released, was the only major film planned from this short-lived studio.

Russian Hill, North Beach, and Telegraph Hill

This shot from *Bullitt* (1968) could be from any number of films featuring hilly chase scenes. *Courtesy of Pacific Film Archive, University of California, Berkeley*

You'll get a workout on this hilly tour, which because of lack of parking and proximity of locations is probably best done afoot (with an occasional assist from a cable car). Begin at the swimming clubs near Aquatic Park overlooking the bay. (We don't really expect you to swim in the always-cold water, though many locals do.) After exploring the traditional tourist areas of the Cannery and Ghirardelli Square, but from a different, cinematic, perspective, climb Hyde Street to the photogenic Russian Hill. Continue down into North Beach, then up to Telegraph Hill with its much-photographed Coit Tower. The tour ends back in North Beach, where you'll likely want to reward yourself with lunch, or at least a foaming cappuccino. Keep your eyes open for directors Philip Kaufman or Chris Columbus, both of whom have offices in the neighborhood.

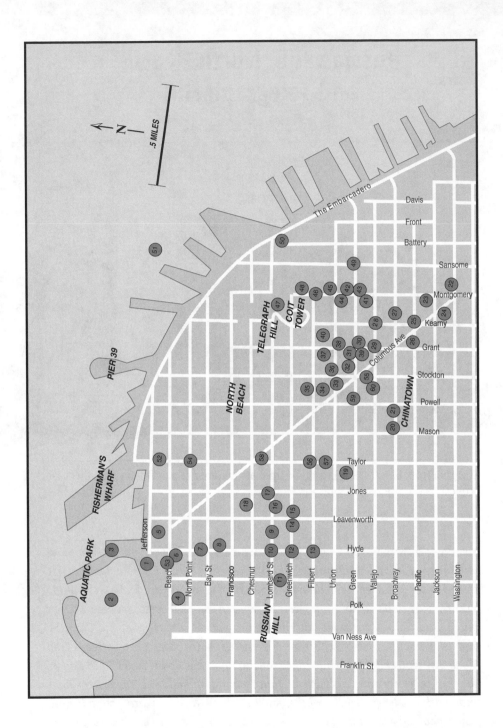

Russian Hill

1. **Swimming Clubs: The Dolphin Club and the South End Rowing Club**
Jefferson Street at Hyde

Cold-water swimmers are an awe-inspiring sight in their orange swim caps just off shore at Aquatic Park, the home of these two San Francisco institutions, both of which are swimming and rowing clubs that enjoy a friendly competition. A fleet of wooden rowing shells monitor organized swimming races from Alcatraz or across the Golden Gate several times a year, including a knee-knocking New Year's Day Alcatraz swim. The South End, which was relocated from south of the Bay Bridge (hence its name) early in the 20th century, has been the frequent host to movie crews filming at Aquatic Park. The protagonist of *Dopamine* (2003), the South Park–based dot-com romance, pops up out of the frigid waters of San Francisco Bay somewhat west of here at Fort Point. A point is made in the screenplay that John Livingston's character was formerly overweight and his life and body are changed by taking up swimming.

2. **Aquatic Park**
Jefferson Street, west of Hyde

Officially the San Francisco Maritime National Historic Park, this scenic area located at the west end of Fisherman's Wharf houses a maritime museum, a library/research facility, and a visitor center. An actual AIDS-benefit bicycle race is featured in the 2001 film *The Wedding Planner* as a throwaway joke when Matthew McConaughey is mistaken for half of a newlywed same-sex couple by gay bicyclists pedaling by the rowing clubs at Jefferson and Hyde Streets. In another scene, in which the traffic pattern is unlikely in reality, the screenplay places McConaughey, in a taxi, in a traffic jam coming up from the bay, from the dead end of Van Ness Avenue, which does not reach the bay.

In *Boys and Girls* (2000), Freddie Prinze Jr. and Claire Forlani take in all the San Francisco sights as they spend the day together. This is established with quick shots of classic tourist destinations: Lombard Street, cable car, City Hall, Fisherman's Wharf, Alcatraz, Ferry Building, Chinatown, Golden Gate Bridge, Transamerica Pyramid, Saints Peter and Paul Church, and Coit Tower. The pair spends considerable time arguing, we mean talking, in Aquatic Park.

"Public phone, hamburger stand, Aquatic Park. Hubba, hubba, hubba, pig bastard," taunts Scorpio, the serial killer, in *Dirty Harry* (1971). Loosely based on the true exploits of the Zodiac serial killer, who terrorized San Francisco in the late 1960s (and who was never caught), this film marked Clint Eastwood's segue from "spaghetti Western" anti-hero to hard-boiled cop who ultimately takes private revenge on the crafty sniper. "Dirty" Harry Callahan went on to appear in four sequels: *Magnum Force* (1973), *The Enforcer* (1976), *Sudden Impact* (1983), and *The Dead Pool* (1988). Don Siegel and Clint Eastwood claim they were on their way to Seattle scouting locations when they stopped in San Francisco and went no farther, not quite realizing that the city would become an intrinsic character in the *Dirty Harry* series. On the way to Aquatic Park, near a tunnel to Fort Mason, Harry is accosted by thugs but he scares them off with his .44 Magnum.

3. **Hyde Street Pier**
The north end of Hyde Street, at San Francisco Bay

A fleet of national historic landmark ships can be visited as part of the National Park Service's outdoor museum at the foot of Hyde

Hyde Street Pier.

The Volkswagen bug that goes off the Hyde Street Pier at the end of *What's Up, Doc?* (1978). *Courtesy of Art, Music and Recreation Center, San Francisco Public Library*

Street, formerly one of the ports of entry for vehicles entering San Francisco from the north via ferry before the construction of the Golden Gate Bridge in the 1930s. Among the ships docked here are the 1886 square-rigger *Balclutha,* the 1896 schooner *C. A. Thayer,* the 1891 scow schooner *Alma,* the 1907 steam tug *Hercules,* and the 1914 paddlewheel tug *Eppleton Hall.*

Too many cars to count ended up in the drink in movies filmed at the end of Hyde Street, among them Herbie *The Love Bug* (1968). In Betty Thomas's 1998 remake of the 1967 Rex Harrison children's classic *Doctor Dolittle*, with Eddie Murphy as the vet who "talks to the animals," "Blossom's Mammoth Circus" was built and filmed at the foot of Larkin and Hyde Streets in 1998.

4.   Ghirardelli Square
900 North Point Street at Larkin

Ghirardelli (pronounced Gear-ar-deli) Square, the frequently mispronounced tourist destination on the northern waterfront, became the nation's first "festival marketplace" thanks to designer Lawrence Halprin in the early 1960s, spawning imitations from coast to coast like Boston's Quincy Market and Baltimore's Harborplace. The trademark sign, which acknowledges the 19th-century chocolate factory on this site, can be read from far out in San Francisco Bay. It is occasionally blurred out of waterfront movie shots, presumably for copyright reasons.

In *Time After Time* (1979), Mary Steenburgen and Malcolm McDowell go to the movies. At the Ghirardelli Cinema, McDowell (as time-traveler H. G. Wells) is cowering under the seat, so terrified is he of the moving images. As they exit, the marquee advertises *Exorcist IV.* This movie house no longer exists.

5.   The Cannery
2801 Leavenworth Street at Beach

Built in 1909 as a fruit-canning plant, this brick complex now houses a hotel, restaurants, and shops catering to tourists. The 1988 film *Dead Pool* depicts a macabre sports pool placing bets on which celebrity is going to die next and crossing names off a list as each of them is killed. A serial killer who preys on famous figures enters the scene, dramatically changing the odds. When "Dirty" Harry Callahan (Clint Eastwood) and aggressive television journalist Samantha Walker (Patricia Clarkson) find their names on the list, the game gets too close to home. It is the fifth and final film in the *Dirty Harry* series. Harry takes Sam to dinner at the Cannery. Afterward a pair of guys accost him and he pulls a gun, then realizes they only want his autograph. Moments later, as Harry and Sam ride the glass elevator to the courtyard, two snipers open fire on them. They fall to the floor and survive the ambush, and Harry quickly dispatches them.

6. Buena Vista Café
2765 Hyde Street at Beach

The original building where the Buena Vista sits today was a boarding-house until 1916, when the landlord converted the first floor into a saloon. Aptly named the Buena Vista ("good view"), it served as a warm meeting place for hundreds of fishermen and handlers who worked for the nearby Sardine Cannery. There they could enjoy a whiskey while scouting the bay for incoming fishing boats, which would mean, "Quick! Finish your drink and get back to meet the boats!" The story of how Irish coffee was reputedly born here begins the night of November 10, 1952. Jack Koeppler, then-owner of the Buena Vista, challenged international travel writer Stanton Delaplane to help re-create a highly touted "Irish coffee" served at Shannon Airport in Ireland. Stan accepted Jack's invitation, and the pair began to experiment immediately. Finally, the recipe was perfected, and has been served to locals and tourists ever since.

Mary Ann Singleton (Laura Linney) calls her mother in Cleveland from a phone booth in this well-known local establishment to tell her mother that she's remaining in San Francisco, in one of the first scenes of the original *Armistead Maupin's Tales of the City* miniseries (1993). In the 1994 feature film *When a Man Loves a Woman*, the opening scene has Andy Garcia and Meg Ryan meeting as strangers, arguing, then kissing madly in front of the restaurant crowd.

7. Hyde Street Cable Car

In an early sequence of *Attack of the Killer Tomatoes*, the 1978 low-budget camp classic, a cable car glides through Russian Hill, down Hyde Street toward Alcatraz in the bay, with bells clanging and seagulls soaring. An identifying caption comes across the screen: "Pentagon, Washington, D.C." And thus the military's involvement in the ridiculous story of how the heretofore peaceful fruits are beginning to grow to enormous size and attacking the population of America. Turns out the tomatoes are being controlled by an evil, power-crazed individual who,

after sufficient damage has been done, plans to "defeat" the killer plants and take over the government. In *Play It Again, Sam* (1972), Woody Allen and Diane Keaton have a conversation on the back of a Hyde Street cable car climbing halfway to the stars from Aquatic Park.

8.   2552 Hyde Street at Bay

Arnold Schwarzenegger lives at this masculine, minimalist address just above Fisherman's Wharf when he's not over at Danny DeVito's house at 722 Steiner in Ivan Reitman's 1994 comedy, *Junior*.

9.   Lombard Street between Hyde and Leavenworth

"The crookedest street in the world" isn't even the crookedest street in San Francisco, which is Vermont, the little-visited curvy lane on the back side of Potrero Hill. *What's Up, Doc?* (1972) and many chase scenes in San Francisco movies have featured the brick-paved street, which was originally a slalom-like solution to driving down the steep residential hill, but has become a traffic-clogged tourist destination because of its eccentric and scenic nature.

10. 2238 Hyde Street at Lombard

The ABC television series *Love on a Rooftop* aired from 1966 to 1971. The opening credits show scenes of Nob Hill, Chinatown, and Washington Square Park, where Peter Deuel and Judy Carne meet over a liverwurst on pumpernickel sandwich. He's an apprentice architect earning $85.37 a week; she's an art student, the daughter of a wealthy car salesman, who has relinquished her world of luxury for Peter. Dave gives Julie his criteria for their new apartment: "cheap, practical, charming, cheap, something with atmosphere, with a view . . . and cheap." He is unhappy when he sees the small, top-floor, walk-up, windowless apartment at "1400 McDoogal Street." Then she shows him the apartment's only asset by taking him up the adjacent stairway to the rooftop's panoramic 360° view of the Bay Area from the top of Russian Hill. Also seen were the neighbors, the Parkers, with Rich Little as an "idea" man who composed menus for a living and Barbara Bostock as his wife. The top of the "View Tower" apartments was the building from which the establishing scene was shot; the elevation and interiors were filmed elsewhere.

11. 2632 Larkin Street at Lombard

FBI Agent Glenn Ford gets a visit from flirtatious Patricia Huston in *Experiment in Terror* (1962). He's following leads trying to protect Lee Remick from Ross Martin. When Ford gets a call from a frightened Huston asking him to come to her apartment as soon as possible, he arrives at this site, only to find that Martin has just murdered her.

12. Tamalpais Building
1201 Greenwich Street at Hyde

In Sam Weisman's 1997 live-action film based on Jay Ward's classic cartoon, *George of the Jungle,* heiress Ursula Stanhope (Leslie Mann) treks off to Africa for adventure, and to get away from her fiancé, who follows her. Returning from Africa, where they have fallen in love, Mann and Brendan Fraser (George) move into her San Francisco apartment, which Fraser refers to as a tree house and where they tell each other to "sleep sweet" as they go to bed. The building has no balconies, so the top of the Vallejo garage above the police station stood in for Mann's balcony with the panoramic view of North Beach from which George does his call to the animals.

13. 1155 Filbert Street at Hyde

In *Bedazzled* (2000), Elliot Richards (Brendan Fraser) rides his bike up one of San Francisco's steepest streets, where he notices Nicole Delarusso (Frances O'Connor) moving into an apartment in this building. He offers to hook up her stereo so she can listen to music while she unpacks, and the next thing we know they're walking around Aquatic Park hand-in-hand.

14. 2201 Leavenworth Street at Greenwich

This is the site of Connie Bradshaw's apartment in the cable miniseries *Armistead Maupin's Tales of the City* (1993). Mary Ann Singleton (Laura Linney) visits, and crashes briefly with, her high school friend (Parker Posey), a swinging single in 1970s SF.

15. 1132 Greenwich at Leavenworth

Police Comissioner Stewart *McMillan and Wife* (Rock Hudson and Susan Saint James) and their housekeeper Mildred (Nancy Walker) enjoyed the great view from their unpretentious home from 1971 to 1976.

16. 949 Lombard at Jones

The Real World, the original television reality show, premiered in 1992, set in the Manhattan neighborhood of SoHo, where seven people who had never met before had to live in a house together for a period of time. It subsequently was hosted by many different cities, and in 1994, the third season was shot

at this San Francisco address with Cory, Judd, Mohammed, Pam, Pedro, Puck, Rachel, and Jo.

17. 900 Lombard Street at Jones

Jimmy Stewart as Scottie and Kim Novak as Madeleine (and, later, Judy) are doomed lovers in the quintessential San Francisco film, Alfred Hitchcock's *Vertigo* (1958). One block below the famous "crookedest street" block of Lombard, the exterior location of Jimmy Stewart's apartment, to which Madeleine comes after her dip into San Francisco Bay, is still recognizable. Interiors were filmed on a sound stage, with the distant Coit Tower ("It led me right to you," purrs Madeleine, standing on Scottie's front porch).

18. San Francisco Art Institute
800 Chestnut Street at Jones

The San Francisco Art Association was founded in 1871, and opened as the California School of Design two years later in offices at 313 Pine Street. In 1877 both organizations moved to new quarters above the California Market at 430 Pine Street. Here, in 1880, Eadweard Muybridge demonstrated his new invention, the Zoopraxiscope, the first public showing of a moving picture. After moving to the former mansion of Mark Hopkins atop Nob Hill, the school was renamed the Mark Hopkins Institute of Arts. After the 1906 fire destroyed the mansion, a new building was erected on the site, and the school was renamed the San Francisco Institute of Art. In 1916 the school was renamed the California School of Fine Arts, and 10 years later moved to its current location at 800 Chestnut Street. The Spanish colonial mission-style building was designed by the firm of Bakewell and Brown, architects of City Hall, Coit Tower, War Memorial Opera House and Veteran's Building, and many other landmark buildings in the area.

Heart Beat: My Life with Jack and Neal was the title of Carolyn Cassady's 1976 memoir about her relationship with Jack Kerouac and Neal Cassady. In 1980 John Byrum brought a high-wattage cast to San Francisco's North Beach neighborhood, hub of the Beat writers' readings, to make a film of this book. Sissy Spacek plays the young wife of Nick Nolte, both of whom are enamored with John Heard. After Allen Ginsberg objected to his thinly veiled portrayal, the character's name was changed to "Ira" and played by Ray Sharkey. Because Carolyn Cassady had been a student at the San Francisco Art Institute, Spacek was filmed descending the staircase from the entrance of the Anne Bremer Memorial Library out into the courtyard, where Nolte and Heard sat on the edge of the fountain waiting for her. Other significant sites used in the film include City Lights Bookstore, 261 Columbus, and Washington Square Bar & Grill at 1707 Powell.

19. Macondray Lane Steps
1801 Taylor Street at Green

The fictional 28 Barbary Lane is the address of the apartment house where much of *Tales of the City* (1993) takes place, in both Armistead Maupin's series of books and the cable miniseries based on

them. Kooky characters smoke dope and savor the lotus blossom of 1970s San Francisco under the watchful eye of Olympia Dukakis as Anna Madrigal. Location shots show characters coming and going up the steep steps, including Mouse (first played by Marcus d'Amico and later by Paul Hopkins) leaving on a stretcher and returning in the arms of his paramour Dr. Jon (William Campbell). Macondray Lane, former home of novelist Maupin, was the basis for Barbary Lane, but the house itself was a soundstage.

20. Above the Broadway Tunnel

Directed by Garry Marshall in 2001, *The Princess Diaries* is a combination ugly duckling tale and Cinderella story of a San Francisco teenager who discovers she is royalty and the granddaughter of Julie Andrews, who is queen of the fictional country Genovia. The crash between the Mustang slipping backward down a steep slope and the fake cable car (on a street with no cable) was filmed on Broadway and Taylor above the Broadway Tunnel. Andrews knights the actor playing the grip operator. In this intersection, director Marshall put *Family Affair*'s Cissy (Kathy Garver) of 1960s television fame in the cable car and gave her one line.

21. The Broadway Tunnel
Broadway between Powell and Larkin

Not the prettiest structure in the neighborhood, the Robert C. Levy Tunnel provides a handy link between North Beach and the western stretches of the city. Filmmakers have usually used it as a source of trouble. Vincent Ward's *What Dreams May Come* (1998), based on a novel by Richard Matheson, stars Robin Williams, Cuba Gooding Jr., and Annabella Sciorra. After driving across the Bay Bridge on a rainy night, road construction at the west end of the tunnel causes an accident, compelling Williams to stop to offer assistance. In the process he is killed in a freak accident. Also in 1998, Thomas Gibson as the evil Beauchamp Day meets his doom in a car wreck in the tunnel after plotting to murder his wife DeDe in *Armistead Maupin's More Tales of the City*. In the 1978 Philip Kaufman remake of *Invasion of the Body Snatchers,* Donald Sutherland and Brooke Adams, trying to escape the evil pod people at

the Broadway Tunnel, hail a cab driven by none other than Don Siegel, the director of the original 1956 version.

22. Belli Building
722 Montgomery Street at Washington

The exterior of the Belli Building, where famous lawyer Melvin Belli had his offices for many years, was used for the building where Hugh Grant's child psychiatrist offices were on the second floor in Chris Columbus's *Nine Months*. The historic building, a San Francisco landmark, is currently in an embarrassing state of disrepair, but in 1995 it was at least filmable.

North Beach

The "Little Italy" of San Francisco, this is the place for a romantic Saturday night date at an Italian restaurant at the foot of Telegraph Hill, followed by an espresso in a Beat-era café and maybe some live jazz.

In *Star Trek IV: The Voyage Home* (1986) the crew walks through North Beach asking people if they know where the "nuclear weapons" are. *Courtesy of Pacific Film Archive, University of California, Berkeley*

Several waves of Italian immigrants have claimed North Beach for their home, and as in New York's Little Italy, they share much of their turf with nearby Chinatown.

Star Trek IV: The Voyage Home, finds Sulu, Scotty, and McCoy walking through North Beach, along Columbus and Grant Avenues, asking people if they know where the "nuclear weapons" are. Apparently several of the passersby were real people, not actors, and their actual responses are used in the film.

Chris O'Donnell as the title character in *The Bachelor* (1999) is pursued by a series of relentless prospective brides through several North Beach locations, including many on Columbus Avenue, among them Danilo's Bakery at Green Street and Bannam Place, as well as Washington Square Park, the heart of North Beach, and two eateries on the Square: Moose's Restaurant at 1652 Stockton and Mama's Restaurant at 1701 Stockton.

"963 Northway, Apartment 207"
North Beach

This is the fictional address of the apartment above Pallucci's Italian Restaurant where Doris Day and her children resided during the third season (1970–71) of *The Doris Day Show* (1968–73). Initially Doris Martin was a widow with two young sons who lived on her father's ranch in Mill Valley. The second season saw her commuting into San Francisco for her job as secretary at *Today's World* magazine. By the third season she and her family moved into a San Francisco apartment, and she began writing for the magazine. The fourth season marked the disappearance of the children, dog, and rest of the cast when she became a carefree, single staff writer.

23. Ernie's Restaurant
847 Montgomery between Jackson and Pacific

This is the upscale eatery where Jimmy Stewart first glimpses the gorgeous Kim Novak, dining with her husband before the Opera, in Hitchcock's *Vertigo* (1958). It later becomes "our place" for Scottie and Judy. A favorite restaurant of Alfred Hitchcock in real life, he held a celebratory party here before the film's premiere. The *Vertigo* interiors of Ernie's, however, were meticulously re-created on a soundstage. When Woody Allen, in *Take the Money and Run*, takes his girlfriend out for a fancy dinner, it is also at Ernie's, still thriving in 1969. The building was transformed into the Essex Club (retaining the monogram "E") in the 1990s.

24. American Zoetrope
916 Kearny Street at Columbus and Jackson

A survivor of the 1906 earthquake and fire, the distinctive, copper-clad Sentinel Building has, since the 1970s, been Francis Ford Coppola's headquarters for his American Zoetrope Studios. The story goes that the director decided on the name of his future studio after receiving a gift of zoetropes from Mogen Scott-Hansen, founder of Lanterna Film Studio and owner of a famous collection of early motion picture–making equipment. Coppola and George Lucas initially planned to house the studio in Marin, but the first home for American Zoetrope was a ware-

house on Folsom Street in 1969. The ground floor of the Kearny building houses Café Niebaum-Coppola, an Italian restaurant that sells many
things with the Coppola brand name.

25. Tosca Café
242 Columbus Avenue at Pacific

In Paul Verhoeven's thriller *Basic Instinct* (1992), at the bar where the cops go to unwind, detective Michael Douglas orders a double black jack on the rocks, admitting that it's his first drink in three months. Wim Wenders's *Until the End of the World* (1991) also features a scene here. Tosca is a real-life hangout for Hollywood celebs in San Francisco. Jeannette Etheridge, owner of the legendary bar, reminisced about how the cast of Philip Kaufman's *The Right Stuff* (1983) sometimes remaining in character as the Mercury 7 astronauts, would come in to unwind during filming. Sam Shepard played the piano and others sang. Jane Dornacker, a local comic and musician who had a *Right Stuff* cameo as Nurse Murch, died in a freak helicopter accident at the age of 38 in New York in October 1986.

In 2004, Niels Mueller accommodated Sean Penn's demand to film *The Assassination of Richard Nixon* in the Bay Area. Based on a true story and set in Baltimore in 1974, the film uses a variety of nondescript locations including the Lucerne Apartments at 766 Sutter Street as the home of Samuel Bicke (Penn), while Tosca serves as the restaurant where his estranged wife (Naomi Watts) works as a waitress.

26. Vesuvio's
255 Columbus Avenue

Vesuvio's, on Jack Kerouac Alley, is next to the historic City Lights Bookstore, best known for publishing the then-radical poets Allen Ginsberg and Lawrence Ferlinghetti in the 1950s. Beat novelist Kerouac was immortalized by a film about his life starring Nick Nolte and Sissy Spacek, *Heartbeat*, in 1980.

Vesuvio's is also a location in the Mike Myers vehicle *So I Married an Axe Murderer* (1993). The exterior of "Café Roads" where Myers performs his poetry is actually Vesuvio Café, even with the cable car running up the street in one scene. The interior scenes were originally filmed at Picaro Café (3120 16th Street at Valencia in the Mission) but Myers apparently requested that they be reshot at the Rococo Showplace (165 10th Street at Howard in SOMA).

Vesuvio's is one of several famous North Beach bars used as a watering hole where Ashley Judd picks up a lover in Philip Kaufman's *Twisted* (2004), only to soon find him murdered. The dream sequence was shot in nearby Adler Alley, with neon jazz signs added.

In Carl Franklin's 2002 *High Crimes,* Ashley Judd and hubby James Caviezel go into San Francisco from their house, supposedly in Marin, but filmed in Calabasas, in Southern California. They dine at Vesuvio's Café (not really a restaurant) at 255 Columbus Avenue and walk over to the Condor Club at Columbus and Broadway in the screenplay. Poor Judd not only doesn't know what county she lives in, but there are some doubts about the identity of the man she is married to.

27. Broadway

North Beach's seedy side is several blocks of nudie bars and porn shops on Broadway east of Columbus Avenue. It is featured as a leading player in a 2000 documentary on the unionization of striptease artists centered around the Lusty Lady Bar, *Live Nude Girls Unite.*

In Lina Wertmüller's *Night Full of Rain* (1977), Giancarlo Giannini remeets Candice Bergen in a singles dance club supposedly set on Broadway, judging from establishing shots of neon storefronts at night in the rain. She is there with another man. He steals her away in order to establish the miserable battle-scarred marriage, which is the core of the movie's plot.

Patty Duke in *Valley of the Dolls* (1967) makes a drunken appearance in San Francisco, which was probably filmed in L.A. A "dolled-up" Neely O'Hara (Duke) flies on impulse to San Francisco and spends some time in a bar. While walking down a sidewalk, she spots a poster of Jennifer (Sharon Tate) on a marquee for a porn movie in a fictitious San Francisco location, seemingly based on Broadway's porn strip in North Beach, and later passes a series of strip clubs including the "Topless A Go Go." Duke's career took a long time to recover from this 1967 fiasco from director Mark Robson, based on the potboiler novel by Jacqueline Susann.

The Roaring Twenties Nightclub, 555 Broadway at Columbus, is a racy bar where Kelly (Lee Remick) is instructed to go meet Red Lynch

(Ross Martin) in Blake Edwards's *Experiment in Terror*. She inadvertently goes off with the wrong man and is nearly killed trying to get out of his car in the 1962 thriller.

In *Swing* (2004) a struggling singer-songwriter inadvertently finds a nightclub frozen in time and learns swing dancing from a beautiful older woman. He is torn between his fiancée, a new attraction, and the people who befriend him in this mysterious club. Interiors of the contemporary jazz club were shot in the Broadway Studios, a dance club at 435 Broadway at Montgomery Street, formerly the infamous Mabuhay Gardens. Local choreographer Cynthia Glinka assembled dancing friends and students as extras for the 1940s and current dance scenes. In addition to teaching the cast to dance, Glinka also had to teach Jacqueline Bisset, who had never swing-danced, how to instruct Innis Casey to swing dance.

28. 430 Vallejo Street at Kearny

This North Beach address is where Goldie Hawn's character lives in *Foul Play* (1978), near Fresno Street. Shy librarian Gloria gets tangled in a complex series of comic/sinister events that culminate in a plot to assassinate the pope. The library scenes are supposed to take place at

the San Francisco Public Library, but these were not filmed there. Other locations in *Foul Play*, which costars Chevy Chase, include Sausalito houseboats, Conzelman Road in the Marin Headlands, Fort Mason overlooking Aquatic Park, and Tiburon. In *Play It Again, Sam* Woody Allen lives at 15–17 Fresno Street, near Vallejo and Kearny. Allen plays a neurotic film buff abandoned by his wife and seeking female companionship, aided and abetted by his best friends, a married couple, and the ghost of Humphrey Bogart. Two weeks before the scheduled start date in 1972, a film strike in New York prevented shooting there. Director Herb Ross refused to make the picture in Los Angeles, because "it was the wrong atmosphere for the story." All the San Francisco locations were found a week before rehearsals were to begin. "Everything was shot on location," Ross maintained, and appropriately so, given Bogart's association with San Francisco. Allen's apartment was actually the home of a young man who was an amateur filmmaker and local film critic.

29. Columbus Avenue at Vallejo

Bedazzled (2000) is the story of a computer programmer (Brendan Fraser) who sells his soul to the devil (Elizabeth Hurley). After Hurley clips the electrical wires connecting the traffic signal control box at Washington Square Park (on Filbert, between Stockton and Powell) all the lights turn green and havoc ensues. On April 9, 2000, a crash involving 18 cars was orchestrated for this film.

At virtually the same multiple intersection (Columbus at Grant and Vallejo) is the Saloon, a hangout for the Ashley Judd character in *Twisted*. Established in 1861, the Saloon is the city's last surviving Barbary Coast bar from the 19th century heyday of this formerly rowdy part of the city. Across the street at 609 Vallejo, Caffe Trieste was used for fantasy sequences of topless women imagined by the temporarily celibate Josh Hartnett in *40 Days and 40 Nights* (2002). The Trieste, a

caffeine-lover's institution since the 1950s, is allegedly where Francis Ford Coppola wrote the screenplay for *The Godfather* (1972).

30. North Beach Video
1398 Grant Avenue at Green

EDtv, Ron Howard's clever and somewhat dark comedy about a desperate cable network that decides to broadcast ordinary guy Matthew McConaughey's every waking moment, turning him into an overnight celebrity and his life upside down, is a remake of the popular 1994 Canadian film *Louis XIX: Le Roi des Ondes*. McConaughey's place of employment was a real-life video store when it was filmed in 1998. It has moved next door, and 1398 Grant is now a Thai restaurant.

In a running gag throughout the movie, local establishments including Moose's Restaurant and Mario's Bohemian Cigar Store, both on Washington Square, are given airtime as subtitled advertisements. Later in the film, as *EDtv* gains nationwide popularity, the sponsors take on a more corporate aspect.

A lot of these North Beach establishments sported new paint jobs shortly after their 15 minutes of fame, perhaps paid for by the compensation property owners received from Hollywood for location shoot rights.

31. Danilo's Bakery
516 Green Street at Bannam Alley

Robin Williams's character, Daniel Hillard, has a bachelor pad upstairs from Danilo Bakery in *Mrs. Doubtfire* (1993) after Sally Field kicks him out of the family house in Pacific Heights. Eugenia Doubtfire's rubber face is crushed by a garbage truck on Bannam Place when it flies out the window. The extremely popular comedy was based on the novel *Alias Madame Doubtfire* by Anne Fine. The film's use of locations and its Oscar-winning makeup, which transformed Williams into a dowdy British housekeeper, helped to reestablish San Francisco as a major movie location in the 1990s.

Escaping the throngs of eager potential brides at Saints Peter and Paul Church a
few blocks away on Washington Square, *The
Bachelor* (1999) Chris O'Donnell orders the
$400 wedding cake from the bakery's store-
front window.

32. Green Valley Restaurant
510 Green Street near Grant

This restaurant (interior and exterior)
appears in *Burglar* (1987), where Whoopi
Goldberg meets G. W. Bailey, only to learn he
has "rolled her over." She escapes through the
bathroom window into Bannam Alley, where
she finds a police motorcycle with keys in the
ignition. She begins a wild chase, which takes
her immediately from North Beach several
miles to Potrero Hill.

33. Fior d'Italia
601 Union Street at Stockton

Fior d'Italia ("Flower of Italy") calls itself the oldest Italian restaurant in the United States. Whether or not that is true, it occupies a prime location on the south side of Washington Square Park. In William Friedkin's *Jade* (1995), David Caruso is waiting in this venerable restaurant for a meeting with Angie Everhart, who promises to provide information. As he watches her walk across Washington Square, she is suddenly hit and run over twice by a black Ford Thunderbird. Caruso jumps into his own car and chases the Thunderbird throughout North Beach, then up Grant Avenue through a Chinese New Year's parade, across the Third Street Bridge, and out to the piers, where the Thunderbird pushes Caruso and his car into the bay.

34. Washington Square Park
Between Union and Filbert, Stockton, and Powell Streets

There is a statue of Ben Franklin in the middle of it, and it is not square, but this has been the heart of North Beach since it was laid out in front of the Saints Peter and Paul Church in the 1950s. In the final

Dirty Harry flick, *The Dead Pool* (1988), a crazy man douses himself in gasoline and threatens to immolate himself unless a recognizable television journalist films him. Enter Patricia Clarkson as the reporter, with Eastwood posing as her cameraman.

35. Saints Peter and Paul Church
666 Filbert Street at Stockton

The Italian Roman Catholic Church was under construction when Cecil B. DeMille used it as a location for his 1923 film *The Ten Commandments*, a morality play about a good and a bad brother. The first portion of the film includes several scenes in two-strip Technicolor. Exteriors of the ornate shrine's facade were used, and a bird's-eye view of 1920s North Beach can be seen in a sequence filmed from the rooftop scaffolding.

Hugh Grant and the pregnant Julianne Moore finally tie the knot in this church in Chris Columbus's *Nine Months* (1995). Barbra Streisand and Ryan O'Neal create havoc in a wedding scene here, as they do all over San Francisco, in the madcap Peter Bogdanovich 1972 comedy *What's Up, Doc?*

The premise of *The Bachelor* (1999) is that after his best buddy screws up and "Would You Marry This Man for 100 Million Dollars?" appears as the front page headline in the fictional *San Francisco Herald*, hundreds of women in wedding dresses fill Saints Peter and Paul Church, eager to marry Chris O'Donnell. Some of the potential brides are actually men in drag.

The nuns from 1992's *Sister Act* (Whoopi Goldberg, Kathy Najimy, Maggie Smith, and others) move some of the action across town from Noe Valley to Saints Peter and Paul Church in the 1993 sequel, *Sister Act II: Back in the Habit.*

After the mentally handicapped couple Juliette Lewis and Giovanni Ribisi get married here in Garry Marshall's *The Other Sister* (1999), Ribisi surprises Lewis with a big brass band playing "76 Trombones" marching through the streets of North Beach, as they drive away together from the steps outside the church.

In *Fearless* (1993), Rosie Perez seeks solace here after the death of her little boy in a plane crash. Fellow survivor Jeff Bridges lives nearby on Telegraph Hill, and he forms an unlikely bond with the grieving mother in Peter Weir's moving screenplay.

In *Getting Even with Dad* (1993), Saul Rubinick and Garland Sartain steal a case of sacramental wine that they have mistaken for a cache of stolen coins. A nun calls the cops and they are caught.

In real life, Saints Peter and Paul Church was the intended site of the wedding ceremony of North Beach native and baseball hero Joe DiMaggio and movie goddess Marilyn Monroe in 1954. But the church denied access to the divorced bridegroom, and the couple was married instead at San Francisco's City Hall. The lack of a religious ceremony did not keep the happy newlyweds from posing for wedding photographs in front of Saints Peter and Paul, however.

36. Dante Building
1606 Stockton Street at Union

In the original *Dirty Harry* (1971), this building, home to a number of North Beach cafés and restaurants, provides the rooftop where a sniper, portrayed by Andy Robinson, who has promised in a letter to next murder a priest or a black man, trains his rifle on an effeminate black man eating an ice cream cone and walking across Washington Square Park. The killer later returns to the site, planning to shoot a priest (actually a disguised police officer serving as bait) coming out of Saints Peter and Paul Church. Harry, standing under a rotating "Jesus Saves" sign, is momentarily distracted, and the killer is able to shoot the officer and escape.

In his autobiography, director Don Siegel describes the enormous effort that went into shooting this one scene. "This was a very dangerous shot and it was my responsibility to go over it with Bruce Sturges and special effects many, many times to ensure that no one would get hurt." The camera lights, as well as those from the revolving neon sign, coupled with the noise of the special effects bullets, precipitated complaints from neighborhood residents when the filming continued after midnight. This is a common occurrence, especially during nighttime filming, and requires support from police.

37. Jasper Place between Filbert and Union

In the 2002 debut episode of cable television series *Monk* with Tony Shalhoub, Detective Adrian Monk is chased by a hit man down Jasper Place in North Beach and escapes. Other authentic city locations include North Beach and Telegraph Hill as well as shots of the Transamerica Pyramid and Bay Bridge. For unknown reasons, location filming did not continue in the series about the neurotic detective.

38. 1462 Grant Avenue at Union

"Meats of the World," where Harriet Michaels (Nancy Travis), who may or may not be a murderer, works as a butcher in the Mike Myers

vehicle *So I Married an Axe Murderer* (1993), was actually Prudente's Italian Deli in North Beach, a storefront business that has since closed.

39. Grant Avenue

In *I Remember Mama* (1948) Barbara Bel Geddes ("He called me a lady, Mama") and Irene Dunne buy flowers together in one scene that was filmed in North Beach. George Stevens's meticulously rendered adaptation of Kathryn Forbes's memoir of growing up in a Norwegian immigrant family in San Francisco remains richly rewarding.

La Bodega
1332 Grant Avenue at Vallejo

One of several famous North Beach watering holes where Ashley Judd, as a self-destructive San Francisco cop, picks up a lover, only to soon find him murdered, in *Twisted* (2004).

40. Varennes Alley between Filbert and Union

Jeff Bridges's life is in upheaval after surviving a plane crash as he is inexplicably drawn to fellow survivor Rosie Perez in Peter Weir's 1993 film of Rafael Yglesias's novel, *Fearless*. Bridges and wife Isabella Rossellini live on a chic little alley on Varennes on the western slope of Telegraph Hill. In one scene he dodges reporters by running down Varennes to Union Street.

41. Vallejo Street at Montgomery

In Peter Hyams's *The Presidio* (1988) a half-clothed Mark Harmon carries Meg Ryan up the steep Vallejo Street hill from this intersection to his home on this block. Hugh Grant and Julianne Moore used the same garden-filled pedestrian block in *Nine Months*. In one scene the neighborhood was decked out for Christmas during a summer location shoot in 1995. A remake of the popular 1994 French film *Neuf Mois,* the Chris Columbus version uses many charming San Francisco locations in telling the tale of the couple's seemingly idyllic relationship torn asunder by an unexpected pregnancy.

Telegraph Hill

42. 1158 Montgomery Street between Union and Green

The exterior for the lonely apartment where Detective Nick Curran (Michael Douglas) lives in *Basic Instinct* (1992) is only a few blocks from police hangout Tosca Bar on Columbus Avenue, and a straight shot out Vallejo to the home of Catherine Tramell (Sharon Stone), the femme fatale who ruins his life. The interior of his apartment, as usual, is a Hollywood set.

43. Montgomery Street at Union Street

The intersection used in this movie is called the "most unfamous San Francisco landmark in cinema" by Hank Donat. The unobstructed view down Montgomery Street from Telegraph Hill toward the Transamerica Pyramid makes it extremely photogenic. In *The Woman in Red* (1984), Gene Wilder as Teddy Pierce finds that his family, friends, and job are all jeopardized when he falls in love with beautiful Kelly LeBrock in a red silk dress. The location also plays the exterior of J-Lo's home in *The Wedding Planner* (2001), and was the residence of Michael Douglas in

Basic Instinct (1992). Douglas lived less than a block from here during his life as Steve Keller in television's *The Streets of San Francisco* (1972–77).

44. 1227 Montgomery Street at Montague

In Philip Kaufman's 1978 remake of Don Siegel's 1956 classic sci-fi thriller *Invasion of the Body Snatchers*, Donald Sutherland starts noticing that people are complaining that their close relatives are in some way "different." The health department worker can afford a Telegraph Hill home with an incredible view at 1227 Montgomery Street at Montague. True to city geography, in one scene Sutherland and Brooke Adams escape out of the back of the house down nearby Castle Street and down the Filbert Steps to Pier 33 on the Embarcadero. This location also appears in *The House on Telegraph Hill* (1951).

45. 296 Union Street at Montgomery

Scottie's erstwhile buddy Midge (Barbara Bel Geddes) lives on Telegraph Hill in *Vertigo* (1958), at a fictional location, which appears to be 296 Union Street at Montgomery. The view from Midge's window was

The Telegraph Hill apartment in which Midge (Barbara Bel Geddes) entertains Scottie (James Stewart) in *Vertigo* (1958) was a set with a backdrop of Russian Hill. *Courtesy of Pacific Film Archive, University of California, Berkeley*

superimposed on a Hollywood set, but it is based on an actual location which appears to be the west-facing side of Telegraph Hill looking down into North Beach and across toward Russian Hill. Here the long-suffering Bel Geddes comforts Stewart as he tries to deal with the dizzying effects of his vertigo. The view in the other direction is seen in establishing shots as Midge and Scottie come and go from her apartment. These

exteriors confirm its location near the top of Telegraph Hill, looking down toward Piers 19 and 23 of the Embarcadero. The *Vertigo* (1958) screenplay was based on *D'entre les morts* by Boilieu and Narcejac.

46. 307 Filbert Street at Montgomery

George C. Scott's character lives here in Richard Lester's *Petulia* (1968), also starring Julie Christie and Richard Chamberlain. Based on *Me and the Arch Kook Petulia* by John Haase, it follows beautiful, unhappily married Petulia (Christie) in pursuit of a recently divorced doctor, straitlaced Scott.

Telegraph Hill is also home to Dennis Quaid in *Innerspace*, Joe Dante's 1987 comic science fiction story of a navy test pilot who, as a result of a miniaturization experiment, is accidentally injected into the body of hypochondriac Martin Short. He and love interest Meg Ryan argue outside his home, with a view of the Transamerica Pyramid.

47. Coit Tower
Telegraph Hill Boulevard, Pioneer Park

In 1931 Lillie Hitchcock Coit donated money for this 210-foot tower, designed by Arthur Brown Jr. as a memorial to the firefighters

of the 1906 earthquake and fire. The Works Progress Administration (WPA) murals inside are a time capsule of the city in the 1930s. (The WPA was created to provide economic relief to citizens during the Great Depression including employment opportunities for artists on relief.)

In the second entry in the *Thin Man* series, bons vivants Nick and Nora Charles investigate murder charges between cocktails and repartee. When William Powell and Myrna Loy drive up a curved roadway to their Telegraph Hill home in *After the Thin Man* (1936), the actual point of arrival is the base of Coit Tower, at the peak of the hill. Watching this revered public monument transformed into the residence of the urbane Charleses delighted some natives and outraged others. A similar cinematic trick is performed in *Pal Joey* (1957), when the grounds of the Tower are transformed into Rita Hayworth's mansion. Based on John O'Hara stories, this Rodgers and Hart musical follows the womanizing antics of Frank Sinatra as he toys with the affections of Hayworth and Kim Novak.

In the 1998 remake of *Doctor Dolittle,* the scenes where the good doctor (Eddie Murphy) confronts a tiger at the top of Coit Tower were apparently faked in Los Angeles with a translight background.

Coit Tower also serves as the phallic beacon to Scottie's (Jimmy Stewart) Russian Hill apartment for Nob Hill dweller Madeleine (Kim Novak) in Hitchcock's masterpiece, *Vertigo* (1958), a twisted valentine to San Francisco. "Coit Tower led me right to you," purrs the seductive Novak. "Well, that's the first time I've ever been grateful for Coit Tower," stammers the blushing Stewart. The geography is a stretch, but the eastward direction is right. Similarly, Kate (Tyne Daly) refers to the phallic tower as "Coitus Interruptus," and calls Clint Eastwood a "cold, bold Callahan with his great big .44," in *The Enforcer* (1976), the third *Dirty Harry* flick.

48. 1360 Montgomery Street

This splendid silvery 1937 deco apartment house is the home of Lauren Bacall in *Dark Passage* (1947). Her stylish townhouse shelters Humphrey Bogart until Agnes Moorehead comes snooping around (in a leopard jacket and matching hat) and trouble ensues. Bogart, unjustly convicted of murder, escapes San Quentin; Bacall picks him up in her station wagon, smuggles him past a police roadblock on the Golden Gate Bridge, and brings him to this house. Another scene shows Bogart, or a body double, with his head bandaged, ascending the steep Filbert Street steps from the eastern base of Telegraph Hill.

In Robert Wise's 1951 noir-thriller *The House on Telegraph Hill*, this block was planted with formal gardens to serve as a background for the action near the landmark restaurant, now closed, called Julius Castle.

Many decades later, Hugh Grant gets his girlfriend (Julianne Moore) pregnant and discovers, after panicking, that he does love her and the child-to-be. The makers of *Nine Months* (1995) covered the front of the former *Dark Passage* building with silk bougainvillea for filming.

49. Philo T. Farnsworth Lab
202 Green Street

A plaque at the corner of Green and Sansome commemorates the birth of television. The State Historical Landmark (#941) was dedicated in 1981. The bronze inscription reads: "In a simple laboratory on this site, 202 Green Street, Philo Taylor Farnsworth, U.S. pioneer in electronics, invented and patented the first operational all-electronic television system on September 7, 1927. The 21-year-old inventor and several dedicated assistants successfully transmitted the first all-electronic television image, the major breakthrough that brought the practical form of this invention to mankind."

Farnsworth filed the first of his television patents a few months after moving to this facility, first named Research Labs and later Television, Inc. In spite of his generally accepted title as "the father of television," Farnsworth, who died in 1971, spent much of his life struggling with RCA over a claim that Russian émigré Vladimir Zworykin was the true inventor of the boob tube that changed all of our lives.

50. Fog City Diner
1300 Battery Street at the Embarcadero

This is where Mike Myers and his cop pal Tony Giardino double-date in *So I Married an Axe Murderer*. After dinner, they fight over the check in Frank Ryan's 1993 comedy. Myers plays a guy who's always

avoided commitment by finding absurd reasons to break up with his girlfriends, but finally meets a beautiful young woman (Nancy Travis), and falls in love. Then he becomes convinced that she's a notorious axe murderer.

51. The Piers

Once cut off from the city by the intrusive Embarcadero Freeway, the Piers were reintegrated with their surrounding neighborhoods after the 1989 Loma Prieta earthquake and the subsequent demolition of the unsafe elevated freeway. The late, unlamented structure can be viewed in many 1960s and '70s movies; try Lina Wertmüller's *The End of the World in Our Usual Bed in a Night Full of Rain* for some good aerial views from 1977 that serve as establishing shots for the San Francisco–based action between Candice Bergen and Giancarlo Giannini.

At the popular tourist destination Pier 39 in *Homeward Bound II: Lost in San Francisco,* this is where the animal stars show each other the "proper method of begging" food from tourists. When they see the sea lions adjacent to the pier, they conclude that "that's what happens to you

if you stay in the water too long: your fur comes off." In the 1996 sequel to *Homeward Bound,* the pets wander through the city having adventures as they try to get home to Marin County.

Pier 43½ sees George C. Scott taking his kids on a Red-and-White Fleet cruise in *Petulia* (1968). *The Birdman of Alcatraz* (1962) opens and closes here, with Edmond O'Brien as author Thomas Gaddis waiting for Robert Stroud (Burt Lancaster), who is leaving Alcatraz after 17 years in prison.

Countless movies have been filmed at various piers. At Pier 41, in Don Siegel's *Lineup* (1958), a suitcase taken by a porter from an arriving ship passenger is tossed into a taxicab, which runs over and kills a cop before crashing, setting the movie in motion. The thriller is an expanded version of a CBS television series (1954–60), which follows the lives of two drug dealers.

Michael "Mouse" Tolliver (Paul Hopkins) and Mary Ann Singleton (Laura Linney) leave on a Mexican cruise from Pier 29, with both of them looking for "Mr. Right" in *More Tales of the City* in 1998.

The Caine Mutiny is the 1954 story of distrust and betrayal on the high seas, starring Humphrey Bogart, Van Johnson, and Fred MacMurray, based on Herman Wouk's Pulitzer Prize–winning novel. Location scenes show the piers along Embarcadero with both the Bay Bridge and the Golden Gate Bridge visible in the background as the USS *Caine* prepares to leave for Pearl Harbor, and again when it returns.

On Pier 7 in *Basic Instinct,* buddies George Dzundza and Michael Douglas have a shouting match about whether Catherine (Sharon Stone) or Beth (Jeanne Tripplehorn) is the murderer. Douglas gets way too involved with murder suspect Stone, who plays the sexy Catherine in the controversial 1992 Paul Verhoeven flick. The charming pedestrian/fishing pier also appears as a romantic backdrop in the 2001 Jennifer Lopez vehicle *The Wedding Planner.*

Fisherman's Wharf is a part of town turned over almost exclusively to tourists and purveyors of souvenir T-shirts. "Why would anyone want to go there?" most locals would ask. Still, the neighborhood retains some vestiges of its days as an actual fishing community from

Pier Seven with a view of the Bay Bridge.

the early 1900s, particularly toward its western end ("Fish Alley") where the morning catch is landed. Dungeness crab remains a certifiable specialty, and *cioppino* is rumored to have been invented in this 'hood, the name for the seafood soup an Italianization of the English word *chop*. The Wharf and its piers have attracted not only many tourists, but also filmmakers over the years.

52. Taylor Street and Jefferson

The Sea Captain's Chest, a Wharf shop, is the spot in front of which a taxicab picks up Lee Remick in Blake Edwards's *Experiment in Terror* (1962). She parks her car in spot number three and uses the phone booth across from Alioto's Restaurant.

Castagnola's Restaurant, a longtime seafood institution at the Wharf, is the backdrop (either real or projected) for a discussion between Stephanie Powers and Ken Berry, as Powers defends her grandmother (Helen Hayes) from his uncle (Keenan Wynn) in their historic preservation versus development struggle in *Herbie Rides Again* (1974), the *Love Bug* sequel from Disney.

In his last James Bond role, in *View to a Kill* (1985), Roger Moore asks for "soft shell crab" at Jefferson and Taylor Streets, and thus meets the CIA agent masquerading as a fish market salesman. As the agent shows Moore the photographs, they stroll past cable cars (not on Fisherman's Wharf in reality).

53. Bowles Hopkins Gallery
747 Beach Street at Hyde

If it is not well known for the classiest art galleries in town, Fisherman's Wharf is heavily populated by art shops catering to tourists. In 1983's *Sudden Impact*, the fourth *Dirty Harry* outing, the actual gallery where Jennifer Spencer's (Sondra Locke) show "Dark Visions" is on display is the Bowles Hopkins. As Locke is leaving the gallery, she is accosted by thugs. She sweetly inquires, "Need a lift? Then shove a jack up your ass."

54. Taylor Street and North Point

A block away, in *Magnum Force* (1973), Dirty Harry (Clint Eastwood) and his colleague watch the Cost Plus store at this intersection through one-way glass. As a theft begins, they engage in a shoot-out with the thugs, thwarting the robbery.

55. Bank of America
1455 Stockton Street at Columbus

Woody Allen tries to pull off a heist at the North Beach branch of the Bank of America in his 1969 comedy *Take the Money and Run*, playing inept petty criminal Virgil Starkwell.

56. Hancock School
940 Filbert Street at Taylor

The kids in *Mrs. Doubtfire* (1993) attend school at Filbert and Taylor, actually the Chinatown branch of City College, with a fine view of Saints Peter and Paul Church in North Beach in the distance.

57. Taylor Street at Union

Mike Myers in *So I Married an Axe Murderer* (1993) lives on Aladdin Terrace off Taylor between Filbert and Union. This tiny alley buried in North Beach serves as the spot where Charlie MacKenzie (Myers) garages his sports car and sits on his roof overlooking the neighborhood.

58. Rocco's Corner
Columbus Street at Chestnut

"This is it!" proclaims the sign at Rocco's, which portrayed the exterior of "Cock of the North," the restaurant where the Mackenzies celebrate their 30th wedding anniversary in Mike Myers's *So I Married an Axe Murderer*. The interior is Edinburgh Castle, 950 Geary Street at Larkin in the Tenderloin.

59. Club Fugazi
678 Green Street at Powell

Club Fugazi was filmed in the original *Armistead Maupin's Tales of the City* (1993) miniseries, when characters watch a modified version of the long-running, belt-em-out musical review *Beach Blanket Babylon*. The San Francisco institution has been packing in the crowds for decades, and it has been housed at Club Fugazi since moving across North Beach from its humble origins in the back room of the venerable Savoy Tivoli bar, which is still alive and well on Grant Avenue.

60. Vallejo Street Garage
755 Vallejo Street at Stockton

Ursula's (Leslie Mann) San Francisco apartment building (the Talmapais atop Russian Hill) had no balconies, so in *George of the Jungle* (1997) the top of the Vallejo garage above the police station stood in for the girlfriend's place, with its panoramic view of North Beach.

Western San Francisco

Bud Cort and Ruth Gordon as *Harold and Maude* (1971) converse at Sutro Baths with the Cliff House in the background. *Courtesy of Pacific Film Archive, University of California, Berkeley*

This tour covers a lot of territory: the entire western half of the 49 square miles that make up the city (and county) of San Francisco. From the comfort of a car, we begin at the westernmost tip of the peninsula with its breathtaking views of the Pacific, then continue east through the Richmond neighborhood (not to be confused with the East Bay city called Richmond). A drive through the wooded Presidio, scenic Crissy Field, and Fort Mason is followed by climbing up the dense and hilly Pacific Heights. We move south through the Western Addition and Hayes Valley, then around the famous Haight-Ashbury and Golden Gate Park. A few sites are scattered in the Sunset district, after which we descend into the Castro, through Noe Valley, ending with one lone site in the Excelsior district.

Sutro Baths, circa 1960s. *Courtesy of San Francisco History Center, San Francisco Public Library*

1. **Sutro Baths**
    Point Lobos Avenue at Merrie Way

Flamboyant entrepreneur Adolph Sutro once lived in an estate overlooking the Pacific Ocean, the architectural footprint of which is now Sutro Heights Park. The name Sutro has dominated this corner of San Francisco since the building of the Sutro Baths, a destination for locals for half a century, with their Victorian glass domes over six salt-water pools. The baths were built on three acres of oceanfront property in 1886, before the western half of the city was developed, but a train link made them accessible to downtowners. Locals and tourists alike frolicked on its slides, trapezes, and high dives, with their views of the Pacific Ocean. There was also a 3,700-seat amphitheater, as well as galleries devoted to both art and natural history exhibits, and three restaurants. Sutro's dream attraction for San Franciscans went into decline when in 1937 his grandson converted the largest swimming tank into a skating rink, which had far less success. The formerly grand site has been a ruin since a 1966 fire. In *The Lineup* (1958), Eli Wallach is to deliver the heroin to "The Man" at the fictional Sutro Museum. Wallach

ends up pushing him off a balcony onto the ice-skating rink to his death, in this expanded version of the CBS television series (1954–60) that follows two drug dealers. In its ruined state, the baths appear in *Harold and Maude* as the site of a staged confrontation between Bud Cort and "suffragette" Ruth Gordon in order to shock Harold's one-armed military uncle. The 1971 black comedy by Hal Ashby, with music by Cat Stevens, has developed a cult following.

2.   Cliff House
1090 Point Lobos Avenue

There have been several versions of the Cliff House at this dramatic location above the Pacific Ocean with its overlook of Seal Rocks. A complete retro design reestablishes the Cliff House as a destination for tourists and locals.

Eric von Stroheim shot scenes for *Greed* at the Cliff House and Seal Rocks in 1925. In the 1938 musical, *Alexander's Ragtime Band*, with Tyrone Power, a title card shows the invitation to the opening of the Rocco Room at the Cliff House featuring Alexander's Ragtime Band, Saturday, May 10th (1919), where Alice Faye performs "Now It Can Be

Told." The Irving Berlin musical chronicles the professional and romantic ups and downs of bandleader Power, nice-guy pianist-composer Don Ameche, and the tough-but-vulnerable singer they vie for (Faye).

In the first *Princess Diaries* (2001) the Queen of Genovia (Julie Andrews) and her San Franciscan granddaughter (Anne Hathaway) visit the Musée Mechanique, which was then housed under the Cliff House, near the Camera Obscura on the deck beneath the restaurant. with a view to the Seal Rocks beyond. On the DVD release, the stars discuss the difficulties of filming outdoors, curiously plagued by flies.

Orson Welles slides through Playland in *The Lady from Shanghai* **(1948).** *Courtesy of Pacific Film Archive, University of California, Berkeley*

3. **Playland at the Beach**
   Great Highway between Balboa and Cabrillo

Originally known as Chutes-at-the-Beach, the late, much-lamented amusement park at Ocean Beach is remembered fondly by longtime locals and was an attraction for filmmakers as well. From 1921 to 1972 the merry-go-round, roller coaster, and concessions (like the locally made It's-It ice cream sandwich) were extremely popular. The famous climax of Orson Welles's *The Lady from Shanghai* (1948) was set in the Hall of Mirrors in the Fun House. The multiple reflections of the beautiful blonde Rita Hayworth make for a stunning scene.

Across the Great Highway is a broad expanse of sand at Ocean Beach, where swimming in the cold water and often-dangerous tides is for pros only. In *Around the Fire* (1998), the final scene of all the hippies reuniting was filmed here. You can glimpse the Cliff House on the hill in the background.

4. The Beach Chalet
Great Highway at John F. Kennedy Drive

Local architect Willis Polk built the Beach Chalet in 1921, and it became home to Lucien Laubaudt's stunning WPA frescoes in the 1930s. Laura Linney as Mary Ann Singleton has an awkward date there with the creepy upstairs neighbor Norman in *Tales of the City* (1993). The then-closed Beach Chalet was still off-limits to the public during the filming, but an impromptu restaurant was created on the lower level. This is now a museum where the public can view the historic frescoes, which are like a time capsule of 1930s life in San Francisco. A restaurant/microbrewery is now located upstairs, with Park Chalet, another restaurant, behind the building.

5. Land's End
El Camino del Mar

Near the Legion of Honor, dramatic, cypress-lined cliffs drop to the Pacific Ocean below.

In the opening scene of 1983's *Sudden Impact*, the fourth *Dirty Harry* flick (and the only one directed by star Clint Eastwood), a man and woman are making out in a parked car during the film's opening when two shots ring out, and the man is later discovered dead. Other nefarious doings happen at Land's End in the original *Tales of the City* (1993); here Barbary Lane resident Norman Neal Williams (Stanley deSantis) falls to his death when his fake necktie gives out.

6.   California Palace of the Legion of Honor
34th Avenue at Clement in Lincoln Park

One of two structures (with the de Young in Golden Gate Park) that form the Fine Arts Museums of San Francisco, the "Legion," as locals call it, was modeled after a historic building, the Légion d'Honneur, near the Musée d'Orsay in Paris. It was a gift of Adolph and Alma de Brettville Spreckels to the city in 1916 as a memorial to the troops killed in World War I and to promote French art in California. A 1990s renovation enhanced its glamorous location atop Point Lobos.

The Legion's most famous cinematic moment comes when, in Alfred Hitchcock's *Vertigo* (1958), Jimmy Stewart follows an entranced Kim Novak into its galleries to watch her staring at the (Hollywood prop) "Portrait of Carlota." She later claims never to have been inside the museum, and we know that Jimmy is in big trouble.

Laura Linney as the naive midwesterner Mary Ann Singleton follows in Kim's footsteps to the Legion in *Armistead Maupin's Tales of the City* (1993), much of which is an homage to the Hitchcock classic. She returns there in a party scene in *Further Tales* (2001), from the same series. Matthew McConaughey plays a scenic game of golf nearby in Lincoln Park, although this scene from *The Wedding Planner* is a long shot, and it may be a body double. McConaughey and Jennifer Lopez check out the flowers, and each other, in a staged flower market set up in front of the art museum in the same film. The 2001 romantic comedy pairs Lopez as a single San Francisco woman who arranges marriages, until she's captivated by one of her prospective bridegrooms.

7. Balboa Theater
3630 Balboa at 38th Avenue

One of the last of a breed of survivors, the Balboa is a neighborhood enterprise that shows first-run movies at bargain prices. Recently restored to a single-screen theater, and renovated with new projection equipment, the theater hosted the Third Annual Film Noir Festival, organized by Eddie Muller.

8. Bank of America
38th Avenue at Balboa

Natasha Richardson as *Patty Hearst* (1988) helps to rob a bank across the street from the Balboa Theater (see page 162). The real-life location of the bank heist is south of Golden Gate Park at 22nd Avenue and Noriega. Paul Schrader filmed the dramatization of the bizarre kidnapping and conversion into bank-robber "Tania" of San Francisco newspaper heiress Patty Hearst, who is now an occasional John Waters actress.

Natasha Richardson as *Patty Hearst* accompanied by Symbionese Liberation Army members make their getaway from the Hibernia Bank in Paul Schrader's 1988 film.
Courtesy of Pacific Film Archive, University of California, Berkeley

9. George Washington High School
600 32nd Avenue at Anza

George Washington High School, a 1934 deco structure designed by Timothy Pflueger, with WPA murals in the lobby, was featured in Blake Edwards's *Experiment in Terror* in 1961. Lee Remick is terrorized by Ross Martin, a man with an asthmatic voice who plans to use her to steal $100,000 from the bank where she works. He threatens to kill her and/or her teenage sister Stephanie Powers if she tells the police. Remick manages to contact FBI agent Glenn Ford, who races around the city following leads. Powers goes to school here.

10. Balboa at 22nd Avenue

In *Play It Again Sam,* the Herbert Ross comedy featuring young Woody Allen in 1972, this intersection is the location where the large sheet of glass is broken in a sight gag. The film about a neurotic film buff abandoned by his wife set the tone for many Allen comedies to come. The Allen character seeks female companionship, aided and abetted by his best friends, a married couple, and the ghost of Humphrey Bogart.

11. Cosmos Company
653–673 Eighth Avenue between Balboa and Cabrillo

The site of Cosmos Company, the first movie studio in San Francisco. In 1912 Thomas Kimmwood Peters, a pioneer newsreel cameraman who filmed the 1906 earthquake and fire, "produced the first motion pictures in San Francisco, a series of old Chinese plays using the Jackson Street Chinese Opera Company as actors," according to a letter he wrote to Mayor Joseph Alioto on April 11, 1969. They had titles like *Adventures of Bow Kung, Trapped by Wireless (for Pathé)*, and *Chinese Stories*.

12. Mel's Drive-In
3355 Geary Boulevard at Commonwealth

Some scenes in *American Graffiti* were filmed here by George Lucas in 1972, although the principal action takes place at the now-defunct Mel's at South Van Ness and Mission. In 1967, Spencer Tracy is not having a good day in Stanley Kramer's *Guess Who's Coming to Dinner.* He pulls in to calm himself by ordering an ice cream flavor that he had there once before. He thinks it's "fresh Oregon boysenberry sherbet" but realizes this is "not the stuff I had before, but I like it." Then he backs into a roadster, and gets into an altercation with its African American driver.

13. St. John's Presbyterian Church
25 Lake Street at Arguello

In *So I Married an Axe Murderer* (1993), this is the church where Mike Myers and Nancy Travis get married. The wedding reception was filmed at the Swedenborgian Church, 2107 Lyon Street at Washington.

14. The Presidio

Originally the Spanish army's base in a New World outpost, the dramatically situated Presidio subsequently reverted to the U.S. Army, which built most of the buildings on its wooded grounds. In 1994 it was taken over by the National Park Service. The flat part of the former military property, until recently the site of Letterman Hospital, has been reborn as a home for George Lucas's sprawling movie production company, the Letterman Digital Arts Center. In addition to movie and television production, the company's global businesses include visual effects, sound, video games, licensing, and online activity.

Civilians got a peek inside the Presidio compound when Sean Connery played an officer in residence, with Meg Ryan as his rebellious daughter, in *The Presidio,* filmed on location here in 1988. Mark Harmon, as a civilian police detective, has a run-in with Colonel Caldwell (Connery), who had been his commanding officer years before when he left the military police over a disagreement over the handling of a drunk driver. A series of murders that cross jurisdictions forces them to work together again. That Harmon is now dating Connery's daughter (Ryan) is not helping the relationship at all. Many Presidio buildings and sites are used as a background for the action, including a tour through the Army Museum (Funston at Lincoln) and the 1930s Mission-style Officer's Club (Moraga at Arguello). Ryan and old family friend Jack Warden stroll through the Military Cemetery, which also is the location of a tearjerker scene with Connery later in the film.

Among the many nonprofits now housed at the former Presidio is the San Francisco Film Society, which produces the annual San Francisco Film Festival and many other cinematic events.

15. Baker Beach

At this popular beach stretched out below the Presidio with Golden Gate views, swimming in the icy waters is for the intrepid only, but fishing is good. In *The Princess Diaries* (2001), a teenage beach party uses an establishing shot with the Golden Gate Bridge in the distance. Then, according to director Garry Marshall, the filming of "Baker Beach" shifted to Los Angeles. The swinging seventies gang from Barbary

Lane gets naked at the far end of Baker Beach in the first installment of *Armistead Maupin's Tales of the City* (1993). In *Dream for an Insomniac* (1996) Ione Skye (daughter of singer Donovan) walks with Mackenzie Astin (son of actors Patty Duke and John Astin) along the beach asking him if he loves his girlfriend. When he equivocates, she gives him a hard time.

16. Golden Gate Bridge

The burnt orange span of the art moderne Golden Gate Bridge has appeared in more films than any other single San Francisco location. Films featuring the famous site include *Flower Drum Song* (1962), *Jagged Edge* (1985), *Guess Who's Coming to Dinner* (1967), *The High and the Mighty* (1954), and countless others. Almost every San Francisco–based film manages to include a view of the city's most famous landmark from one angle or another. It is hard to imagine how much the opening of the bridge in 1937 must have changed the Bay Area, allowing commuters easy access to San Francisco from the north, without getting on a boat, for the first time. The single-span suspension bridge was a neces-

sity because of the incredible depths of the underwater gorge beneath the Golden Gate; there was no place to plant a central pier.

A few examples of creative uses of the Golden Gate Bridge by film-makers follow:

- In 1955, a giant octopus threatens to destroy San Francisco, and in fact makes quite a mess of the south tower of the bridge, in *It Came from Beneath the Sea.*

- Gregory Peck and his submarine crew come to San Francisco to investigate reports of a nuclear cloud wiping out the world's population. Through the periscope, Peck finds the Golden Gate Bridge eerily silent and unpopulated in Stanley Kramer's *On the Beach* (1959).

- In 1974 Herbie *The Love Bug* drives up the cables to one of the piers of the bridge with Helen Hayes inside.

- Christopher Reeve's Man of Steel keeps a school bus full of kids from falling off the bridge after an earthquake on the San Andreas Fault snaps cables and fractures part of the roadway (in remarkably convincing models) in 1978's *Superman*.

- Albert Brooks drives his convertible across the bridge in *Mother* (1996), in a scene reminiscent of *The Graduate*, as Simon and Garfunkel sound-alikes sing "Mother Henderson" on the soundtrack. He is on his way from L.A. to Sausalito to move back in with his mother, played by Debbie Reynolds in her first feature film role in 25 years.

- In Chris Columbus's *Bicentennial Man* (1999), set in the future, the bridge has both an upper and a lower deck, an engineering challenge which might become a reality someday.

17. Fort Point
Long Avenue

The fort was constructed by the U.S. Army Corps of Engineers between 1853 and 1861 to prevent entrance of a hostile fleet into San Francisco Bay. It was threatened with demolition during the construction of the Golden Gate Bridge, until the towering structure was eventually built around it. Between 1933 and 1937 the fort was used as a base of operations for the construction of the bridge. During World War II, the fort was occupied by about 100 soldiers who manned searchlights and rapid-fire cannons mounted atop the structure as part of the protection of a submarine net strung across the entrance to the Bay. Fort Point, only the third system brick fort on the West Coast, became a National Historic Site on October 16, 1970. It currently houses a museum and is one of the few pre–Civil War structures in the city.

The great cinematic moment of Fort Point, directly beneath the south end of the Golden Gate Bridge, is, of course, the plunge into the San Francisco Bay of the mysterious Madeleine (Kim Novak), followed by retired detective Scottie (Jimmy Stewart), in Alfred Hitchcock's *Vertigo* (1958). In 1977 Mel Brooks staged a wacky Hitchcock homage at Fort Point in *High Anxiety* by having his own character attacked by a metal-mouthed villain while he's trapped in a Tippi-Hedren-in-Bodega-Bay phone booth at Kim Novak's Fort Point. Richard Lester's *Petulia* (1968) sees George C. Scott passing Fort Point on a Red-and-White Fleet ferry cruise with his kids. Commuters Martin Mull and Bill Macy from groovy bedroom community Mill Valley also come and go past familiar Bay sites on the Red-and-White Fleet in the Marin County spoof *Serial* (1980).

In 1999 Robin Williams flirts with a fellow android in a scene filmed at Fort Point in *Bicentennial Man*. In this sci-fi comedy, Williams

George C. Scott and Julie Christie underneath the Golden Gate Bridge in a scene from *Petulia* (1968). *Courtesy of Art, Music & Recreation Center, San Francisco Public Library*

is purchased by the Martin family as a household robot, programmed to perform menial tasks. Within a few days the family realizes that they don't have an ordinary droid as Andrew begins to experience emotions and creative thought. Over two centuries, Andrew learns the intricacies of humanity. Rupert Burns's (Oliver Platt) studio was located at Fort Point.

The lead in the indie film *Dopamine* (2003), John Livingston, pops out of the bay in a wet suit at Fort Point, an unlikely spot for swimmers, who favor the sheltered cove at Aquatic Park. Surfers prefer the white water near the rocks beneath the fort. The screenplay of *Dopamine* explains that software artist Rand (Livingston) was a fat kid until he discovered swimming.

In 1967 an abandoned Fort Point was used for the final sequence of the neo-noir classic *Point Blank*. Based on the novel *The Hunter* by Richard Stark (pseudonym used by Donald E. Westlake), the story involves reclaiming $93,000 that was stolen from Lee Marvin during a heist. Carroll O'Connor stands in the middle of the interior courtyard waiting for the helicopter to land and deliver the purloined money. Marvin watches from various positions throughout the fort. After the money is delivered and the helicopter takes off, O'Connor is shot, by Keenan Wynn. He calls for Marvin to come get his money, but there is only silence, and a final shot of Alcatraz, where the story began.

18. Crissy Field/Marina Green

Landfill from the 1915 Pan-Pacific Exposition in this part of the city turned wetlands into an airfield from 1919 to 1936. Crissy Field Beach and Golden Gate Promenade have been popular destinations for locals since their restoration as a wildlife sanctuary in the 1990s. Locals enjoy the wildlife preserve, the beach, dog-walking, and running paths of Crissy Field. Both it and the nearby Marina Green (Marina Boulevard, from Fillmore to Scott Streets) have frequently been used as movie locations.

Before its rebirth, in 1955, scientists track the undersea movement, with radar, of a giant octopus threatening San Francisco from Crissy Field in *It Came from Beneath the Sea*. Robin Williams in drag frolics with the kids in a *Mrs. Doubtfire* montage in 1993. *Doubtfire* director Chris Columbus returned two years later to film *Nine Months* (1995) here: the opening scene where Julianne Moore and Hugh Grant are pic-

Robin Williams as Mrs. Doubtfire, in a film by the same name, takes his kids bicycling through Crissy Field with its views of the Golden Gate Bridge. *Courtesy of Pacific Film Archive, University of California, Berkeley*

nicking to celebrate five perfect years together. When Moore raises the issue of marriage and children, Grant is knocked down by a kite, and Tom Arnold offers mouth-to-mouth resuscitation. Crissy Field and its beaches are used as scenic backgrounds, with distant views of Golden Gate Bridge, for several Keanu Reeves scenes as he ponders his future with or without Charlize Theron, in 2001's *Sweet November*. *Doctor Dolittle 2*, the 2001 sequel to Eddie Murphy's remake of the Rex Harrison musical, was the first movie to film at the new West Crissy Field picnic area.

Cow Hollow/Marina

19. Palace of Fine Arts
3301 Lyon Street at Bay Street

The landmark domed structure, a masterpiece by Bay Area architect Bernard Maybeck, is the last survivor of the Panama-Pacific International Exposition in 1915. Originally constructed of temporary materials, it was made more permanent several decades after the fair closed. It is an extraordinarily romantic indoor/outdoor space of a central rotunda surrounded by a graceful peristyle of Corinthian columns,

interspersed with a quiet lagoon and fountains. It now houses a science museum—called the Exploratorium—and a theater.

Scottie and Judy (Jimmy Stewart and Kim Novak) take a romantic walk along the lagoon by the Palace of Fine Arts while they are "courting" in the second half of Hitchcock's *Vertigo* (1958). Their stroll inspires many other cinematic couples, including Mary Ann and Burke (Laura Linney and Colin Ferguson), who stroll by the building in *More Tales of the City* (1998). The Palace is the scene where Tom Hanks gives Robin Wright his Medal of Honor in *Forrest Gump* (1994). In *The Bachelor* (1999) Chris O'Donnell and Renée Zellweger celebrate their first year together with a candle in a cupcake. Later, O'Donnell is in a rowboat with James Cromwell (in reality there are no boats in the lake) when he learns that the priest had been married for 26 years; O'Donnell realizes that he truly loves Zellweger. In *Woman on Top*, the 1999 story of a sexy Brazilian television chef, Penelope Cruz appears in a special segment of her show, "Passion Food Live!" which is being shot with the Palace of Fine Arts as the background. In *Boys and Girls* (2000), Freddie Prinze Jr. and Claire Forlani have yet another heart-to-heart talk here about their relationship and whether she might be a girlfriend substitute for him.

In a break from the action of *The Rock* in 1996, Sean Connery goes to meet his estranged daughter (Claire Forlani again) at the Palace of Fine Arts and is recaptured by Nicolas Cage. She supposedly lives at "32 Stenson Drive" in San Francisco, but no such address exists. In *The Other Sister* (1999), Juliette Lewis, as the mentally handicapped Carla, is fiercely seeking independence from her overprotective parents, Diane Keaton and Tom Skerritt. Underneath the columns Lewis and Keaton have the "sex talk" and Lewis's loud and graphic conversation embarrasses Keaton. Later, when Lewis and Giovanni Ribisi discuss their wedding, Lewis assures him that her mother will NOT be planning her wedding; she will be doing it herself.

20. Marina Green/East Harbor

In the original *Dirty Harry* (1971), this is the location of the pay phone booth where Clint Eastwood is instructed to wait for the call from the extortionist who promises that Harry will be "bounced all over town" to make sure he's alone. The extortionist then accepts the bag containing $200,000 in cash in exchange for the 14-year-old girl he has kidnapped.

21. Fort Mason Center
Marina Boulevard at Buchanan Street

This former military fort is home to museums, theaters, artists' studios, and other non-profits, as well as Greens, the renowned vegetarian restaurant with a great view of the Golden Gate Bridge.

The rave scenes in Greg Harrison's *Groove* were filmed in a darkened Pier One warehouse at Fort Mason in 2000. *Red Diaper Baby*, a one-man stage play starring Josh Kornbluth, was shot entirely at the Magic Theater in Fort Mason Center in 2004.

22. Café Cantata
2026 Union Street at Buchanan

In *Bullitt*, Jacqueline Bisset and Steve McQueen dine at this popular restaurant/café until he is interrupted by a phone call. The quintessential San Francisco chase flick was filmed all over the city in 1968.

23. "Erskine's Photo Studio"
2040 Union Street

In the television series *Phyllis*, Phyllis Lindstrom (Cloris Leachman) moves from Minneapolis to her hometown of San Francisco following the death of husband Lars. The spin-off of *The Mary Tyler Moore Show* ran from 1975 to 1977. Phyllis worked as assistant to photographer Julie Erskine (played first by Barbara Colby, then Liz Torres) in the first season. The address is one of many retail establishments in the now-urban and urbane Cow Hollow, whose pastoral name comes from its use in the 19th century as a bovine grazing area. The weekly opening theme song by Stan Daniels is an unusual exercise in Broadway style razzle-dazzle, which ultimately becomes a joke at the title character's expense.

> "Who makes the fog surrounding the Golden Gate simply
>   disappear?
> *Phyllis. Phyllis.*
> Who makes the warning bells on the cable cars play "The Gang's
>   All Here"?
> *Phyllis. Phyllis.*
> Who charms the crabs at Fisherman's Wharf right out of their
>   shell?

Who lights the lamps of Chinatown just by walking in view . . .
   who?
Phyllis. Phyllis. Phyllis. It sure isn't you!"

24. Metro Theater
2055 Union Street at Webster

The Metro was built by Samuel L. Levin and opened on April 23, 1924, as the "Metropolitan." It was a key link in the chain of theaters run by San Francisco Theatres Inc., which consisted of the Alexandria, Coliseum, Metro, Harding, Balboa, Vogue, and later the Coronet. The interiors and exteriors were extensively remodeled before it reopened in June 1941 as the "Metro." In 1957 it was the site of the first San Francisco International Film Festival, where the opening night feature was director Helmut Kautner's feature, *Captain from Köpenick*, which won the festival's Golden Gate award.

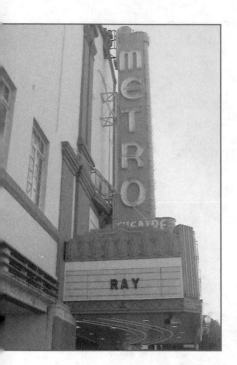

25. 2100 Green Street at Webster

In the 1998 remake of the Rex Harrison children's classic about a veterinarian who can "talk to the animals," this is the home of *Doctor Dolittle* (Eddie Murphy) and his family. His offices are a block away at 2107 Union at Webster.

26. 2340 Francisco Street at Divisadero

In *Time After Time* (1979), a desperate Malcolm McDowell, as time-traveling H. G. Wells, tries to drive his first car chasing David Warner and Mary Steenburgen around town, in an homage to *Bullitt*. This is the exterior of Steenburgen's apartment, but the interiors are a set. Its actual proximity to the Palace of Fine Arts, also used in the chase sequences, must have been a plus.

Pacific Heights

The neighborhood of Pacific Heights is among the most desirable, and expensive, real estate in the city. The views over San Francisco Bay are unmatched. Ironically, *Pacific Heights* (1990) was filmed across town on 19th Street on Potrero Hill.

27. 2601 Lyon Street at Green

This building portrays Grove High School in *The Princess Diaries* (2001). The Heather Matarazzo character, Lily Moscovitz, Anne Hathaway's best friend, is picked up and dropped off here by chauffeur Hector Elizondo. The setting for the film was changed from New York in Meg Cabot's novel to San Francisco, where director Garry Marshall's grandchildren live.

28. 2930 Vallejo Street at Lyon

Sharon Stone as Catherine Trammel called this address home, but the house was identified in *Basic Instinct* (1992) as "162 Divisadero," which would place it in the Castro, if the address existed. This property sold in 1998 for $7.25 million. Stone was frequently seen about town while she was a Sea Cliff resident and married to Phil Bronstein, the editor of the *San Francisco Chronicle*.

29. The Simmons House
2898 Vallejo Street at Baker

Richard Chamberlain, the villainous engineer responsible for the self-destruction of San Francisco's tallest skyscraper, lives here with wife Susan Blakely in *The Towering Inferno* (1974) until that fateful night. This is where architect Paul Newman goes to visit contractor William Holden, but meets up with his daughter and son-in-law Chamberlain. It is apparent that they have cut costs by authorizing the installation of wiring that might be up to code but is not what the architect ordered.

This mansion was also featured as "Caulfield's Detective Agency" in the NBC series *Partners in Crime* in 1984. The first series to be filmed entirely in the city since *The Streets of San Francisco* (1972–77), *Partners in Crime* starred Lynda Carter and Loni Anderson as ex-wives of a murdered detective who go into business together.

30. 2700 Vallejo Street at Divisadero

In *Bullitt* (1968), this is the home of Walter Chalmers (Robert Vaughn), the smarmy bureaucrat who treats Frank Bullitt (Steve McQueen) with condescension. It's also where, in *Pleasure of His Company* (1961), Fred Astaire disrupts Debbie Reynold's plans to marry Tab Hunter.

Entrance to the cul-de-sac Raycliff Terrace.

31. 634 Raycliff Terrace
Between Pacific Avenue and Broadway, Divisadero, and Broderick

Spencer Tracy and Katharine Hepburn live on fictitious "Claremont Drive" in Pacific Heights in Stanley Kramer's *Guess Who's Coming to Dinner* (1967). The Draytons' upscale house has a terrace with views of Angel Island, the Golden Gate Bridge, and the San Francisco Bay, all background matte paintings. Exteriors were shot in Pasadena, California, and 90 percent of the movie was shot on one set. Tracy, who had been in poor health, died 10 days after filming wrapped.

32. 2301 Scott Street at Washington
This was Sydney Kovak's (Loni Anderson) home in the short-lived TV series *Partners in Crime* (1984). Pretty good for a struggling bass player.

The cast and director of *Guess Who's Coming to Dinner* (1967) on the soundstage set of the Pacific Heights terrace with its illuminated backdrop. *Courtesy of Pacific Film Archive, University of California, Berkeley*

33. Alta Plaza Park
Steiner Street at Clay

In Coppola's *The Conversation* (1974), this is the site of the brief dream sequence in which Cindy Williams is running up the steps of the park in the fog, eluding Gene Hackman, who is pursuing her. *What's Up, Doc?* (1978) features a madcap chase scene on the steps of Pacific Heights' usually serene Alta Plaza Park, chipping the concrete steps. The nearby Fire Station #38 at California and Laguna is the first to respond to the disaster downtown in *The Towering Inferno* (1974).

34. 2640 Steiner Street at Broadway

Sally Field and Robin Williams live here in the early scenes of Chris Columbus's *Mrs. Doubtfire,* the extremely popular comedy based on the novel *Alias Madame Doubtfire* by Anne Fine. The film's use of locations and its Oscar-winning makeup job, transforming Robin Williams into a dowdy British housekeeper, helped to reestablish San Francisco as a major movie location in the 1990s. Field keeps this Pacific Heights house when Williams moves to North Beach, but he returns in drag. Rumor has it that the owners of this elegant home were not happy with the filmmakers.

35. 2311 Broadway
Between Fillmore Street and Steiner

This was the Salingers' house in the television show *Party of Five,* which ran on Fox from 1994 to 2000, about five kids who lose their parents but manage to keep the family restaurant and their own lives together.

2311 Broadway (*Party of Five*).

36. 2230 Sacramento Street at Buchanan

This is the "Adamson Mansion," actually an apartment building fictitiously called 1001 Franklin, in the screenplay of *Family Plot* (1976), Hitchcock's last movie. The building is used as the home of Karen Black and William Devane. Exteriors only were filmed there, with some interiors in the garage. The city is never identified as San Francisco in *Family Plot*, and Los Angeles was also used interchangeably in the editing.

37. Spreckels Mansion
2080 Washington Street at Octavia

Created in the massive beaux arts style, the Spreckels Mansion, referred to as "Parthenon of the West," was built by sugar king Claus Spreckels for his new wife, Alma deBretteville Spreckels, and is now owned by author Danielle Steel.

In the 1957 Rodgers and Hart musical *Pal Joey*, former burlesque queen and now wealthy socialite Rita Hayworth offers to fund "Chez Joey," the chic nightclub Frank Sinatra wants to open, at this location. Apparently Rita Hayworth demanded top billing, with newcomer Kim Novak's name to appear after Sinatra's. Sinatra is said to have acquiesced diplomatically, saying he didn't mind being in the middle of that sandwich. Hayworth, Columbia's third choice (after Marlene Dietrich and Mae West) to play the older woman, was actually three years younger than Sinatra.

38. Hotel Majestic
1500 Sutter Street at Gough

An elegant hotel and restaurant are housed in this former mansion built in 1902 at the edge of Pacific Heights. According to the press material of the hotel, the Majestic was reportedly the permanent residence of actresses (and sisters) Joan Fontaine and Olivia de Havilland for nearly a decade. (Although this claim is made in the hotel's promotional literature, the staff could neither confirm nor deny it.) It occasionally hosts film crews (reportedly the makers of *Sweet November* in 2001, among others, stayed here) and other Hollywood celebs like Nicolas Cage.

39. Hayes Street at Laguna

A quiet spot in the Hayes Valley commercial strip has a startling cinematic history. Famed early director Eric von Stroheim filmed *Greed,* an adaptation of the classic Frank Norris novel *McTeague,* here in 1925. Doc McTeague is a simple man whose wife's obsession with money drives him to madness. His dentist office is supposed to be at California

and Polk, but Polk Gulch, rebuilt after the 1906 earthquake, looked too modern. This two-story building had the perfect round corner room, so von Stroheim rented the entire building and had his cast move into the rooms to make the actors feel "inside" the characters. The intersection became von Stroheim's microcosm of flats, corner saloon, grocery, and post office. Von Stroheim's 42 reels of film were finally pared by the studio to 18. Other *Greed* locations include Cliff House, Seal Rocks, Bush and Sutter, and the B Street Station in Oakland. The structure is currently an assisted living facility for the frail elderly, over an Indian restaurant.

40. "Slut Central"
422 Oak Street at Laguna

In *Vegas in Space*, a 1991 release that could have been made only in San Francisco, this six-room flat was the residence of drag queen stars Doris Fish, "Tippi," and Ginger Quest. The "plot" involves three soldiers who are ordered to take a pill to change their gender before being sent undercover as showgirls on a secret mission to the women-only planet of Clitoris's capital city, "Vegas in Space." Once they arrive, they must maneuver through complex politics and decadent parties to uncover a plot to disrupt the most important pleasure planet in the universe.

Known as "Slut Central" after the then-renowned drag troupe, Sluts A-Go-Go, the flat was where the bulk of the film was shot between March 1983 and July 1984. Because the rooms were so small, much of the film was shot with fisheye lenses in order to get more than just one drag queen in the frame, according to director Phillip R. Ford. The dining room became the spaceship interior, Prince Angel's "Doom Room," and the "Girl's Quarters." The front room (later "Tippi's" bedroom) became "Mt. Venus," with a terrestrial landscape painted by Doris, where Queen Veneer demonstrated the "Color Dial" for Captain Tracy Daniels. Ginger Quest's bedroom served as the "Storage Room," where the film's shock-finish final scene was photographed. The living room became the throne room, or "Pink Flush Room," where Empress Nueva held court, and also where the preclimax "Cocktail Party" scene was shot. "We blew the Victorian flat's circuits repeatedly until our clever and resourceful director of photography Robin Clark learned how to 'tie-in' directly to the PG&E

lines outside." The few exteriors were shot around the city: the black and white "Mount Venus" exterior on the peak of Corona Heights Park; the long "Plas-world SpacePort Mall" at Project Artaud on Florida Street; and the "Vanity Lounge" climax at 544 Natoma, a South-of-Market performance space. "Queen Veneer's Gothic Detention Center" was shot at the Farm, a combination commune–performance space under Highway 101 near Potrero and Cesar Chavez Streets. The table-top miniature effects, the title starfield, and numerous cutaways and inserts were shot at 3567 18th Street. Now referred to as "The House of Fish," Doris Fish herself never lived there.

41. 312 Fillmore Street at Haight

This is the apartment where sexy Brazilian television chef Penelope Cruz stays with her best friend, transgendered Monica (Harold Perrineau Jr.), in *Woman on Top* (1999). "We painted the trim on this apartment, redid the lobby and added the murals and an elevator inside," according to scenic artist Tom Richardson. It was truly amazing (and completely impossible in reality) how quickly and effortlessly Cruz could get downtown and to other neighborhoods from this location.

42. Alamo Square Victorians
700 Steiner Street between Fulton and Grove

The much-photographed "postcard Victorians" were the opening scene in the weekly television series *Full House* (1987–95). Set in San Francisco, the sitcom stars Bob Saget as Danny Tanner, who becomes a single father when his wife is killed in a car accident. His brother-in-law Jesse (John Stamos) moves into the house to help Danny raise his three daughters. This series made the Olsen twins a household name.

In the original *Armistead Maupin's Tales of the City* (1993) miniseries, Russian Hill landlady Anna Madrigal (Olympia Dukakis) meets bastard businessman Edgar Halcyon (Donald Moffat), who is crying on a park bench in Alamo Square with a view of the postcard Victorians. She offers him a sandwich on foccacia bread, starting a sunset-years romance.

The Victorians are dwarfed by futuristic buildings in the sci-fi comedy *Bicentennial Man* (1999), as Robin Williams and Embeth Davidtz play chess in Alamo Square.

The Shannon Kavanaugh House
722 Steiner Street at Fulton

Jan (Glenn Close) and Nick (Mandy Patinkin) live in this Victorian in 1985's *Maxie*. He's a librarian and she works as the secretary to the local Catholic bishop. Stripping wallpaper, they discover a message that was left more than 60 years ago by Maxie. Next-door neighbor Ruth Gordon tells them that Maxie Malone, a flapper who once lived in the house, had a bit role in a silent film and then died tragically. Watching a video of Maxie's film, Jan is overcome by her restless spirit.

The house on the corner is also the home to Danny DeVito's character in *Junior* (1994), a comedy about a straight-laced scientist (Arnold Schwarzenegger) whose aggressive colleague persuades him to try injecting sperm into his body to become pregnant. Schwarzenegger becomes a better man by giving birth, and then refuses to give up his baby. The home's interior, with pink and white floral wallpaper, etched Victorian

glass, and curved doorways, was partially re-created in Hollywood, but actual house interiors were also used.

720 Steiner Street

In *Invasion of the Body Snatchers* (1978), Brooke Adams lives with her husband, until he begins to act very strangely, in this house across from Alamo Square, which was used for both interiors and exteriors. Robert Duvall, in priest garb, is briefly seen strangely swinging on a children's swing in Alamo Square in the Philip Kaufman remake of Don Siegel's 1956 sci-fi thriller.

The 700 block of Steiner Street backdrop is almost as popular as the Golden Gate Bridge as an establishing shot, and the many projects that have panned past the postcard Victorians include the following:

- Television series: *Trapper John, M.D.* (1979–86), *Hotel* (1983–88), *Partners in Crime* (1984), *The Streets of San Francisco* (1972–77), *Hawaii Five-O* (1968–80), and *Midnight Caller* (1988–91).

- Feature films: *Foul Play* (1978), *Woman in Red* (1984), *Patty Hearst* (1988), *Fat Man and Little Boy* (1989), and *Never Die Twice* (2001).

43. Southern Pacific Hospital
1400 Fell Street at Baker

In *D.O.A.* (1950), seeking a second diagnosis after having been told he's doomed to die, Edmond O'Brien comes to this facility (built in 1908 and a San Francisco Historic Landmark), only to have the dire diagnosis confirmed.

44. 628 Cole Street at Haight

In *Boys and Girls* (2000), Ryan (Freddie Prinze Jr.) and Jennifer (Claire Forlani) are college students whose love-hate relationship focuses on their respective boyfriends and girlfriends until they sleep together, which ruins everything. No way would a pair of UC Berkeley undergraduates be able to afford this apartment. It's hard to tell, but apparently they were supposed to be living in Berkeley, with the scenes of Telegraph Avenue actually shot around the corner along Haight Street.

45. 1672 Haight Street at Cole

In 1987's *Burglar* this is "Haight Street Books" where Bernie (Whoopi Goldberg) works, right next to the Poodle Factory, the dog grooming shop where her best friend works. Odd that a bookstore also sells keys. In the Hugh Wilson flick, Bernice "Bernie" Rhodenbarr is a burglar by trade, and she runs a bookstore as well. Her friend Carl Heller is a dog groomer. After a successful burglary, it's discovered that a dead body was in the house she burgled. The only one who can be placed at the scene of the crime, she has to use her criminal skills to clear her name of

the murder as well as avoid getting charged with the burglary. Based on the book *The Burglar in the Closet* and other Burglar novels by Lawrence Block, two of the principal characters underwent major changes: Bernard "Bernie" Rhodenbarr, a white male bookstore owner/burglar originally to be played by Bruce Willis, became Bernice "Bernie" Rhodenbarr, played by Whoopi Goldberg, and lesbian dog groomer Carolyn Kaiser, Bernie's best friend, became gay dog groomer Carl Heller, portrayed by Bobcat Goldthwait.

46. Kezar Stadium
Frederick and Stanyan Streets

The 1989 Loma Prieta earthquake severely damaged the stadium, which was subsequently demolished and totally rebuilt. In the original *Dirty Harry*, a key scene was filmed at the old stadium in 1971.

Kezar Stadium, 1929. *Photo courtesy of the San Francisco History Center, San Francisco Public Library*

A doctor from Park Emergency Hospital around the corner from Kezar calls the police with an important tip: a guy with a knife wound was treated and released. "I think the groundskeeper lets him live there . . . Kezar Stadium." As Harry (Clint Eastwood) points his Magnum at Scorpio, the floodlights are switched on, illuminating the stadium so that the hero can see and shoot the villain. As Scorpio whimpers for justice, the camera spirals away into the night sky.

47. 305 Hugo Street at 4th Avenue

This arts-and-crafts home is featured as the exterior of Mike Myers's parents' residence in *So I Married an Axe Murderer.* The 1993 comedy is about a guy who's always avoided commitment by finding absurd reasons to break up with his girlfriends. When he finally meets the beautiful Nancy Travis and falls in love, he becomes convinced that she's a notorious axe murderer. In a pre–Austin Powers stunt, Myers plays both father and son, Charlie and Stuart Mackenzie, who live here.

Brenda Fricker is Mrs. Mackenzie, part of the very Scottish clan that welcomes Travis to their home.

Golden Gate Park

A bleak, and frequently foggy, section of San Francisco that had been mostly sand dunes was transformed in the late 19th century into one of the country's great urban spaces, thanks to the vision of a Scotsman named John McLaren. Designed by Frederick Law Olmstead, it is now a landscaped park with lakes and waterfalls, jogging paths, and cultural institutions, that runs half the seven-mile width of the city from Ocean Beach to the "panhandle" of the Haight-Ashbury.

Though the Starship Enterprise is supposed to have landed in Golden Gate Park in *Star Trek IV: The Voyage Home* in 1986, most of the scenes were actually shot in Will Rogers State Park in Los Angeles.

Filmmakers from Charlie Chaplin (*The Jitney Elopement,* 1915) to Woody Allen (*Take the Money and Run,* 1969) have shot scenes in the scenic, wooded urban environment of Golden Gate Park.

48. The Academy of Sciences/Steinhart Aquarium
Concourse Drive

Founded in 1853, the Academy of Sciences is the city's most popular science museum, and the Steinhart Aquarium, one of the world's largest, is an institution and a popular destination for kids and grown-ups alike. In 2005, the Academy underwent a total transformation by Italian architect Renzo Piano, so the scenes from the films in which it appears cannot, alas, be revisited.

Steinhart Aquarium, 1948. *Courtesy of the San Francisco History Center, San Francisco Public Library*

H. G. Wells (Malcolm McDowell), transported from Victorian London to an Academy of Sciences exhibit devoted to his life, enters the strange world of San Francisco in the late 1970s. *Courtesy of Pacific Film Archive, University of California, Berkeley*

The Academy appears as the exterior of the museum where the time machine is on exhibit as part of the "H. G. Wells: A Man Before His Time" exhibition in *Time After Time* (1979). Whoopi Goldberg, as 1987's *Burglar*, is warned to "disappear" in the roundabout of the Academy of Sciences.

One of the most popular sections of the Academy is the aquarium, filmed by Orson Welles in *The Lady from Shanghai* (1947), with an intentionally eerie effect from the illuminated tanks. In 1999, *The Bachelor* Chris O'Donnell pursues old girlfriend Brooke Shields to a benefit gala at Steinhart and proposes. In 2000, when the third installment of *Armistead Maupin's Tales of the City* was shot partly on location, former rivals Mary Ann and DeDe (Laura Linney and Barbara Garrick) meet in the aquarium for a tête-à-tête.

49. The Music Concourse
Concourse Drive at Martin Luther King Jr. Drive

The park and its 1899 bandshell (the Spreckels "Temple of Music," designed by the Reid Brothers, who also gave us the Fairmont Hotel and the New Mission Theatre), which separate the Academy of Sciences from the De Young Museum, were used as a film location in *The Wedding Planner* (2001) as, what else, an outdoor wedding scene. Woody Allen and Diane Keaton have a tête-à-tête on a park bench here as their friendship begins to become a romance in *Play It Again, Sam* (1972).

50. Japanese Tea Garden
Hagiwara Tea Garden Drive

Since 1894, this Victorian version of the quiet contemplativeness of a tea garden has been drawing American tourists who seek the Japanese experience without the airfare. First an attraction at Golden Gate Park's Midwinter Fair, the gardens are lined with trees, shrubs, flowers, ponds, bridges, a pagoda, and a Buddha. Cherry blossom time in the spring is particularly magical. In one of America's sadder episodes, the Hagiwara family, who long ran the concession (and are credited with the invention of the fortune cookie), were deported in 1942. A plaque near the entrance commemorates them.

In 1968, a scene from *Petulia* was filmed in the tea garden, and in *The Wedding Planner* (2001) Jennifer Lopez and Matthew McConaughey have a scene in Golden Gate Park, with the Japanese Tea Garden visible in the background. Later in that film, Mr. Right (McConaughey) and Miss Wrong (Bridgette Wilson) have a conversation under a bridge inside the tea garden. The M. H. de Young Memorial Museum next door was rarely used for movie shoots in its previous incarnation before being

completely rebuilt in 2005 by Swiss architects Herzog and de Meuron. But in *Getting Even with Dad* (1994), Ted Danson, McCauley Culkin, and Glenne Headley do tour the old art museum, which remarkably has a copy of Georges Seurat's *Sunday Afternoon on the Island of the Grand Jatte* hanging in one of its galleries.

51. Conservatory of Flowers
John F. Kennedy Drive at Conservatory Drive West

The picturesque glass-and-wood greenhouse is the oldest building in Golden Gate Park (1878). The magical jungle of flowers, palms, and ferns recently underwent an extensive renovation, after severe damage from a winter storm in 1995. The Conservatory provides a lovely backdrop for the action in several films, including aerial views in Mel Brooks's *High Anxiety* (1977) and from-the-ground views in *Armistead Maupin's Further Tales of the City* (2001). Establishing shots from the lat-

ter miniseries show Pru Giroux (Mary Kay Place) walking by the Golden Gate Park landmark with her poodle, although most of the other park scenes were filmed in Canada. In the same film, the third of the *Tales* series, Laura Linney and Barbara Garrick have a conversation in a car with the Conservatory in the background. In the 2000 romantic comedy *Playing Mona Lisa,* Ivan Sergei invites Alicia Witt to meet him for pizza. She gets confused when she discovers the point of rendezvous is the Conservatory of Flowers. When she inquires about the pizza, a delivery guy on a scooter arrives. They take the pizza into the Conservatory, past the sign that says Danger: Keep Out.

52. Bank of America
22nd Avenue at Noriega

Formerly a Hibernia Bank, this is the actual site of a 1970s Symbionese Liberation Army (SLA) robbery, which included kidnapped newspaper heiress Patty Hearst, whose adventure as a fugitive from the law was dramatized in *Patty Hearst*, starring Natasha Richardson. Only an ATM remains at this former Bank of America location, in the outside wall of what is now a video store. A bank in the Sunset District was used for location filming by director Paul Shrader in 1988.

53. Surf Theater
4520 Irving Street at 45th Avenue

In this theater at the beginning of *Play It Again, Sam* (1972), Woody Allen is mesmerized by the final scene of *Casablanca*. His idol Humphrey Bogart follows Allen from the 1930s movie screen into his 1970s San Francisco life, giving the nebbishy protagonist advice on life and love. Built in 1926 as the Parkview, the theater was renamed the Sunset in 1937, and remodeled and renamed the Surf in 1957. It was owned by independent cinema mogul Mel Novikoff until it closed in 1985.

54. San Francisco Zoo
2701 Sloat Boulevard at 45th Avenue

The zoo is a local destination for kids and adults alike, with its more than 1,000 species of birds and mammals, many of them endangered.

Dustin Hoffman follows Katherine Ross to the San Francisco Zoo in *The Graduate* (1967). In Mike Nichols's film, Hoffman sees Ross on a bus, runs after it, and follows her to the zoo where she's meeting a boyfriend. After wandering around the zoo, they finally find him. "We thought you said to meet at the monkey house," Hoffman complains. *Courtesy of Pacific Film Archive, University of California, Berkeley*

55. Mount Davidson Park
Dalewood Way at Lansdale Avenue

This is San Francisco's highest point, at 938 feet above sea level. It is also almost dead center geographically within the city's seven-by-seven miles. Although it is not a famous tourist destination, the location features an embattled cross, which is a tribute to the Armenian war dead. A series of crosses have been mounted on the peak since the first one appeared in 1923, and the present 103-foot high concrete shaft was designed in 1932 by George Kelham, the architect of the Old Main Library (now the Asian Art Museum) and the reconstructed Palace Hotel (post-earthquake, 1906). Controversy swirled around the cross in the late 20th century, when objections were raised about the presence of a Christian symbol on publicly owned land. In 1997, the highest bidder acquired the property on which it stands, and the cross and its surrounding park became the property of the Council of Armenian American Organizations of Northern California. In Don Siegel's *Dirty Harry* (1971), Clint Eastwood, on his way up to the summit, is confronted by Scorpio. Harry is ordered by the serial killer to "put [his] nose right up against the cement" of the cross. In the ensuing struggle Harry plunges his concealed switchblade into Scorpio's thigh.

56. Forest Hills MUNI Station
Laguna Honda at Woodside

In *Dirty Harry*, this is Clint Eastwood's first destination on the deadly wild goose chase back and forth across the city, demonically directed by the Scorpio killer. From here "Dirty" Harry Callahan is directed to take the K Ingleside train and exit at Church and 20th Streets.

57. Twin Peaks
Twin Peaks Boulevard

The scenic overlook from the double hilltops at the center of the city has been filmed many times, often as a backdrop with no actors, as in *Vertigo*, where the panoramic view of 1957 San Francisco shot from this high point signals Scottie's (Jimmy Stewart) recovery from depression at nearby St. Joseph's Hospital in Buena Vista Park. Mary Ann (Laura Linney) and DeDe (Barbara Garrick) drive up to the city overlook and have a windswept talk in *Further Tales of the City* (2001).

View from Twin Peaks.

58. 100 St. Germain Avenue at Glenbrook Avenue

In Blake Edwards's *Experiment in Terror* (1962), immediately after pulling into her garage at this address, Lee Remick is apprehended by Ross Martin, who explains his plan to have her steal $100,000 from the bank where she works. He threatens her and her sister if she calls the police, telling her that he knows her every move.

59. Buena Vista Park
Haight Street at Buena Vista

This 36-acre wooded hillside city park is surrounded by some of the city's finest architecture, and sports stunning views toward the north. Its reputation as a hippie haven in the 1960s and a gay sex camp in the 1970s and 1980s has been overturned by concerned citizens groups in the Upper Haight. A scene from the lyrical interracial romance in *Golden Gate* (1994) between Matt Dillon and Joan Chen was filmed in the park. The Walden House, located at the northern (and bottom) end of the green space, which helps to maintain Buena Vista Park, poses as a Catholic boys' school in *40 Days and 40 Nights* (2002).

Joan Chen and Matt Dillon overlook San Francisco's dramatic coastline in *Golden Gate* (1994). *Courtesy of Pacific Film Archive, University of California, Berkeley*

60. St. Joseph's Hospital
351–355 Buena Vista Avenue East

Now a condominium complex, this really was a hospital in 1958 when poor deranged Scottie (Jimmy Stewart) checks in after he is unable to keep Madeleine (Kim Novak) from self-destruction in Hitchcock's *Vertigo.*

Two Hitchcock locations from *Vertigo* at the corner of Gough and Eddy are long gone. Scottie follows Madeleine to the "Old McKittrick Hotel" at 1007 Gough Street, where Ellen Corby protects the tenants' privacy while putting olive oil on her rubber tree leaves at the front desk, an actual-location interior. The Victorian structure, scheduled for demolition at the time of filming, was the fictional home of the mysterious Carlota Valdes. The site is now tennis courts of an apartment building below St. Mary's Cathedral. In a shot of Stewart looking up at the "McKittrick," the church of St. Paulus is seen behind him on the southeast corner. St. Paulus burned down in the 1990s.

The Castro Neighborhood

The predominantly gay and lesbian neighborhood began its growth as a political force under City Supervisor Harvey Milk. Milk's assassination in 1978 by former City Supervisor Dan White, who opposed gay rights as represented by Milk, is documented in *The Times of Harvey Milk* (1983). Milk's camera shop and campaign headquarters were located on Castro Street between 18th and 19th in a store front that is now a soap-and-lotion shop. A plaque in the sidewalk, a mural of Harvey looking out a window, and the name of the MUNI Plaza at Castro and Market Streets commemorate this charismatic leader.

The annual Gay Pride Parade does not usually start or end in the Castro, but stretches out along lower Market Street every June. The 1993 telling of Randy Shilts's *And the Band Played On* features footage of a candlelight AIDS vigil between Castro and Market Streets as well as 1981 footage of a pride parade used as a "Halloween Parade."

In *Kamikaze Hearts,* lesbian porn-star drug addicts play themselves in scenes from their lives in this 1986 cinema verité documentary. Tina "Tigr" Mennett rides in a convertible along a recognizable stretch of Market Street between Noe and Sanchez.

61. The Castro Theatre
429 Castro Street between 17th and 18th Streets

This historic movie palace is much beloved, and attended, by San Francisco film aficionados because of its unique programming of both classic movies and new work in cutting-edge film festivals such as Berlin and Beyond, the Jewish Film Festival, and the International San Francisco Gay and Lesbian Film Festival. A mighty Wurlitzer adds to the neighborhood appeal, inducing audiences to sing along to "San Francisco" between screenings. Local architect Timothy Pflueger is responsible for the design of this 1923 theater, Oakland's Paramount, and many others, as well as a 1930s renovation of the closed New Mission Theatre. The ornate Spanish baroque facade only hints at the opulence of the interior, with its auditorium ceiling cast to resemble the inside of an Arabian nights tent with richly ornamented ropes and swags. Renovations by the Nasser family, who have owned the theater for decades, include new projection equipment, carpeting, and seats.

Matthew McConaughey pursues Jenna Elfman into the Castro's lobby and beyond (to a fictional ladies' room) in the last reel of *EDtv*

(1999). (He has just completed an unlikely two-minute sprint from his workplace, North Beach Video, which is all the way across the city.)

62. Mecca Restaurant
2029 Market Street at Delores

This tony restaurant is used to show Diane Lane's life in the City by the Bay in *Under the Tuscan Sun* (2003). Frances Mayes's apparently idyllic life in everybody's favorite city takes an unexpected turn when a divorce and writer's block drive her away from San Francisco. But she and the city both look great in the opening scenes before the action moves on to central Italy.

Castro/Mission

63. Mission Dolores
Dolores Street at 16th Street

Scottie Ferguson (Jimmy Stewart) follows the mysterious Madeleine Elster (Kim Novak) through the historic 1782 adobe church

into the graveyard, where she ponders the headstone of Carlota Valdes, a movie prop that was later removed, in Hitchcock's classic *Vertigo* (1958). The 18th-century adobe structure, one of the oldest buildings in San Francisco, and part of a chain of California missions where Father Junipero Serra and his merry men converted the locals to Christianity, is open to the public as a museum, next door to a more contemporary Spanish baroque basilica.

64. Dolores Park
Between 18th and 20th, Dolores, and Church Streets

Named for the nearby Mission Dolores and the beautiful palm-lined boulevard (Dolores Street) that runs up and down the hills along its eastern edge, this park sports some of the most dramatic views of the downtown skyline and is frequently used by local performance troupes.

In the 2001 version of *Sweet November*, the remake of a 1968 Sandy Dennis/Anthony Newley vehicle, Charlize Theron and Keanu Reeves have three scenes with Dolores Park used as a scenic background. The director inserted a fake building resembling a greenhouse at the end of the 19th Street pedestrian bridge in order to hide a statue.

The J-Church MUNI light-rail train climbs past Dolores Park, affording a vista of the city. Brian De Palma opens and closes his 1989 Vietnam feature *Casualties of War* with scenes of Michael J. Fox riding a J-Church train. He sees an Asian woman who reminds him of an incident some years prior, when a five-man patrol of American soldiers kidnapped a young Vietnamese woman from her village, forced her to march with them, and then raped and killed her. Reportedly based on a true story, most of the film is a flashback to the dehumanizing reality of combat.

"Dirty" Harry Callahan (Clint Eastwood), although directed by the Zodiac killer to take the K Ingleside train to Dolores Park, should actually take the J-Church line to Church Street and 20th.

The upscale neighborhood of Noe Valley was festooned with trash and graffiti so Saint Paul's Catholic Church would appear to be in a run-down section of town for *Sister Act* (1992). *Courtesy of Pacific Film Archive, University of California, Berkeley*

65. St. Paul's Church
Church Street at Valley

The Gothic revival church in 1992's *Sister Act* is home to Mother Superior Maggie Smith, Kathy Najimy, and the rest of the nuns. There Whoopi Goldberg as a fugitive seeks refuge by pretending to be a nun.

66. Fire Station #43
Brazil Avenue and Athens Street

In the Excelsior neighborhood, Princess Anne Hathaway and her artist mother live in a renovated firehouse in the first *The Princess Diaries* (2001). During a visit from "Queen" Julie Andrews, we see exteriors.

Marin, Sonoma, Napa, and Mendocino Counties

Frightened children run past Potter School in the Sonoma County town of Bodega in Hitchcock's *The Birds* (1963). *Courtesy of Pacific Film Archive, University of California, Berkeley*

This driving tour covers sites in the counties of Marin, Sonoma, Napa, and Mendocino, and readers will likely want to allow several days. After crossing the Golden Gate Bridge, the views from the Marin headlands and from the town of Sausalito are spectacular. In the shadow of the majestic Mount Tamalpais, head north through the small inland towns of Mill Valley, Larkspur, San Rafael, Nicasio, Fairfax, and San Quentin before cutting over to the dramatic coastline. In Sonoma County, begin in the quaint town of Petaluma, advance to Santa Rosa, then return to the coast to the towns of Bodega and Bodega Bay. East of Sonoma is Napa County, renowned for its winemaking, but less well

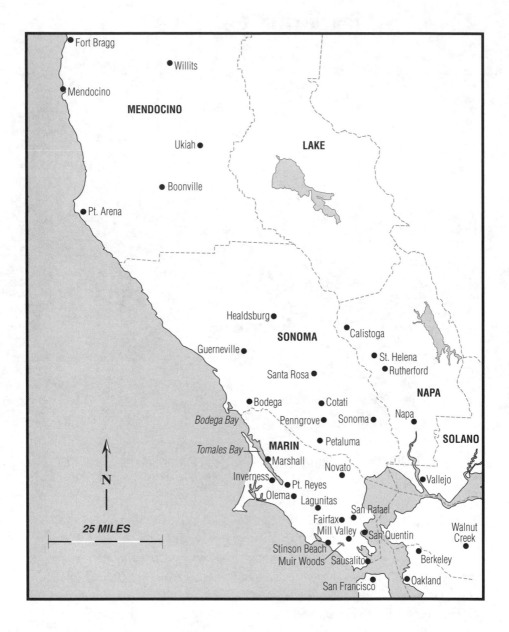

known for its contributions to movies. Mendocino, the northernmost county represented in this book, boasts a long and rich history of moviemaking centered in the scenic coastal towns of Point Arena, Mendocino, and Fort Bragg.

Marin County

Just across the Golden Gate Bridge from the city are the Marin Headlands. The spectacular views of the city and the bay make them a favorite spot for tourists and filmmakers. For example, Robert Iscove filmed Freddie Prinze Jr. and Claire Forlani using the dramatic backdrop in *Boys and Girls* in 2000.

Fort Baker, just to the east of the Golden Gate Bridge, is the fictional location of the lighthouse used in climactic scenes in the neo-noir romantic suspense thriller *Final Analysis* (1992), in which Kim Basinger behaves very badly. (The actual lighthouse is located considerably farther south in San Mateo County's Pescadero.) On a bluff overlooking Fort Baker, politically correct Marin residents Martin Mull, Sally Kellerman, and Tuesday Weld scatter the ashes of one of their own in *Serial,* the tongue-in-cheek send-up of self-important Marinites in 1980.

Sausalito

Sausalito, the closest so-called bedroom community across the bridge in affluent Marin County, has attracted a number of filmmakers with its splendid views of the city and its laid-back attitude. The Sausalito Ferry shepherds herds of tourists and commuters across San Francisco Bay to and from the Embarcadero Ferry Building at the foot of Market Street.

Ironically, *Sausalito* is more an idea and an ideal than a location in the 2000 movie named for it, although one scene featuring its water-

front main street appears in the film. Most of the action—a romance between divorced mom Ellen (Maggie Cheung) and Mike (Leon Lai)—takes place in San Francisco in this Hong Kong production by Andrew Lau. In 1972, Woody Allen and company were in Sausalito to shoot the Herbert Ross film *Play It Again, Sam*, and the first day of shooting was at the Trident (now Horizons) Restaurant. The scene where the self-conscious, clumsy Allan (Woody Allen) is introduced to a potential blind date and puts his hand in the salad took 37 takes to get right. This film is about a neurotic film buff (Allen), who has been abandoned by his wife and seeks female companionship, aided and abetted by his best friends, a married couple, and the ghost of Humphrey Bogart.

Suburbanite Martin Mull rides his bicycle all the way from Mill Valley to the Sausalito Ferry for his morning commute into the city in *Serial* (1980), based on the novel by Cyra McFadden. The film version also stars Sally Kellerman, Bill Macy, Tom Smothers, and Tuesday Weld. Many of the characters are seen coming and going through the streets of Sausalito and Mill Valley. *Good Neighbor Sam* Bissell (Jack Lemmon) also commutes from Marin County (although his tract home was likely

filmed in Southern California). He gets a morning ride across the Golden
Gate Bridge with his wife Dorothy Provine, who drives along the Marina
Green (in rear projection shots) and into the Financial District, before
depositing him near his advertising agency, somewhere around Union
Square. The David Swift comedy from 1964 features all-American husband Lemmon getting duped into posing as the husband of his sexy
neighbor Romy Schneider in order to help her collect some insurance
money. Complications ensue when his employer makes this faux couple
his models on a billboard campaign, risking the reputation of his client's
wholesome product: milk.

Another commuter from a Marin location was Doris Day, during
the run of the television series *The Doris Day Show* from 1968 to 1973.
The fictional address where widowed Doris Martin lived with her two
young sons is 32 Mill Valley Road, on her father's ranch in Mill Valley.
The second season saw her commuting into San Francisco for her job as
secretary at *Today's World* magazine and living in a North Beach flat.

In the 1996 comedy *Mother*, Albert Brooks decides to move back
home to Sausalito from L.A. and reinvent his childhood room in his
mother's Sausalito home. Mother is played by Debbie Reynolds, her first

film in 25 years. Brooks and Reynolds drive by many Sausalito locations, like the ferry pier and Ondine restaurant, as they "bond" in the car during "the experiment," as Brooks calls his neurotic relocation. Reynolds's home appears to be in Sausalito. Mother and son spar over groceries at the Sausalito Mollie Stone's Supermarket.

Larkspur

Another Marin town, Larkspur, is the setting of the scene of the final confrontation between Harry Callahan (Clint Eastwood) and serial killer Scorpio in the original *Dirty Harry* (1971). The final chase through the Hutchinson Company Crushed Rock Quarry Plant, the climax of the movie, takes place where the condo complex at Larkspur Landing is now, behind the mall. Scars on the rock wall around the condos on Old Quarry Road might be remnants of the quarry. Harry repeats his grim offer: surrender or gamble ("Do I feel lucky?"). Scorpio reaches for his gun and Harry shoots him, propelling his body backward into the small lake.

San Rafael

San Rafael is the home of Industrial Light & Magic, which has provided postproduction visual effects services to the entertainment industry since 1975. ILM is renowned for its model making, matte painting, computer-generated imagery, digital animation, and a variety of other related processes required in the production of visual effects. Since *Star Wars* was first released in 1977, over 200 feature films have utilized ILM's facilities, including many that have earned "Best Visual Effects" and Oscars for technical achievement from the Academy of Motion Picture Arts and Sciences.

Lucasfilm, at Nicasio's Skywalker Ranch, was founded by George Lucas in 1971. In addition to motion picture and television production, the company's global businesses include visual effects, sound, video games, licensing, and online activity. Lucas is expanding his empire with the Letterman Digital Art Center on the former grounds of the San Francisco Presidio. The new facility, which occupies a large piece of prime San Francisco real estate, houses many of the Lucasfilm divisions, establishing a premiere digital entertainment facility in the Bay Area.

St. Vincent's School in Marinwood is the site of the wedding of the doomed couple played by Annabella Sciorra and Robin Williams in *What Dreams May Come* (1998). The picturesque school is a home for emotionally troubled boys and also serves several Marin County non-profit organizations.

Marin County Civic Center
3501 Civic Center Drive, at the San Pedro Exit of Freeway 101

A posthumous work of architect Frank Lloyd Wright, who died in 1959, the unusual building is not his proudest achievement, and a recent paint job is not flattering. It is the only government building designed by Wright to be completed, and its futuristic shapes have inspired directors of sci-fi features.

Ethan Hawke, Uma Thurman, and Jude Law head the cast of *Gattaca* (1997), a film that uses the eccentric architecture of the Frank Lloyd Wright building to good advantage. The film's title comes from the initials GTCA (guanine, thymine, cytosine, and adenine), the components of DNA. Ethan Hawke dreams of becoming a crew member on an expedition to a moon of Saturn. Using an illegal DNA broker, he makes

a deal with a man with better genes (Jude Law) so that they can both go into space. George Lucas's early sci-fi thriller *THX 1138* (1971) was also filmed partially in the interior of the Civic Center buildings.

The Barry Levinson feature *Bandits* (2001) uses several Marin County locations. It is loosely based on a true story of two bank robbers, Bruce Willis and Billy Bob Thornton, who break out of prison and begin a bank robbing spree. They become known as the "sleepover bandits" because they kidnap bank managers the night before their robbery, spend the night with their families, and then all go to the bank in the morning to get the money. When a bored housewife (Cate Blanchett) decides to run away from her failing marriage, she joins the criminals. Initially attracted to Willis, she also ends up in bed with Thornton, and a complicated romantic relationship begins. Bay View Bank at 305

Anselmo Avenue is the "San Andreas Bank" where one of the many rob-
beries takes place. When a pair of cops come by wondering where Dottie,
the drive-up window girl is, Thornton in a blond wig goes into explicit
detail about why she's out sick. The bank's real name is visible in one
brief scene. In another scene, filmed at the Fireside Motel (115 Shoreline
Highway in Mill Valley), the trio hole up in #19 in this vintage bungalow
court right off the highway. When Blanchett and Willis return from a
shopping spree, Thornton, incensed that they've gone shopping for dis-
guises, wants Blanchett to leave.

Fairfax

In Fairfax, at the Marin Town and Country Club (Pastori Avenue at Center Boulevard), Blake Edwards filmed a scene in his 1962 thriller *Experiment in Terror*. The only location not in the San Francisco city limits, this
is where Toby and her boyfriend go swimming after school.

   In Samuel P. Taylor State Park, on the part of Sir Francis Drake
Boulevard that runs through Lagunitas, several outdoor concert scenes

were filmed in 1998's *Around the Fire*. John Jacobsen filmed the story of Simon, a Manhattan transplant who discovers flowers, hippies, and LSD.

In *Dirty Harry* (1971), after crossing the Golden Gate Bridge with the children commanded to continue singing "Row, row, row your boat," the bus driver, played by local actress Ruth Kobart, is ordered to exit Highway 101 at the Sir Francis Drake Boulevard exit in Larkspur. Supposedly on the way to the Santa Rosa Airport, the exit they take is about 45 miles too early.

San Quentin

San Quentin, California's oldest and best known correctional institution, has appeared as itself in several films. In 1999's *True Crime*, Clint Eastwood, as a burnt-out journalist for the *Oakland Tribune*, is assigned to write a routine story about the last hours of a man on death row. He drives through demonstrators at the prison gates at the end of the main

street in one scene. Many exterior scenes were filmed there, but the interiors are shot at Manex studios.

In 1958's *I Want to Live*, Susan Hayward as Barbara Graham awaits her fate at San Quentin, after she is transferred from "Covina." We see a crowd of people run out of a café and swarm her car as it enters the gates. We follow the car as it approaches the prison. After the execution (on a replica set constructed on a sound stage) we see Edward Montgomery (Simon Oakland) in the same location just outside the gates, reading a letter from Graham. The closing credits roll over this same shot.

In Woody Allen's *Take the Money and Run* (1969), 100 San Quentin prisoners were paid a small fee to work on the film during the prison sequences. The regular cast and crew were stamped each day with a special ink that glowed under ultraviolet light so the guards could tell who was allowed to leave the prison grounds at the end of the day. Allen's first feature as writer, director, and star, this mock documentary tells through interviews and flashbacks of how Virgil Starkwell becomes America's most dangerous and most wanted criminal.

Muir Woods

In an acknowledged nod to *Vertigo* (1958), H. G. Wells (Malcolm McDowell) in *Time After Time* (1979) visits Marin's lovely dark and deep Muir Woods in order to explain where and when he was born. Apparently they didn't get all the footage they needed on one day of shooting, so a few scenes were grabbed elsewhere, according to director Nicholas Meyer.

At the end of Bill Condon's *Kinsey* (2004), Alfred Kinsey (Liam Neeson) and his wife (Laura Linney) go to San Francisco to solicit funding from philanthropist Huntington Hartford for further research. After their unsuccessful attempt, a dejected Neeson suggests stopping in the "woods" (on their way to the airport!?). The film ends with a lovely scene in the redwoods. This was always Condon's original scripted ending to the film, but because of an increasingly tight budget and short shooting schedule, it was scrapped. A less effective ending of Mr. and Mrs. Kinsey sitting on a park bench was shot just outside Gramercy Park in New York City, where the rest of the film had been made. Realizing that the new ending was not powerful enough, the producers sought additional funding to shoot the original ending. According to Kinsey's biographer, Jonathan Gathorne-Hardy, the Kinseys at one point "sought solace in Muir

Woods," after a long day taking sex histories in San Francisco. Interestingly, American Zoetrope was briefly on board as the fiscal agent for the film. Funding secured, Condon brought his crew to film Neeson and Linney in a spectacular gathering of redwoods. The scene may have been set in Muir Woods but was filmed in Big Basin, in the same spot where *Vertigo* was filmed 45 years previously.

Novato

Novato had its moment of Hollywood glory when Richard Donner filmed *Radio Flyer* with Lorraine Bracco, John Heard, and Elijah Wood here in 1990. A premiere benefit was held at the Pacific Rowland Theater in 1992. Locations include Novato High School, a theater on Grant Avenue in downtown Novato, and the Vintage Oaks Shopping Center. The fantasy about an abused boy whose toy wagon becomes a magic rocketship was also filmed in nearby Nicasio.

Marshall

The *Bandits* (2001) trio find themselves in Nick's Cove in the charming hamlet of Marshall, off Highway One on the east side of Tomales Bay. This was one of many locations used along the northern California coast, including Bodega Bay, Dillon Beach to the north, and Half Moon Bay to the south. Valley Ford in Sonoma County was where the crash involving two cars and a Clover Stornetta milk truck was filmed.

Stinson Beach/Point Reyes

The opening scene of a long expanse of beach in John Carpenter's *The Fog* (1980) is identified as Stinson Beach. In this slasher flick, made just after Carpenter's success with the first *Halloween* (1978), citizens of west Marin/west Sonoma are terrorized by meat hook–wielding ghosts of shipwrecked sailors who are cloaked in the shroud of a dense fog. Much of the action in the small coastal town dubbed San Antonio Bay was filmed in Point Reyes Station and Olema. The director calls the peninsula with Point Reyes "the second foggiest point in the U.S., after Nantucket." Carpenter's wife Adrienne Barbeau plays the heroine, who is a disc jockey for radio station KAB (1340 on the dial) in the Point Reyes

The town of Point Reyes was used as a location in the horror movie *The Fog* (1980).
Courtesy of Pacific Film Archive, University of California, Berkeley

Lighthouse, of all places. She lives with her son in a house on the water in Inverness, on Tomales Bay. The church where Hal Holbrook is a priest was actually in Altadena, Southern California, per director comments on the DVD. Only Bodega Bay, farther north in Sonoma County, plays itself.

John Carpenter bought a "hilltop retreat" in Inverness during filming of 1980's *The Fog,* and he shot *Village of the Damned* (1995) here 15 years later virtually in his backyard, with Christopher Reeve, Kirstie Alley, and Mark Hamill. Inverness, Nicasio, and Point Reyes all stand in for the fictional Midwich.

Sonoma County

The lyrical beauty of Sonoma County, particularly its noncommercialized western extremes, is equally intense in the winter, when the rains turn the countryside an electric green, and in the summer, when the parched hills are bathed in golden light. Vineyards whose product now rival the wines of neighboring Napa dot the landscape, and quaint small towns seem like a throwback to an earlier time. Moviemakers have frequently seized upon any or all of these qualities of Sonoma County as a quintessential, and probably mythical, version of America in the 20th century.

A dazed Humbert Humbert (Jeremy Irons) weaves back and forth in his woody on a country road in an area described by director Adrian Lyne as "Sonoma County," clearly in the rainy season, in the opening scene of *Lolita*. The 1997 remake of Stanley Kubrick's classic film (which starred James Mason as Humbert) raised eyebrows with its frank portrayal of the physical love affair between a lascivious professor and a teenage girl. Both films were based on one of the 20th century's great novels, by Vladimir Nabokov.

Penngrove/Cotati

The Farmer's Daughter features scenes filmed in both Penngrove (the Pioneer Hotel) and Cotati (Scott Ranch on Old Adobe Road) in 1947. The heartwarming Loretta Young vehicle, in which a smart, opinionated Swedish maid from the country teaches those city politicians a thing or two, was the basis of the Inger Stevens television series in the 1960s.

Petaluma

The heart of the town of Petaluma, Western Avenue at North Petaluma Boulevard, appears in the recent remake of *Lolita* and also in *Peggy Sue Got Married* (1986). It is used also as the all-American town in a scene from Lawrence Kasdan's *Mumford*, filmed in various Sonoma towns in 1999. The clever screenplay tells the tale of Dr. Mumford (Loren Dean), who moves to a town that shares his name and changes the lives of his patients (Hope Davis, Jason Lee, Mary McDonnell) with his unorthodox advice. The Mumford house, shared with tenant Alfre Woodard, is on Liberty Street in Petaluma.

This is a rich cinematic block, since the white Victorian across the street (226 Liberty) is Kathleen Turner's childhood home in *Peggy Sue Got Married* (see page 226). Director Francis Ford Coppola filmed the 1986 fantasy of time travel mostly in Petaluma and Santa Rosa. In a scene in front of the house, a tipsy "teenage" Peggy Sue (Turner, actually

226 Liberty Street, Petaluma.

Downtown Petaluma.

an adult who is having a nostalgic visit to her past), tells her father (Don Murray), who has just brought home a brand new Edsel, "Oh Dad, you were always doing things like that!" Another Liberty Street address appears in *Basic Instinct,* the erotic slasher flick starring Michael Douglas and Sharon Stone in 1992. "26 Albion Road, Mill Valley" is actually 26 Liberty Street, Petaluma, home of Stone's sweet old lady friend, Hazel Dobkin, who was in San Quentin for having murdered her husband and children. The car chase in *Basic Instinct* takes place on Petaluma Boulevard from B Street to East Washington. Other recognizable sites in Paul Verhoeven's film are the iron-front buildings and St. Vincent's Church in the vicinity of Howard, Sixth and Liberty Streets, and Western Avenue.

Kathleen Turner is seen in downtown Petaluma, crossing in front of the distinctive corner Carithers department store, now a Couches Etc., at Kentucky and Western in *Peggy Sue* (see page 226). Turner's future husband, "teenage" Nicolas Cage, tries to break free of the *cage* of his family's business, a retail store ("Bodell Appliances") at 120 Petaluma North. But fate does not intend for him to be a rock-and-roll musician, and the business stays in the Bodell family. The altered storefront is now unrecognizable.

Petaluma High School was used for The Hop in George Lucas's *American Graffiti* in 1973, although other Bay Area high schools were also used for location shooting, including Tamalpais in Mill Valley and Buchanan Field in Concord, to tell the bittersweet story of a group of high school kids (Ron Howard, Cindy Williams, Richard Dreyfus, Harrison Ford, and others) about to break up forever after their graduation.

The former Gilardi's Liquors at 844 Bodega Avenue, Petaluma.

The *Graffiti* scene where the kids try to score some booze was filmed at Gilardi's Liquors, still a retail establishment, but with a different name, at 844 Bodega Avenue on the west side of Petaluma.

Petaluma kids experimenting with space travel are the focus of *Explorers*, a 1985 fantasy that is supposed to take place in a Maryland town. It includes very early performances by Ethan Hawke and River Phoenix, who wind up in the Petaluma River downtown when their homemade spacecraft returns to earth. A lovely Victorian house with a turret at 920 D Street, on one of Petaluma's most charming residential drags, was used as young Amanda Peterson's home in this flick from director Joe Dante, of *Gremlins* fame.

The Nosecchi Dairy at 5345 Bodega Avenue outside Petaluma is the long driveway leading to the Brenner ranch supposedly located on Bodega Head (see Bodega Bay) in Hitchcock's classic terror flick *The Birds*

920 "D" Street, Petaluma.

The Petaluma River.

(1963). Farther along the route from Petaluma toward the coast, according to the authors, is the site of Dan Fawcett's farm in the Hitchcock film: the Bianchi Ranch. The "first ranch on right side of Bodega Avenue heading north toward Bodega Bay after leaving Valley Ford," it is where Jessica Tandy is struck dumb by the sight of her neighbor with his eyes pecked out.

The Petaluma Speedway (100 Fairgrounds Drive) stands in for the Lansing (Michigan) Speedway where the early version of the Tucker automobile is tested for endurance. Although primarily set in Ypsilanti, Michigan, and Chicago, *Tucker: The Man and His Dream* (1988) was shot at locations throughout Marin, Sonoma, Solano, San Mateo, Contra Costa, and San Francisco counties. In some scenes Jeff Bridges apparently wears cuff links once owned by the real Preston Tucker. Producer George Lucas and director Francis Ford Coppola each came to own one of the 50 Tuckers originally produced.

Santa Rosa

Hayley Mills as *Pollyanna*, the "glad girl" orphan who cheers up Jane Wyman as her crabby Aunt Polly and everyone else in town, lived in a mansion at 1015 McDonald Avenue. The third floor of the actually flat-topped Victorian (the Mableton Mansion) was added by art director Peter Ellenshaw with a matte painting for dramatic scenes involving Pollyanna's bedroom and a tall tree. The Disney classic is a remake of a Mary Pickford silent film based on a novel by Eleanor Porter. The 1960 version co-stars Agnes Moorehead, Karl Malden, Richard Egan, Nancy Olson, and James Drury. Over 300 girls auditioned for the part of Polly-anna; Hayley Mills was signed just days before filming started. Her first scenes were shot on a hillside outside Santa Rosa with Karl Malden.

In Alfred Hitchcock's thriller *Shadow of a Doubt* (1943), the principal action takes place at the "Newton House" at 904 McDonald

Avenue at 14th Street in Santa Rosa. Creepy uncle Joseph Cotten visits a northern California town, raising suspicion that he is a murderer on the lam. Uncle Charlie tries to kill Young Charlie (Teresa Wright) with car exhaust fumes in the garage, which still stands on 14th Street. Otherwise the house was used for exteriors only. Santa Rosa's Central Courthouse Square is featured prominently in the cinematic view of this quintessential American small city that represented quaint "goodness" to Hitchcock. Many of the buildings no longer exist after two earthquakes and misguided redevelopment efforts that tore down the theaters, courthouse, churches, library, and other buildings. The train station from *Shadow of a Doubt* was real and still exists in central Santa Rosa.

In 2003, Railroad Square and its station were used in the Steve Martin/Bonnie Hunt remake of *Cheaper by the Dozen* (2004). This is the story of a couple with 12 kids who leave their apparently perfect lives in

"Midland" for the big city of Chicago (played by a Hancock Park mansion in Los Angeles). Everything seems OK until the parents are consumed by ambition (his job as a university football coach and hers as a writer of books like *Cheaper by the Dozen*), which takes them away from their parental duties, and the kids begin to get even. After one of the neglected dozen runs away from home, the tear-stained reunion scene happens at this train station. The director refers on the DVD to this as the first day of shooting in "Petaluma," which is where the rural house is located.

Smile is a look at the great American tradition of the beauty pageant, set in Santa Rosa, as teenage girls (young Melanie Griffith among them) compete to be Young California Miss. The scene of most of the action is Santa Rosa Veterans Memorial Building. The 1975 film stars Barbara Feldon and Bruce Dern. The final competition with audience was filmed at the Old Cal Theater on B Street in Santa Rosa.

Santa Rosa High School poses as "Buchanan High School," the site of Peggy Sue's reunion in Coppola's *Peggy Sue Got Married* (1986). It is also the site of flashback scenes to the high school days of classmates Kathleen Turner, Joan Allen, and company. Housewife and mother Turner passes out at her 25th high school reunion and becomes a teenager again, messing with fate through her time travel. She has a chance to dump Nicholas Cage, but doesn't.

Town of Sonoma

In western, coastal Sonoma County, filmmakers have focused on gloomier aspects of the often genteel Pacific shores. John Carpenter's *The Fog* (1980) puts lethal weapons into the hands of phantom sailors who terrorize coastal "San Antonio Bay," actually a compilation of west Marin towns. In one marina scene, "San Antonio" residents go north to Bodega Bay, which plays itself.

In the terror flick *I Know What You Did Last Summer* (1997), teens Sarah Michelle Gellar, Freddie Prinze Jr., and others make a pact to keep an accidental killing a secret. A year later, they begin receiving letters stating, "I know what you did last summer," and the body count goes up. Set in coastal North Carolina, many of the beginning scenes, including the opening credits, the accident, and the bonfire on the beach, were filmed along the Sonoma Coast, between Fort Ross and Marshall and near Jenner, south of Goat Rock, on Highway 101.

Bodega Bay

Bodega Bay's legendary moment, of course, comes with the visit of Alfred Hitchcock and his actors (Rod Taylor, Suzanne Pleshette, Jessica Tandy, Veronica Cartwright, and Tippi Hedren) in the 1962 thriller *The Birds*, based on a short story by Daphne du Maurier (*Rebecca*), who originally

Bodega Bay from Bodega Head.

set the action in England. Hitchcock was both praised and condemned for his ambiguous thriller, in which bloodthirsty birds inexplicably attack the citizens of the sleepy coastal hamlet. Visitors are frequently disappointed to find that the quaint village was mostly created in Hollywood, but The Tides complex of restaurants and piers still exists, although dramatically altered after two fires destroyed the one that appears in *The Birds* and a subsequent structure. From The Tides, Hedren rents the boat to surprise Taylor with a gift of love birds (hint hint) and is attacked by a seagull mid-harbor. Inside the restaurant complex is a gift shop where one can buy Hitchcock posters and *Birds* memorabilia.

The Brenner ranch where Taylor lives with mom (Tandy) and sis (Cartwright) was located on the road leading to Bodega Head. The ranch house and barn were only facades constructed around old shacks that once occupied the site currently housing the Bodega Bay Marine Laboratory on Bay Shore Road. They were used only for exteriors. The pier at which Hedren arrives was constructed and later demolished by the film crew at a site across the harbor from the town.

The scene in which the children run screaming from the Bodega Bay School as they are attacked by birds is on Taylor Street in "Old Town" Bodega Bay. There is no schoolhouse at the top of Taylor Street.

Children flee *The Birds* (1963) down Taylor Street toward the harbor in Bodega Bay.
Courtesy of Pacific Film Archive, University of California, Berkeley

Taylor Street to Bodega Harbor.

Bodega

The Potter School House is located about six miles away in the inland town of Bodega, and the footage was spliced together in a Hollywood editing room. The "Bodega Bay School" on Bodega Lane near Bodega Avenue, where Suzanne Pleshette taught, Tippi Hedren smoked by the jungle gym, and from which bird-pecked kids ran in terror, is now available for tours and also has a gift shop with kitschy *The Birds* souvenirs. Pleshette's home next door was also a facade.

At a calmer moment, in 1968, the Potter School House and the nearby Church of Saint Teresa of Avila stand in for Kentucky when Francis Ford Coppola films immigrants Fred Astaire and Petula Clark as an Irish father and daughter searching for "Rainbow Valley" in the film

The Potter School House, Bodega.

Potter School House and Church of Saint Teresa of Avila, Bodega.

version of the 1940s Broadway musical *Finian's Rainbow*. The actors pass by the small town of Bodega during the opening credits.

Monte Rio

In the small resort town of Monte Rio on Sonoma County's Russian River, Michael Kurtiz filmed Bing Crosby, Danny Kaye, Rosemary Clooney, and Vera-Ellen in *White Christmas* (1954). The story goes that because Crosby refused to travel very far from where he was vacationing at the nearby Bohemian Grove, the Village Inn hotel found in nearby Monte Rio was enlisted to portray the winter resort.

Luciano Pavarotti, Kathryn Harold, and Eddie Albert float above the scenic vineyards of Napa in a hot air balloon at the end of *Yes, Giorgio* (1982). *Courtesy of Pacific Film Archive, University of California, Berkeley*

Napa County

Although neighboring Sonoma County is giving Napa a run for its money, Napa is the heart and soul of the California wine industry. An incredibly rich strip of land running north and south between two mountain ridges, Napa Valley and its hospitable climate were discovered to be a natural match for grape growing in the 19th century. The rest is history.

Filmmakers love the inviting climate, the beautiful rolling terrain, and the golden light of the valley. It is an easy day trip from San Francisco, and many of the almost 300 wineries have tasting rooms that welcome visitors.

Disney's 1960 film version of the Eleanor Porter novel *Pollyanna* was filmed on numerous locations in Napa and Sonoma Counties, which were then woven together in Hollywood to resemble one New England town. Young Hayley Mills takes on the role of the "glad girl" previously played by Mary Pickford in a silent film version. The old Bale Grist Mill, at a state park on Highway 29 (3801 St. Helena Highway), open to the public as a museum, appears as backdrop in the early scene under the credits as Disney child star Kevin Considine rolls a wagon wheel hoop by it. Location filming took place August 1–16, 1959, and locals including those from women's clubs and car clubs served as extras.

St. Helena

The "Harrington" train station where *Pollyanna* arrives at the beginning and leaves at the end of the film named for her is the St. Helena train station on Railroad Avenue. The Vermont town of Beldingsville in the novel is renamed Harrington but still set in the Northeast. When David Swift, a television director, was given the project by Disney, he was amazed that he could ask for anything he wanted. "I asked for a train, and there it was."

In 1998, Disney remade another Hayley Mills classic. *The Parent Trap* is about twin girls who don't know about each other and bring their divorced parents together once they figure it out. Dennis Quaid's "dad" character's gorgeous hillside home, played by the Staglin Family Vineyard, is surrounded by grapes. Also starring in the remake are Lindsay Lohan as the twins and Natasha Richardson as "mom." You can see many views of the vineyard and villa, which always seem to be bathed in the golden light of late afternoon. You can also see Staglin Family Vineyard wine bottles in many scenes in the movie, as well as in the film credits at the end. Francis Ford Coppola's nearby Niebaum-Coppola Winery (on Route 29 near Rutherford) was also used for location filming.

The Staglin Family Vineyard, St. Helena.

In *A Walk in the Clouds* (1995), Mexican director Alfonso Arau (*Like Water for Chocolate*) presents Napa Valley as the magical place that it is, as the local vintners try to get the crop in against all odds. Many scenes were filmed in vineyards that are difficult to identify, but in one scene Keanu Reeves confronts his prospective father-in-law Giancarlo Giannini in the redwood cellar of Charles Krug Winery (on Highway 29 north of St. Helena).

Falcon Crest used exteriors of Spring Mountain Winery. The television series about a North Carolina vintners dynasty, led by tough boss Jane Wyman, ran from 1981 to 1990. It competed fairly successfully against similar soap opera formulas like those of *Dynasty* and *Dallas*. A remarkable parade of guest players showed up on *Falcon Crest*, including Kim Novak, Rod Taylor, Gina Lollobrigida, Mel Ferrer, and Lana Turner. Open to the public during the run of the television show, the historic 1885 mansion nestled into the western slope of Napa Valley outside St. Helena is now a private property. It can be glimpsed from a distance by driving west from St. Helena, at the only traffic light (Madrona Street), then turning right after three blocks onto Spring Mountain Road, and going up a small road to the right to 2600 Spring Mountain Road for an

Distant view of Spring Mountain Winery.

overview of the mansion and its property, which can be viewed across a reservoir owned by Napa County. (But please respect the owners' privacy.)

Niebaum-Coppola Winery
1991 St. Helena Highway, Rutherford

This massive stone winery, built by 19th-century seafarer and fur trader Gustav Niebaum, was bought by Francis Ford Coppola in 1995. The carved wooden staircase leads upstairs to a movie museum. Among the fascinating artifacts are Don Corleone's massive desk from the Academy Award–winning *The Godfather*, two original *Tucker* cars, the giant martini glass that held Natassja Kinski in *One from the Heart*, costumes from *Bram Stoker's Dracula*, various Oscars and other awards, and other memorabilia from Coppola's distinguished career.

An artifact of particular interest to movie buffs is the riverboat from *Apocalypse Now* (1979), which has rested in the vineyard above the château for many years. Coppola reshot a few final scenes at the estate

to complete the film. Coppola's movie career and the winery have been intertwined since the beginning. Rubicon, the estate's proprietary red wine made primarily from Cabernet Sauvignon grapes, has appeared in several Coppola films and can always be found wherever Coppola is on location.

Mendocino County

In April 1904, the Miles Brothers Photographers of San Francisco came to the Mendocino coast, commissioned by Abbie Krebs, owner of the Caspar Lumber Company, to make a film showing how lumber was produced. Hollywood, in the person of well-known early filmmaker Fred J. Bulshofer, came 12 years later to shoot *The Promise* (1916), the first of 17 silent films shot here, ending with *In Search of a Hero* directed by Duke Worne in 1925. In spring 1943, footage for *The Uninvited* was shot here, but neither Ray Milland nor Ruth Hussey came to the area. Films and television shows continue to capitalize on the area's unspoiled natural beauty and the relatively rustic look of its towns. The area is warmly receptive to film crews, who often infuse the local economy and use willing residents as extras.

Frenchman's Creek (1944) starring Joan Fontaine was filmed around the Albion and Big Rivers. In 1948, Jane Wyman won an Oscar for her performance as *Johnny Belinda*. Directed by Jean Negulesco, the story takes place in a small fishing village on the island of Cape Breton. Built in 1867 of local redwood for $10,000, the interior and exterior of the Presbyterian Church at 44831 Main Street were used in the wedding scene, in which members of the church choir appear as extras.

In 1954, Elia Kazan directed James Dean, Jo Van Fleet, and Julie Harris in downtown Mendocino in *East of Eden*. Then filming moved to Salinas, where the John Steinbeck novel was actually set, before being completed on the Warner Bros. back lot. In 1963, trees were planted and a village constructed at Anchor Bay for the filming of *Island of the Blue Dolphins,* Scott O'Dell's bestselling children's novel.

Norman Jewison came to the area in the fall of 1965 for three months to shoot *The Russians Are Coming, The Russians Are Coming,* starring Carl Reiner, Eva Marie Saint, Alan Arkin, Brian Keith, Jonathan Winters, Paul Ford, Theodore Bikel, and Michael J. Pollard. Actually set in Gloucester, New England, it is the first feature film shot in its entirety in the area, including Fort Bragg, Noyo Bay, Cleone, Westport, Mendocino, Little River, and Albion. The comedy tells the story of a Soviet submarine captain who comes up for a look at America (off the coast of a small island in Maine) and runs aground. When he sends his two English-speaking crewmen to procure a boat with enough power to pull them off, they don't exactly blend in and the town becomes convinced that it is being invaded. The decade brought two more film crews: *The Spirit Is Willing* (1966) starring Sid Caesar, Vera Miles, and John McGiver; and *The Dunwich Horror* (1969) with Sandra Dee, Dean Stockwell, and Ed Begley.

In the summer of 1970, director Robert Mulligan filmed Herbert Raucher's novel *Summer of '42,* starring Jennifer O'Neill and Gary Grimes, here. The Mendocino Volunteer Fire Department at 44700 Little Lake Street appears as the "Packett Island Fire Department." The town of Mendocino, as well as 10-Mile Beach in Fort Bragg, stand in for the New England setting in the story of a 14-year-old boy eagerly awaiting his first sexual encounter, who finds himself developing an innocent

Fearing that *The Russians Are Coming, The Russians Are Coming* (1966), blundering butcher Paul Ford mobilizes his community in front of the fake facade of "Gloucester Island City Hall" erected at Noyo. *Courtesy of Pacific Film Archive, University of California, Berkeley*

love for a young woman awaiting news of her soldier husband's fate in World War II. This was followed by *Slither* (1972) starring James Caan, Peter Boyle, Sally Kellerman, and Louise Lasser.

In 1978, Ellen Burstyn reprised her role from the Broadway production of Bernard Slade's play *Same Time, Next Year,* costarring with Alan Alda. Heritage House, in Little River, portrays the romantic inn where they meet by chance over dinner in 1951. They find themselves in the same bed, wondering later how this could have happened since both are married to other people. They nevertheless agree to meet on the same weekend each year. That same year, Bette Davis and Gena Rowlands shot the CBS television movie *Strangers: The Story of a Mother and Daughter* (1978) at 600 Kelley Street, Main Street, Noyo Harbors, and the Fort Bragg Library.

Cujo, based on the Stephen King novel, is one of the better of the many horror films shot in the area. In 1978 Mendocino temporarily became "Castle Rock," Maine, where Dee Wallace and her child are trapped in a car while being attacked by a rabid dog. Sean Penn vies for Elizabeth McGovern's affections in Richard Benjamin's romantic *Racing with the Moon,* set in 1943 and filmed in 1983 in Fort Bragg and Mendocino.

In the CBS television series *Murder, She Wrote*, which ran from 1984 to 1989, Angela Lansbury plays Jessica Fletcher, who lives at Blair House on Mendocino's Little Lake Street, portraying 698 Candlewood, "Cabot Cove," Maine. Tom Bosley and Jerry Orbach costar as Lansbury, the school teacher and murder mystery writer, helps solve crimes in the quiet community, where nearby Fort Bragg's Noyo Harbor stands in for Cabot Cove, Maine; the Masonic temple becomes the Cabot Cove Playhouse; and the Mendocino Fire House becomes Cabot Cove's.

Dark Mansions, a 1985 ABC pilot that was never picked up, starred Michael York, Lois Chiles, and Paul Shenar. The titular twin mansions set on a bluff near Seattle are actually both the Greystoke Mansion in Hollywood, with the Heritage House's meadow and bluff below serving as the grounds. When Richard Benjamin shot *Overboard* in late spring 1987, he left an estimated $3 to $4 million in the appreciative Noyo and Mendocino communities. In the film, rich bitch Goldie Hawn hires country carpenter Kurt Russell to build a closet on her yacht. When the two don't see eye to eye, she sets sail, leaving him unpaid. When Hawn falls overboard, and is fished out of the sea, she suffers from amnesia. Russell tells her she's his wife, getting a free housekeeper and mother for his four kids. By the time her memory returns she realizes she has fallen in love with Russell and his boys.

The following year, Michael Micklis portrayed John Belushi in *Wired* (1989). Part of the biopic, based on Bob Woodward's book, uses MacKerricher Park as the cemetery site in Martha's Vineyard where Belushi was buried.

After she discovers that her boyfriend has betrayed her, Julia Roberts begins working as a private nurse for Campbell Scott, who is suffering from blood cancer. They rent a house in northern California where they fall in love, knowing he hasn't long to live. For Joel Schumacher's 1990 film *Dying Young,* also starring Colleen Dewhurst and Ellen Burstyn, a house and water tower were erected on Mendocino's Main

Street specifically for shooting exteriors. The house was demolished after filming completed, while the water tower remained.

Two years later, against the backdrop of Point Arena, Mel Gibson and Isabel Glasser played 1930s young lovers in *The Rest of Daniel.* By the time Steve Miner's film was released in 1992 it had been renamed *Forever Young.* In *Pontiac Moon* (1994), starring husband and wife Ted Danson and Mary Steenburgen, Mendocino became the fictitious west coast town "Meridian Bay."

In 2001, an episode of *The Fugitive,* an update of the 1960s television series, used Mendocino Savings Band as "Emerson Savings and Loan" in the small northern California town of "Cliffside." That same year Jim Carrey played a Hollywood scriptwriter during the 1950s suspected of being a Communist. After a freak car accident leaves him with amnesia, he ends up living in *The Majestic,* a run-down movie theater in a small California town. Also featuring Laurie Holden, Martin Landau, James Whitmore, and David Ogden Stiers, most of the filming was done in Ferndale, with additional scenes at the Skunk Railroad Depot in Fort Bragg, Point Cabrillo Lighthouse near Caspar, and Big River Beach at Mendocino.

Alcatraz, Angel, Treasure, and Mare Islands and Alameda and Contra Costa Counties

Gibson Gowland as McTeague serenades Zasu Pitts as Trina against the San Francisco Bay in Eric von Stroheim's *Greed* (1925). *Courtesy of Pacific Film Archive, University of California, Berkeley*

This tour requires ferries to get to Angel Island and Alcatraz. A car is necessary to get to Treasure Island via the Bay Bridge and Mare Island adjacent to Vallejo. (Some areas of these former naval bases may not be accessible to tourists.) From the Bay Bridge the tour leads through Emeryville to Berkeley, and into Oakland. From Oakland it goes west to the island of Alameda and then south down to Niles. Then it cuts over northeast to Antioch and Danville in Contra Costa County, and ends at the Caldecott Tunnel on the way back to the Bay Bridge.

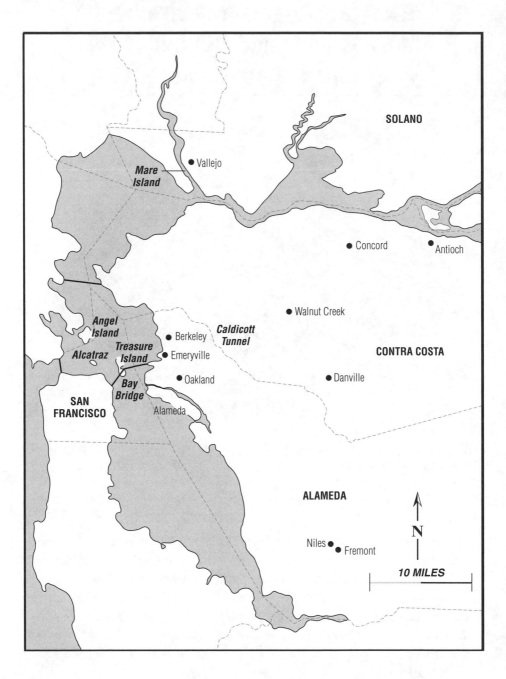

SOLANO

Vallejo

Mare
Island

Concord

Antioch

Walnut Creek

Angel
Island

Caldicott
Tunnel

CONTRA COSTA

Alcatraz

Treasure
Island

Berkeley

Emeryville

Oakland

Danville

Bay
Bridge

SAN
FRANCISCO

Alameda

ALAMEDA

Niles Fremont

N

10 MILES

The Islands

Part of the area's charm is the islands in its bay. Rich with history and vistas, they have become an intrinsic part of its cinematic reputation. In addition to the photogenic Alcatraz and Angel Island, the former military installations at Treasure Island and Mare Island play significant roles in film production.

Alcatraz Island

In 1775 the Spanish explorer Juan Manuel de Ayala was the first to sail into what is now known as San Francisco Bay, and named one of the three islands *Alcatraces*. Over time, the name became Alcatraz, usually defined as meaning "pelican" or "strange bird." In 1850, a presidential order set aside the island for possible use as a United States military reservation. The U.S. Army built a fortress at the top of the island in the early 1850s and made plans to install more than 100 cannons, making Alcatraz the most heavily fortified military site on the West Coast. The island was also the site of the first operational lighthouse on the West

Coast of the United States. By the late 1850s the first military prisoners were being housed on the island; its role as a prison would continue for more than 100 years. In 1909, the army tore down the fortress, leaving its basement level to serve as the foundation for a new military prison. From 1909 through 1911, the military prisoners on Alcatraz built the new prison, which was designated the Pacific Branch, U.S. Disciplinary Barracks for the U.S. Army. It was this prison building that later became famous as "The Rock."

In 1933, the Federal Bureau of Prisons transferred the island to the U.S. Department of Justice for use as a maximum-security, minimum-privilege penitentiary to deal with the most incorrigible inmates in federal prisons. While several well-known criminals such as Al Capone, George "Machine Gun" Kelly, Alvin Karpis (the first "Public Enemy #1"), and Arthur "Doc" Barker did time on Alcatraz, most of the 1,576 prisoners incarcerated there were not well-known gangsters, but prisoners who refused to conform to the rules and regulations at other federal institutions, were considered violent and dangerous, or were escape risks.

On March 21, 1963, after 29 years of operation, Alcatraz closed because the institution was too expensive to continue operating. Many ideas were proposed for the island, including a monument to the United Nations, a West Coast version of the Statue of Liberty, and a shopping center/hotel complex. In 1969, the island made news when a group of Native Americans claimed it as Indian land with the hope of creating a Native American cultural center and education complex on the island. Much damage occurred including graffiti, vandalism, and a fire that destroyed the lighthouse keeper's home, the warden's home, and the Officer's Club, before federal marshals removed the remaining Native Americans from the island in June 1971. Some of the damage was repaired in the process of making the area safe for tourists before Alcatraz Island reopened to the public in fall 1973 becoming a popular visitor site and prime location for movies.

Based on the novel *The Hunter* by Richard Stark (a pseudonym of Donald E. Westlake), *Point Blank* (1967) is a neo-noir classic about reclaiming $93,000 that was stolen from Lee Marvin during a heist. Through a number of lightning-quick, elliptically assembled shots, Marvin, his best friend John Vernon, and Marvin's wife Sharon Acker successfully intercept a clandestine money drop-off taking place on Alcatraz. When Vernon finds that his share of the spoils isn't satisfactory, he and Acker plug Marvin full of holes in a prison cell. Left for dead, he somehow manages to survive the ambush and, with a stomach full of lead, returns to San Francisco by floating on his back along the treacherous Alcatraz currents. A year later, a mysterious informer tells him how to find his wife and Vernon, but Marvin's motivation isn't revenge; he simply wants his $93,000. Director John Boorman filmed throughout the abandoned correctional facility, a wonderfully atmospheric setting. Early in the film Keenan Wynn meets Marvin on a Red & White Cruise of the bay, listening skeptically to the tour guide explaining about the various attempted escapes from Alcatraz.

One of those escapes was orchestrated by Frank Morris, who, because he had escaped from prisons before, was sent to the "inescapable" Alcatraz. In *Escape from Alcatraz* (1979), directed by Don Siegel, Clint Eastwood plays the famous escapee. The actual cells that had been home to the real-life inmates Frank Morris, John Anglin (Fred Ward), and John's brother Clarence (Jack Thibeau) were cells #138, #140, and #144 in B Block ("Michigan Avenue") along the bottom row. The cells used in the film, however, are located in the C Block, middle cells on the Broadway side along the bottom row. During filming, tourists were still allowed onto the island, and a new boatload would arrive every half hour. They became so much of a distraction that the majority of filming was moved to night shoots. The boat bringing Eastwood to Alcatraz in the very beginning of the movie (MV *Warden Johnston*, named after the first warden of Alcatraz) was actually used to transport prisoners to and from Alcatraz and was not a mock-up. The boat was built by prisoners in McNeil Island in Washington for this specific purpose, and was used for much of the time Alcatraz was in service as a prison.

Don Siegel reminisces about using Alacatraz as a location in his 1993 autobiography, *A Siegel Film*. In 1954, Siegel, with producer Walter Wanger, inspected three maximum security prisons—Alcatraz, San Quentin, and Folsom—looking for a location for *Riot in Cell Block 11* (1954), which was ultimately shot at Folsom State Prison. "I was very depressed by what I saw at Alcatraz," he writes. "It was impregnable and totally escape proof. All the prisoners had single cells and most of them should have been in an insane asylum." When he returned in 1978, Alcatraz was being run by the Department of Parks and Recreation Commission. Siegel noted, "It needed extensive refurbishing, but it was shootable."

Nor was *Escape from Alcatraz* Clint Eastwood's first visit to the island. In *The Enforcer* (1976), the third installment of the *Dirty Harry* series, Eastwood and his new partner Tyne Daly must track down the People's Revolutionary Strike Force (based on the Symbionese Liberation Army) who have kidnapped the mayor and are demanding $2 million ransom. When they learn the mayor is being held on Alcatraz Island, Eastwood and Daly take a fireboat there to try to rescue him. The final showdown is shot throughout the interior and exterior of the former prison.

Mike Myers takes a tour of Alcatraz in *So I Married an Axe Murderer* (1993). Various exteriors and interiors of the former prison were used in the scenes where John "Vicky" Johnson guides the tour through the cell block.

Murder in the First (1995) was inspired by a true story of a petty thief incarcerated and subsequently sent to Alcatraz in the 1930s after an attempt to escape from prison. He is placed in solitary confinement, where the maximum stay is supposed to be 19 days, but Kevin Bacon spends years alone, cold and in complete darkness, only to emerge a madman and a soon-to-be murderer. The story follows rookie lawyer Christian Slater attempting to prove that Alcatraz was to blame, and that Bacon should not be executed. Although the movie took place in the late 1930s, all exterior shots of Alcatraz show the burned-out shell of the warden's house. The warden's house on Alcatraz didn't burn down until 1970, seven years after it was closed as a prison, during the Native American occupation of the island.

In *The Rock* (1996), a group of renegade marine commandos seizes a stockpile of chemical weapons and takes over Alcatraz, with 81 tourists as hostages. Their leader, Ed Harris, demands $100 million in ransom as restitution to families of soldiers who died in covert operations and were thereby denied compensation. He is threatening to launch 15 rockets carrying deadly VX nerve gas into the San Francisco Bay area. An elite SEAL team, with support from an FBI chemical warfare expert (Nicolas Cage) and a former Alcatraz escapee (Sean Connery), is assembled to penetrate the terrorists' defenses on the island. Much actual footage of Alcatraz exteriors, interiors, and views was mixed with sets. (Because he didn't want to travel from the mainland to the island every day, Connery reportedly insisted the producers build a cabin for him on Alcatraz.) At the film's end when Cage allows him to escape, Connery directs him to the closet in his room at the Pan Pacific Hotel (500 Post at Mason) for some clothes.

Perhaps the most famous film set on Alcatraz, *The Birdman of Alcatraz*, was shot on Hollywood sets. The real Robert Stroud, who lived in cell #42 in the D Block, was not allowed to keep birds in the prison. Far from the sympathetic character portrayed by Burt Lancaster, Stroud was an unremorseful killer. Finding a latent talent for medical research while incarcerated, he did in fact keep birds during his time at Leavenworth. Stroud never read the Thomas E. Gaddis book based on his life or saw John Frankenheimer's 1962 movie. At the end of the film, Lancaster as Stroud says, "If you San Franciscans had any civic pride you'd blow that place out of the Bay instead of advertising it. What an eyesore." He goes on to ask Gaddis, "You know what they used to call Alcatraz in the old days? Bird Island."

Other projects set on and/or shot on the Rock include the 2004 television series *Dead Famous* (2004), *Down Time* (2001), *Electric Dreams*

Burt Lancaster as Robert Stroud, *The Birdman of Alcatraz* (1962), on a Hollywood set. Stroud never kept birds at Alcatraz. *Courtesy of Pacific Film Archive, University of California, Berkeley*

(1984), *The Magic of David Copperfield IX: Escape from Alcatraz* (1987), *The Rock* (1967), *Slaughterhouse Rock* (1988*), Star Wars: Episode V—The Empire Strikes Back* (1980), *Terror on Alcatraz* (1986), and *We Sold Our Souls for Rock 'n' Roll* (2001).

Angel Island

Now a park run by the State of California, the picturesque island has a sad history as a spot for the detention of prisoners of war (beginning with the Spanish-American War), a quarantine camp, and an immigration station (from 1910 to 1940). At the end of Don Siegel's *Escape from Alcatraz* (1979), a scene where guards search for the three escaped convicts takes place on Angel Island. When they find yellow chrysanthemums, the warden recognizes the flowers as a signal from Frank Morris (Clint Eastwood) that the convicts have actually survived. The warden nevertheless declares, "They drowned," and throws the flowers into the water.

Treasure Island

One of three former military bases, along with Mare Island and Alameda Naval Air Station, Treasure Island Naval Station is being developed for further film production. The 400-acre island, with three hangars larger than football fields, is conveniently located for use by local production crews. Much of Edward Dmytryk's film of Herman Wouk's *The Caine Mutiny* (1954) was shot on Treasure Island during 15 months in the early 1950s. The prolonged production resulted from a conflict with the U.S. Navy, still in residence, which thought it would be negatively portrayed due to the unsavory subject matter. Filmmakers reached a compromise by including a statement on screen that there has never been a mutiny on a U.S. Navy ship.

In January 1997 filming on *Flubber* began on soundstages at Treasure Island, including a huge set for the basketball stadium interior, as well as Robin Williams's laboratory and the interior of the mansion. Williams plays the Fred MacMurray role in this remake of Disney's *The Absent Minded Professor* (1961), about a kooky academic who invents a high-bouncing blob that revolutionizes basketball, among other things. Treasure Island was host to a remarkable deco-style World's Fair in

Treasure Island in San Francisco Bay.

1939–40, where the great Mexican muralist Diego Rivera created his mural entitled *Pan American Unity* before an awestruck public. (It is now on display at City College of San Francisco.)

Williams returned to Treasure Island for *Patch Adams* in 1998. Based on a true story, the film stars Williams as a troubled man with experiences on both sides of mental health care. Filming was done on Treasure Island soundstages, where a 20,000-square-foot hospital set doubled as the Medical College of Virginia. Exteriors were shot at the University of North Carolina at Chapel Hill with additional school scenes shot at UC Berkeley's Wheeler Hall and LeConte Hall.

The *Nash Bridges* television series (CBS, 1996–2001) used Building 180 for production offices and the elaborate set of Don Johnson's character's apartment near Chinatown. Johnson's 1970 Hemi Barracuda was frequently spotted cruising many neighborhoods of San Francisco with a camera mounted on the hood.

Copycat in 1994 was the first film that used Treasure Island hangar space for shooting and production offices. The interior of the lavish house inhabited by agoraphobic psychiatrist Sigourney Weaver was constructed in Building Two. The following year *Jade,* directed by William Friedkin and starring David Caruso, Linda Fiorentino, and Chazz Palmintieri, made use of the facilities. Island space was used for the live-action segments of *James and the Giant Peach* (1996), based on Roald Dahl's popular children's book.

For *Metro* (1997), the Eddie Murphy police action thriller, a complete police station interior was constructed, as well as rain machines to achieve San Francisco's famous moody appearance. In addition, Treasure Island has played a role in the production of the following films: *A Smile Like Yours* (1997), *Twisted* (2004), *Sweet November* (2001), *Groove* (2000), *Sausalito* (2000), *Bicentennial Man* (1999), *The Parent Trap* (1998), *What Dreams May Come* (1998), *Nothing Sacred* (1997), *Phenomenon* (1996), *Indiana Jones and the Last Crusade* (1989), *Chu Chu and the Philly Flash* (1981), *Indiana Jones and the Raiders of the Lost Ark* (1981), and *Dirty Harry* (1971).

In late 2004 Chris Columbus announced he would be shooting the film version of the Broadway musical *Rent* on Treasure Island. By April 2005 crews were filming on Treasure Island, and throughout San Francisco, which was dressed to appear as New York.

Mare Island

Since its closure in 1996, the former Mare Island Naval Shipyard, located in the city of Vallejo, has been successfully utilized by the film industry on a variety of projects. The island contains several large buildings that have been used as soundstages on such projects as *Jack* (1996), *Sphere* (1998), *Flubber* (1997), and MTV's *Road Rules* (1994–present). Mare Island's unique "looks" have also been used in location filming in such feature films as *Metro* (1997), *What Dreams May Come* (1998), and *Patch Adams* (1998).

An early film crew arrived on April 2, 1929, with 12 trucks of machinery, dynamos for lighting effects, and properties for scenery. Director Raoul Walsh and the three principal actors Victor McLaglen, Edmond Lowe, and Lya De Putti (later replaced by Lily Dalmita) went directly to Mare Island for preliminary details before beginning work on a scene of *The Cock-eyed World* (1929). There they worked on the transport *Henderson* for the final scenes of the film, the sequel to *What Price Glory?* (1926). Several dozen Boy Scouts were hired as extras as well as a few men and women of Vallejo during the four days of shooting.

Among other films that have used the facilities at Mare Island are: *50 First Dates* (2004), *In Control of All Things* (2004), *Twisted* (2004). *Get Money* (2003), *Yamashita: The Tiger's Treasure* (2002), *Bandits* (2001),

Police confront a student riot at Henry J. Kaiser Jr. Auditorium, Oakland, in *The Strawberry Statement* (1970). *Courtesy of Pacific Film Archive, University of California, Berkeley*

Disneyland's Golden Dreams (2001), *Obstacles* (2000), *Tucker: The Man and His Dream* (1988), and *Destination Tokyo* (1943).

Alameda County

Referred to as the "East Bay" by the San Francisco–centric Bay Area, Alameda County has starred in a surprising number of films, whether as itself or standing in for other locations.

Bay Bridge

The San Francisco–Oakland Bay Bridge consists of two major segments connecting Yerba Buena Island with each shore. The western segment, terminating in San Francisco, consists of two suspension bridges end-to-end with a central anchorage. The eastern span, terminating in Oakland, consists of a truss causeway, five medium span truss bridges, and a double tower cantilever span. Construction began on July 9, 1933,

and the bridge was opened to traffic on Thursday, November 12, 1936, at 12:30 P.M. The total cost of construction for the bridge was $79.5 million. After damage during the 1989 Loma Prieta earthquake closed the bridge for a month, construction crews repaired a fallen section of the roadway, and the extent of the structure's vulnerability was emphasized. After more than a decade of study, work began in 2002 on a replacement for the cantilever portion of the bridge, with completion not expected for a decade.

Follow the Fleet was filmed in 1936, the year the Bay Bridge was completed. When the fleet puts in at San Francisco, sailor Fred Astaire tries to rekindle the flame with his old dancing partner, Ginger Rogers, while Astaire's buddy Randolph Scott romances Rogers's sister Harriet Hilliard (later Harriet Nelson, of Ozzie and Harriet fame). The sisters look out their apartment window, supposedly at Hyde and Geary Streets, watching the fleet leaving the bay at night. Night footage of the Bay Bridge is hard to positively identify.

John Huston's classic 1941 noir detective caper, The Maltese Falcon, is set in San Francisco but not shot on location. In the first scenes, the Bay Bridge is shown in establishing shots, with "San Francisco" written in white over the gray image.

During the opening title sequence of *Experiment in Terror*, Lee Remick is driving a light Ford Fairlane convertible west across the Bay Bridge's upper deck, which in 1961 had two-way traffic. The stark pho-

Fred Astaire and Ginger Rogers in *Follow the Fleet* (1936), one of many films set in but not shot in San Francisco. *Courtesy of Pacific Film Archive, University of California, Berkeley*

tography and haunting score by Henry Mancini portray the city, glistening in the distance, as a menacing place.

In *The Graduate* (1967), director Mike Nichols makes a legendary Bay Bridge faux pas. Dustin Hoffman is supposed to be driving east across the bridge to Berkeley to track down Katherine Ross, who is attending the University of California at Berkeley. The eastbound lanes, actually on the bottom of this double-decker bridge, were deemed not photogenic enough, so he is shown driving his red convertible the wrong way: west, away from Berkeley.

Oliver Stone's *Salvador* (1986) tells the semi-biographical story of journalist Richard Boyle (James Woods). As the film starts, Boyle is very down on his luck: he makes little money, and after his family gets evicted from their scummy San Francisco apartment, his wife leaves him. Rather than attempt to get his life together, Woods recruits his similarly wild friend Jim Belushi to head south with him. Ultimately Woods convinces Belushi that El Salvador is the place to be, as he entices him with stories of cheap, quality prostitutes and dismisses tales of political unrest and violence. As they leave San Francisco this pair is also shown driving westbound on the upper deck of the Bay Bridge.

Another confusing wrong-way on the bridge scene appears in Harold Ramis's 2000 remake *Bedazzled*. Elizabeth Hurley as the Devil drives her car, a Lamborghini Diablo, the wrong way (east) on the upper deck. This scene was shot early in the morning of April 9, 2000. The "DV8" Club (with the Bay Bridge superimposed above it) was filmed in San Pedro, in Southern California.

High school student Nia Long lives with her mother Whoopi Goldberg in the East Bay in *Made in America* (1993). When she starts to question who her real father is, she and Will Smith ride their motorbike across the Bay Bridge (accurately) into San Francisco en route to the Bay Area Cryobank (on Nob Hill). When they arrive Long pretends that they are there because Smith wants to make a deposit while she sneaks a look at her sperm donor's record.

Brendan Fraser as *George of the Jungle* (1997) refers to the Bay Bridge as the "biggest rope bridge George has ever seen." This is the site of the dramatic sequence in which George heroically rescues a parasailor trapped in the suspension cables.

The last scene of *Groove* (2000), the independent film directed by Greg Harrison in 2000, shows Hamish Linklater driving home to San

Francisco's warehouse district from Berkeley after "connecting" with Lola Glaudini. It has been suggested that this is the only use of the Bay Bridge toll plaza in a feature film.

Pixar Animation Studios
Emeryville

Since its incorporation in 1986, Pixar has been responsible for many important breakthroughs in the application of computer graphics for filmmaking. After more than nine years of creative and technical achievements, *Toy Story* was released in November 1995 to critical acclaim and became the highest grossing film of the year. Following the successes of *A Bug's Life* (1998), *Toy Story 2* (1999), and *Monsters, Inc.* (2001), *Finding Nemo* (2003) became the highest grossing animated film of all time. *The Incredibles* was released in November 2004, earning over $630 million and winning the 2005 Oscar for Best Sound Editing.

Emeryville is also a location in the film *Harold and Maude* (1971), Colin Higgin's offbeat dark comedy about a suicidal young man and a free-spirited older woman who find each other through their mutual interest in strangers' funerals and fall in love. In one scene Bud Cort and Ruth Gordon sit overlooking the funky 1970s sculpture park in Emeryville's mud flats at the edge of the bay. There is little left of this former ever-changing art site just off Highway 80 at the intersection with Highway 580.

Saul Zaentz Film Center
2600 10th Street at Parker, Emeryville

The Film Center evolved from Fantasy Records, a company specializing in jazz and blues. In 1972, Saul Zaentz and his Fantasy partners ventured into feature film, producing *Payday* in 1973, following with *One Flew Over the Cuckoo's Nest*, co-produced with Michael Douglas in 1976. The latter film's success encouraged Fantasy to add a new building to their facility. Opened in 1980, the Fantasy Building included a fully equipped dubbing stage and editing suites for picture and sound. A second film mixing stage was added in 1989, along with additional editing rooms and many facility updates. Among Saul Zaentz's many award-winning producing credits are *Three Warriors* (1978), *Lord of the Rings* (1978), *Amadeus* (1984), *The Unbearable Lightness of Being* (1988), and *The English Patient* (1996).

Berkeley BART Station
2160 Shattuck Avenue, Berkeley

George Lucas adapted *THX 1138*, his first film, from a 17-minute short he made at the University of Southern California called *Electronic Labyrinth THX-1138-4EB*. (The title is believed to be Lucas's San Francisco telephone number, 849-1138—the letters THX correspond to letters found on the buttons 8, 4, and 9.) In the futuristic society located beneath the surface of the Earth, drugs are used to control people, sex is outlawed, and the only recreation is the acquisition of objects. THX 1138 (Robert Duvall) stops taking drugs, and falls in love with LUH 3417 (Maggie McOrnie). They are both thrown in jail where they meet SEN 5241 (Donald Pleasence) and plan an escape. Lucas originally was all set to shoot the film in Japan until he realized he didn't have enough money to get there. The film, the first for Francis Ford Coppola's Ameri-

The ladder that Robert Duvall climbs to the upper world is actually rebar in place before the track for BART was installed. He is crawling horizontally, and the image was rotated 90 degrees in the final cut of *THX 1138* (1971). *Courtesy of Pacific Film Archive, University of California, Berkeley*

can Zoetrope, was recut by officials at Warner Bros. who did not like the finished product and reduced the marketing budget. To provide the large number of extras required, George Lucas contacted the Synanon drug rehabilitation facility, where he found many recovering drug users, their heads shaved as part of the program, who were willing to work for $30/day.

Bay Area Rapid Transit system was nearing completion and allowed filming to take place throughout the tunnels, computer center, tracks, and stations. The scene of bodies on slabs in the morgue was filmed at the Berkeley BART station.

University of California at Berkeley

Berkeley's premier cinematic attraction is the University of California campus. The roots of UC Berkeley go back to the gold rush days of 1849, when the drafters of the state constitution planned a university. In 1868, the governor signed into law the Organic Act that created the University of California, a merger between the private College of California and the Agricultural, Mining, and Mechanical Arts College. The new university used the former College of California's buildings in Oakland until South Hall and North Hall were completed on the Berkeley site, and in September 1873 the university, with an enrollment of 191 students, moved to Berkeley.

At the turn of the 20th century, one of the university's most generous benefactors, Phoebe Apperson Hearst, conceived of and financed an international competition for campus architectural plans. Won by Emile Bénard of Paris, this brought Berkeley not only a building plan but worldwide fame. John Galen Howard, the supervising architect charged with implementing the Bénard plan, developed a classic style of architecture that makes the campus so photogenic.

In his first major film role, Dustin Hoffman is a naive college graduate in *The Graduate* (1967), who is seduced by Anne Bancroft, a middle-aged woman, and then falls in love with her daughter, Katherine Ross. When Hoffman drives from Los Angeles to Berkeley to try to find Ross and win her back, Theta Delta Chi at 2647 Durant is the fraternity where he tries to find the fellow who threatened to steal her away. Several shots of the UC Berkeley campus are interspersed with those of University of Southern California in Los Angeles and Stanford University in Palo Alto. A few Telegraph Avenue location shots have Dustin Hoffman

sitting in Café Mediterranean, across from Moe's Books, waiting for a glimpse of Ross.

Shots of the campus appear in Paul Schrader's 1988 dramatization of the bizarre kidnapping and conversion into bank robber of San Francisco newspaper heiress *Patty Hearst,* played by Natasha Richardson. Hearst herself later appeared in John Waters's films.

In the opening scene of Richard Benjamin's *Made in America* (1993), Whoopi Goldberg is seen riding her bicycle past the Campanile and Wheeler Hall, through Sather Gate, across Sproul Plaza, and south down Telegraph Avenue. It appears as if her shop, African Queen, is located on Telegraph Avenue, but it's actually at 2998 College Avenue. Goldberg is raising her teenage daughter Nia Long, who accidentally discovers that she was the product of artificial insemination, and in a raid on a sperm bank computer, learns that her biological father is Hal Jackson (Ted Danson), a white car dealer who makes a fool of himself in his television ads and is a committed bachelor with no interest in a family.

Later in the film, Goldberg and Danson go for a romantic walk across the campus, passing Sproul Hall, back through Sather Gate, Stephens Hall, and the Faculty Glade. Rumor has it that in 1993 while making the film, Goldberg and Danson had an affair.

The following year, in *Junior* (1994), Arnold Schwarzenegger and Danny DeVito portray scientists working on a new drug that will reduce the chances of a woman's body rejecting an embryo, the primary cause of a miscarriage. When their research funding is withdrawn, and human experimentation is denied to them, DeVito convinces Schwarzenegger to test the drug by allowing himself to be impregnated. Schwarzenegger uncharacteristically and unexpectedly becomes attached to "his" unborn baby in Ivan Reitman's comedy. Inexplicably the University of California campus is called "Leland University" after Leland Stanford, the founder of nearby rival Stanford University.

Freddie Prinze Jr. and Claire Forlani are childhood friends, now college students, in *Boys and Girls* (2000). He is intent on earning his degree and she is out for fun. Their love-hate relationship focuses on their respective boyfriends and girlfriends, until they sleep together, which seems to ruin everything. Bowles Hall was used for "Carmen Hall," the all-male dorm where Prinze and Jason Biggs are roommates. Because the many scenes around the University of California campus (including Wheeler and Mulford Halls, the Campanile, Sather Gate, Doe Library, Kleeberger Field, and Valley Life Science Building) were shot while classes were in session, the students seen are actually registered students walking around. By the way, Berkeley does not offer degrees in Latin (which Forlani is studying) or Structural Engineering (Prinze's major), although Classics and Civil Engineering are options.

Berkeley Art Museum
2626 Bancroft Way, Berkeley

Mr. Ricco (1975), an urban action thriller, features Dean Martin as an aging San Francisco defense attorney risking his life to prove the innocence of his client, a black militant accused of murder, when he stumbles into an SFPD police brutality cover-up. The film's shootout finale takes place at the Berkeley Art Museum. The museum was founded in 1963 when artist and teacher Hans Hofmann donated 45 paintings and $250,000 to the university. The unusual museum build-

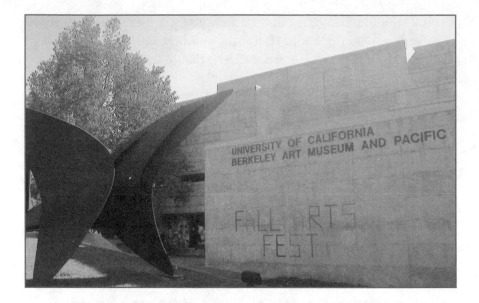

ing is the result of an architectural competition won by San Francisco architect Mario Ciampi and associates Richard L. Jorasch and Ronald E. Wagner. Construction began in 1967, and the building opened on November 7, 1970.

Lawrence Berkeley Lab
1 Cyclotron Road, Berkeley

Lawrence Berkeley National Laboratory (Berkeley Lab), a leader in science and engineering research for more than 70 years, is located on 200 acres in the hills above the Berkeley campus of the University of California, overlooking the San Francisco Bay. A brief scene from George Lucas's *THX 1138* (1971) was filmed there.

Claremont Resort & Spa
41 Tunnel Road, Berkeley

The Claremont Resort & Spa opened in 1915 and gained a reputation as a retreat for wealthy San Franciscans to escape the fog on "the sunny side of the bay." Nestled into 22 acres of beautifully landscaped gardens and rolling hills, it boasts panoramic views of the bay and San Francisco skyline. During the 1930s and 1940s, the hotel was a center for ballroom dancing and big band music, featuring, among others, Tommy Dorsey and Count Basie. In 1993, Chris Columbus used the resort for swimming pool scenes featuring Robin Williams as *Mrs. Doubtfire*, Sally Field, the children, and Pierce Brosnan. "Can you say liposuction?" Williams, as the nanny, quips to the kids, when Brosnan appears in his swim trunks.

2998 College Avenue
Between Ashby and Webster, Berkeley

Site of Whoopi Goldberg's afrocentric bookshop African Queen in *Made in America* (1993). This is where her "real African Queen" assistant, Paul Rodriguez, lip-synchs to Judy Garland, and where Whoopi inadvertently locks in two middle-aged white women who end up embracing African culture. In one scene the marquee of the nearby Elmwood Theater advertises a Paula Prentiss retrospective. Paula Prentiss is director Richard Benjamin's wife.

Telegraph Avenue

This stretch of the long avenue that runs from Berkeley through Oakland is where Preston Tucker leads the police on a chase through downtown Oakland to demonstrate the speed capability of the Tucker automobile in *Tucker: The Man and His Dream* (1988). It is also the location of the parade of Tuckers at the film's finale. *Made in America* (1993) also uses this photogenic section of town in some of its chase sequences.

Founded in 1852, Oakland is the county seat of Alameda County, the third largest city in the San Francisco Bay area, and home of the Port of Oakland, one of three major shipping ports on the West Coast. Oakland's former reputation as a high-crime city with a crumbling public education system is being rapidly reversed. Its warm weather, hillside neighborhoods with stunning views, and a substantial offering of shopping districts and diverse restaurants have led real estate prices to skyrocket. Oaklanders are understandably frustrated by the continued misuse of the most famous quote about their city, by Gertrude Stein, who said, "There's no there there." This didn't have anything to do with the city itself; rather, it only reflected that her childhood home had been torn down. The quote has been turned on its head, with a downtown statue simply titled, "There." And as for the Oakland Film Commission, headed by Ami Zins, it is extremely knowledgeable and cooperative in assisting local filming projects.

Temescal Library
5205 Telegraph Avenue, Oakland

This branch of the Oakland Public Library was used in a very brief scene in *The Assassination of Richard Nixon* (2004) starring Sean Penn as a worn-out office furniture salesman, and Naomi Watts as his estranged wife. Based on the true story of a Baltimore man who, in 1974, hijacked an airplane with the intent of crashing it into the White House, the script is by director Niels Mueller and Kevin Kennedy. Penn frequently annoys Watts by showing up at her house on Locksley Street, and argues with his sole friend Bonny Simmons (Don Cheadle) at his auto repair shop at 16th Street and Peralta. Foreign Body Mechanics, 2428 Webster; Geoffrey's Inner Circle, 410 4th Street; and Innovative Bank, 361 14th Street, Alameda are among the film's other locations in Berkeley, Oakland, Sacramento, and San Francisco.

Mountain View Cemetery
5000 Piedmont Avenue, Oakland

With its stately avenues and winding roadways, its native live oaks and imported Italian stone pines, its simple columbarium and elaborate mausoleums, Mountain View Cemetery is a prime example of early American culture and the lively spirit of early California. Designed by Frederick Law Olmsted in 1863, Mountain View is the resting place of famous figures like author Frank Norris, artist Thomas Hill, architects Julia Morgan and Bernard Maybeck, and railroad builder and banker Charles Crocker.

In *What Dreams May Come* (1998), after the death of their two children, Dr. Chris Nielson (Robin Williams) and his wife Annie (Annabella Sciorra) have a difficult time continuing their lives. When Chris is killed in a car accident, it is the last straw for Annie. The scene of grief-stricken Annabella Sciorra visiting the graves of Robin Williams and their children was shot in Mountain View Cemetery.

Oakland Technical High School
4351 Broadway, Oakland

Where Nia Long and Will Smith are classmates in *Made in America* (1993). In the final graduation scene, when Long, who will be going to MIT, is presented with the Westinghouse Award, she in turn awards it to her mother, Whoopi Goldberg, and her father, Ted Danson.

Paramount Theater
2025 Broadway at 20th, Oakland

The Paramount Theater, designed by renowned San Francisco architect Timothy L. Pflueger and completed in late 1931, was one of the first Depression-era buildings to incorporate and integrate the work of numerous creative artists into its architecture.

After its initial brief blaze of "movie palace" glory in the 1930s, this remarkable auditorium suffered three decades of neglect and decline until it was rescued by the Oakland Symphony, the City of Oakland, and numerous private donors. In 1973, after being meticulously restored to its original splendor, it was entered in the National Register of Historic Places. The Paramount Theater, one of the finest remaining examples of art deco design in the United States, is now home to the Oakland Ballet and the Oakland East Bay Symphony, and hosts a year-round schedule of popular music concerts, variety shows, and, oh yes, movies.

In 1972 Michael Ritchie filmed much of *The Candidate* (1972) in the Paramount Theater. The story tells of charismatic Californian lawyer Robert Redford fighting for the little man. His integrity gets him noticed by the Democratic Party machine, and he is persuaded to run for the Senate against an apparently unassailable incumbent. The ornate movie palace had fallen into disrepair and closed in 1970. The lobby was used as Redford's campaign headquarters, where people like Robert Shields and Natalie Wood, playing themselves, appeared. The auditorium was used for the rally scenes. Shortly after filming completed, the dramatic restoration of the facility began.

Francis Ford Coppola shot much of his 1988 picture *Tucker: The Man and His Dream* in the Bay Area. The true story of Preston Tucker, the maverick car designer, and his ill-fated challenge to the auto industry with his revolutionary car concept offered distinct parallels to director Coppola's own efforts to build a new movie studio of his own. In addition to Jeff Bridges as Tucker, the cast includes Joan Allen, Martin Landau,

Frederic Forrest, Mako, Christian Slater, Peter Donat, Dean Stockwell, Dean Goodman, and an uncredited Lloyd Bridges. The Paramount Theater is featured as one of the stops on the "nice long publicity tour" that Tucker is urged to take, proudly demonstrating his Tucker automobile.

That same year, Robert Zemeckis used the Paramount in *Who Framed Roger Rabbit?* (1988), which combined live action and animation. The groundbreaking technology boasted a clever plot involving the social upheaval in Hollywood between humans and "toons." In one scene Roger Rabbit and Bob Hoskins watch a "Goofy" cartoon from the front row of a balcony, with a theater full of kids below. The cartoon femme fatale, "Dolores," enters later during a black-and-white newsreel. The equally deco "Maroon Cartoon" studios appear on screen in the newsreel. The opulent theater was also used in 2002 as a setting in *Comedian* in which veteran comic Jerry Seinfeld and newcomer Orny Adams perform in concert.

2201 Broadway, Oakland

When former rock star and San Francisco nightclub owner Johnny Boz is found murdered in his bed in *Basic Instinct* (1992), Detective Michael Douglas is assigned to the case. The prime suspect is Sharon Stone, an attractive and manipulative novelist who had been seeing Boz. Police psychiatrist Jeanne Tripplehorn, Douglas's ex-girlfriend, is brought in on the case when it is discovered that the murder was copied directly from one of Stone's novels. Douglas starts to get too involved with the seductive Stone, much to Tripplehorn's consternation, who was once a college roommate of Stone's. This nondescript building in Oakland is where Tripplehorn has asked Douglas's colleague, George Dzundza, to meet her. He ends up getting stabbed to death in the elevator on the fourth floor, before Douglas confronts Tripplehorn in the movie's denouement.

First Baptist Church
534 22nd Street at Telegraph Avenue, Oakland

When Robin Williams is killed in a car accident in *What Dreams May Come* (1998), his funeral is held here.

Latham Square Building
1611 Telegraph Avenue, Oakland

The Matrix Reloaded (2003) and *The Matrix Revolutions* (2004) did extensive filming in the downtown Oakland area. The parking garage underneath the 508 16th Street entrance to this building is where the car crashes out of the garage and heads west on 16th Street. The painted fence in the background was put up to cover the bottom of the Cathedral Building on Telegraph Avenue so that this block could be reused later. The reflections of the Latham Square Building and the north side of the Rotunda Building are visible. The chase then heads east on 16th Street, before heading west, then east again. At various times, the Dalziel Building is visible out the window, as is the Fox Theater.

Oakland Tribune Tower
401 13th Street, Oakland

Clint Eastwood works as a second-rate journalist for the Oakland Tribune in *True Crime* (1999). The interiors, featuring Christine Ebersole as a compassionate colleague, were shot on the sixth floor of 2201 Broadway, a few blocks away. The pressroom was filmed at the *Contra Costa Times* at 2640 Shadeland Road in Walnut Creek.

"Frank Beachum's house"
1035 8th Avenue, Oakland

The house in Oakland where Isaiah Washington and Lisa Gay Hamilton live in *True Crime* (1999). When she tells him that they're out of A-1 Steak Sauce he goes to the convenience store to pick up a bottle, and trouble ensues.

City Center, Oakland

In the final scene of *True Crime* (1999), Clint Eastwood encounters the freed Isaiah Washington as Frank Beachum with his family in front of the 1988 red aluminum sculpture, entitled "There," by Roslyn Mazzilli. Washington gives him a salute of thanks for saving his life, and Eastwood ruefully returns it, as the end credits roll.

Oakland City Center Marriott Hotel
1001 Broadway, Oakland

This centrally located hotel was used in *Bee Season* (2005), based on Myla Goldberg's bestselling novel, with a screenplay by Naomi Foner. In the film, Juliette Binoche begins a downward emotional spiral as her husband, Richard Gere, avoids their collapsing marriage by immersing himself in daughter Flora Cross's quest to become a spelling bee champion. Her brother, Aaron, is played by Max Minghella, son of Academy Award–winning director Anthony Minghella. Shot entirely in the Bay Area in 2004 by directors Scott McGhee and David Siegel, other locations include: Police Department at 455 7th Street, Our Lady of Lourdes Catholic Church at 2800 Lakeshore Drive, and Altenheim Senior Living at 1720 MacArthur Boulevard.

City Hall
Frank Ogawa Plaza at Broadway and 14th Street

Constructed in 1914 in the beaux arts style with granite veneer and terra cotta ornamentation, City Hall is currently registered as a National Historic Landmark. It is 18 stories tall, consisting of a 3-story podium, a 10-story office tower, and a 91-foot high ornamental clock tower.

The building suffered significant damage in the October 1989 Loma Prieta earthquake, forcing the city to move all operations and necessitating a major restoration and seismic upgrade. Francis Ford Cop-

pola used exterior and interiors of Oakland's City Hall for the offices of the corrupt senator Homer Ferguson in *Tucker: The Man and His Dream*. An uncredited Lloyd Bridges, father of Jeff Bridges, who plays Preston Tucker, was cast in the role of Ferguson in the 1988 film.

Haiku Tunnel, the 2001 film version of San Francisco–based Josh Kornbluth's hit one-man comedy show, depicts a neurotic male secretary who is a terrific office "temp" but a horrible "perm." When his new boss at the law firm of Schuyler & Mitchell (aka "S & M"), a tax attorney who just may be Satan, gives him 17 "very important letters" to mail out, he doesn't, and the ensuing complications bring him face-to-face with a lifetime of personal demons. These law offices, reportedly a stand-in for Pillsbury, Madison, & Sutro, where Kornbluth worked as a legal secretary, were set in downtown San Francisco, but many of the scenes were actually shot in Oakland.

Scenes were shot at City Hall in 2003 under the working title *Heart of the Possible*, a story of personal dilemmas and political conflicts unfolding against the backdrop of a modern Democratic National Convention, but the film was released as *Convention* (2003). Frank Ogawa Plaza also appears in *Happily Even After* (2003) in which a troubled young man's older sister hires a mysterious young woman to help him.

City Hall is glimpsed in *Poetic Justice* (1993) starring Janet Jackson. Other Oakland locations used include 1720 Filbert Street at 18th Street, the Lakeside Motel (122 East 12th Street), Lakeside Drive, and 14th Street. Saeed Dobahi Market (1000 18th Street) and the area around 18th and Market Streets also appear in the film about a young girl named Justice who, after witnessing the murder of her boyfriend, decides to forget about college and become a South Central Los Angeles hairdresser. Composing poetry is the only way for Justice to cope with her depression. (Justice's poetry was written by longtime San Franciscan Maya Angelou, who makes a cameo appearance as Aunt June.) On her way to a convention in Oakland, Justice is forced to ride with Lucky (Tupac Shakur), a postal worker whom she has not gotten along with in the past. After various arguments, they gradually discover that they have more in common than they thought, and begin to fall in love.

Hotel Oakland
270 13th Street between Harrison and Alice Streets, Oakland

Tucker: The Man and His Dream (1988) recounts the true story of Preston Tucker, the maverick car designer, and his ill-fated challenge to the auto industry with his revolutionary car concept. This building is where the interiors of the dramatic courtroom scene were shot.

Constructed between 1910 and 1912 for over $3 million, the block-square Hotel Oakland became a prominent social center during the next decade. Presidents Wilson, Coolidge, and Hoover were guests, as were other celebrities, including Amelia Earhart, Sarah Bernhardt, Jean Harlow, and Mary Pickford. The exterior of the building and all two-story spaces on the main floor are on the National Register of Historic Places. It is now used as a home for the elderly.

Broadway Auto Row
14th Street and Madison, Oakland

The site of Ted Danson's car dealership, where he is shooting a commercial with a bear when Nia Long confronts him with the fact of his paternity, and where later, he is making another commercial atop an elephant when Whoopi Goldberg wreaks havoc with the filming, in *Made in America* (1993).

Alameda County Courthouse
1225 Fallon Street at 13th Street, Oakland

True Crime, directed by and starring Clint Eastwood, was shot locally in 1999. Eastwood plays a womanizer, a (barely) recovering alcoholic, who can scarcely accomplish the assignments he is given as a journalist for the *Oakland Tribune*. He's assigned to write a routine story about the last hours of a man on death row, Isaiah Washington, convicted of the shooting death of a pregnant clerk in a convenience store. Both the city editor and the editor-in-chief James Woods know Eastwood is a hotshot with a habit of turning routine stories into federal cases, and they warn him against trying to save Washington at the 11th hour. But Eastwood becomes convinced the wrong man is going to be executed. "When my nose tells me something stinks—I gotta have faith in it," he tells Washington. At this location, Frances Fisher, Eastwood's former partner, appears as lawyer Cecilia Nussaum, on the steps of the Alameda County Courthouse.

Lake Merritt, Oakland

Lake Merritt was an arm of the San Francisco Bay until Oakland mayor Dr. Samuel Merritt donated money in 1869 to begin building a dam at the 12th Street Bridge, across the "neck" of the inlet, in order to make a lake for Oakland. It was called "Merritt's Lake" for many years, until gradually becoming known as Lake Merritt.

Nia Long and Will Smith ride his motorbike around Lake Merritt in one scene of *Made in America* (1993). Then a runaway elephant carrying Ted Danson throughout Oakland and following, it turns out, the bell on Whoopi Goldberg's bicycle, dumps him in the drink.

In *What Dreams May Come* (1998), the last scene, where the two (toy) boats collide on the lake and the owners smile at each other, was shot here on July 1, 1998. When the little girl giggles and offers the little boy a sandwich, the scene echoes how Robin Williams and Annabella Sciorra first met.

Bee Season (2005) used the parking area near the Lake Merritt Boathouse. Filmed entirely in Oakland, other *Bee Season* locations include: Children's Hospital and Research Center, 5700 Martin Luther King Way; Henry J. Kaiser Auditorium, 10 10th Street; and KwikWay Drive-In, 500 Lakepark Avenue.

Morcom Amphitheater of Roses
Jean Street at Grand Avenue near Lake Merritt, Oakland

Bikini Planet is a 2002 sci-fi comedy adventure spoof of B-movies from the 1950s and '60s like *Queen of Outer Space* (1958), starring Zsa

Zsa Gabor, in which astronauts must save the earth from the invasion led by Princess Nibbi. Directed by Derek Zemrak, with a script by Brian Zemrak, the low-budget film features locations scouted by Scott Trimble including Hayward, Livermore, and Pleasanton. Eight acres of plush forested Victorian gardens secluded in the midst of a hilly residential neighborhood were the site of the alien planet scenes shot here in March 2001.

Martin Luther King Way (formerly Grove Street)
At 5th Street, Oakland

In the two *Matrix* sequels, underneath the intersection of Highways 880 (Nimitz Freeway) and 980 in downtown Oakland. At the northeast corner of 5th Street and Martin Luther King Way, Trinity's car crashed through the fence. The Chinese truck that appears in *The Matrix Reloaded* (2003) previously appeared in another Keanu Reeves movie, *Sweet November* (2001), as a Korean BBQ truck. Trinity and Morpheus drove east underneath the Nimitz Freeway. The location managers worked extensively with various agencies in the city of Oakland to temporarily move out hundreds of Oakland Police Department vehicles that normally park under here.

Jack London Square, Oakland

Jack London was born in San Francisco on January 12, 1876, and 10 years later the family settled near the waterfront. At a very young age London helped support his family by delivering newspapers, sweeping saloon floors, setting up pins in a bowling alley, and working at other odd jobs. At age 15 he bought his first boat, the *Dazzler,* which he used to rob oyster beds along the San Francisco Bay for nearly a year. He borrowed the entrance fee for college from the proprietor of Heinold's First & Last Chance Saloon, still operating today at Jack London Square, its floor still slanted because of damage after the 1906 earthquake. London entered the University of California at Berkeley at age 20, quitting after one semester. After unsuccessfully attempting to support himself by writing, he eventually settled on work in a steam laundry to make ends meet.

In 1897 he joined the Yukon Gold Rush to the Klondike. His first book, *The Son of the Wolf,* a collection of his Klondike tales, was published by Houghton Mifflin Company in 1900. That same year he married Elizabeth (Bess) Maddern and they settled in Oakland. In 1901 and again in 1905, London ran unsuccessfully for mayor of Oakland as a Socialist candidate. In 1906 he bought a ranch near Glen Ellen in the Sonoma Valley, where he resided until his death on November 22, 1916, from an acute attack of uremia, a kidney disease. His cabin was moved to Jack London Square in 1970, and stands near the water today.

Jack London Square is a collection of shops, restaurants, hotels, theaters, and historic buildings, including the Overland House restaurant, built in 1887 at the terminus of the transcontinental railroad. The waterfront is where Captain Thomas Gray, grandfather of the famous dancer Isadora Duncan, began the first ferry service to San Francisco in 1850.

The shots of *Mrs. Doubtfire* (Robin Williams) in the 1993 film appearing on television were actually filmed at KTVU Television Studios, at the south end of Jack London Square.

Port of Oakland
530 Water Street, Oakland

The Port of Oakland was the first major port on the Pacific Coast of the United States to build terminals for container ships. In 1852 large shipping wharves were constructed along the Oakland Estuary, which was dredged to create a viable shipping channel. The shipping channel was deepened 22 years later to make Oakland a deep water port. In 1962, the Port of Oakland began to admit container ships, greatly increasing the amount of cargo loaded and unloaded. By the late 1960s, the Port of Oakland was the second largest port in the world in container tonnage. Depth and navigation restrictions in San Francisco Bay limited its capacity, however, and by the late 1970s it had been supplanted by the Ports of Los Angeles and Long Beach as the major container port on the West Coast. In the opening scene of *Bee Season* (2005), a helicopter carries the letter A and places it into the Oakland sign.

Posey-Webster Tube
Between Oakland and Alameda

The Webster Tube is an underwater tunnel that goes below the Oakland Inner Harbor channel that separates Oakland from the island of Alameda. The Posey Tube is the neighboring tunnel that takes traffic back north from Webster Street in Alameda to Harrison Street in Oakland.

In George Lucas's *THX 1138* (1971) the final chase scenes of escaping Robert Duvall were filmed in "every tunnel in the area," including this one. Because shooting was done at night, neighbors often called the cops to complain, and a couple of times shooting was shut down. The Posey-Webster Tube also appears in both *Matrix II* (2003) and *Matrix III* (2004).

Alameda

The 1968 comedy *Yours, Mine and Ours* stars Henry Fonda and Lucille Ball, who live in officers' quarters, and features additional scenes shot at the base commissary. In April 1995 a car chase scene involving Sandra Bullock's character in *The Net* (1996) was shot at Glascock Avenue and the Park Street Bridge, which connects Oakland to Alameda.

Carl Franklin shot much of his 2002 film *High Crimes* in the Bay Area. The thriller stars Ashley Judd as a high-powered lawyer who finds her world turned upside down when her husband, James Caviezel, is arrested and tried for murdering Latin American villagers while he was in the Marines. Judd realizes that to navigate the military justice system, she'll need help from the somewhat unconventional lawyer Morgan Freeman. The fictional San Lazaro Marine Corps Base was mostly filmed at the former Alameda Naval Air Station. During four days of filming there, the base was brought back to life with tanks, jeeps, signage, hundreds of military extras, and extensive repair and painting. Now known as Alameda Point, businesses such as Manex Studios and ESC Entertainment, as well as many other nonfilm businesses, have been located here. The exterior of the Brig was filmed at Building 16 (the former hospital) at the corner of West Essex and Saratoga Streets at Alameda Point, while the interior was built at Sunset Gower Independent Studios in Hollywood. The second floor of Administration Building 1 at 950 West Mall Square was the site of the military courtroom hallway while the courtroom itself is a set built at Sunset Gower Independent Studios.

This is also the site of the major freeway sequence in *The Matrix Reloaded*. This 2003 sequel to *The Matrix* (1999) claims to have earned over $735 million worldwide, making it the most commercially success-ful R-rated movie in history. Directed by Andy and Larry Wachowski, the science fiction action thriller was shot back to back with the third installment of the trilogy, *The Matrix Revolutions* (2004). Although most of the film was shot in Australia, a freeway in Akron, Ohio, was report-edly the first choice for the location to shoot the 14-minute chase scene involving cars, motorcycles, and trailer trucks. When it was determined it would take one hour to back up all cars necessary to prepare for the start of a take, a 1.4-mile, three-lane loop highway was built specifically for the scene on the decommissioned Alameda Point Navy Base. It was destroyed when filming was completed. General Motors donated 300 cars for use in the production of the movie, all of which were wrecked by the end of filming. The sequence took almost three months to shoot, longer than many films' entire shooting schedule.

According to Oakland city officials who worked with the filmmak-ers on the downtown Oakland shots, colors on the set were tightly con-trolled for a futuristic look: sidewalk curbs were painted over to remove all red and blue colors, and there could be no greenery or other plant life, so filming was done over the winter before tree leaves sprouted in the spring. Among the Oakland locations used were 16th Street, 5th Street, the Nimitz Freeway, and the Webster Tube to Alameda. On the freeway chase, a signboard marks the exit to a place called Paterson Pass. This reference to the production designer, Owen Paterson, was one of many inside jokes using crew members' names.

The meeting between the Oracle (Gloria Foster) and the ensuing fight with Agent Smith (Hugo Weaving) were shot on a soundstage con-structed from an old aircraft hangar at the former Alameda Naval Air Station at Alameda Point, as were the Zion rave scenes.

Oakland Zoo
9777 Golf Links Road off Highway 580, Oakland

In *True Crime* (1999), director and star Clint Eastwood takes his real-life daughter Francesca Ruth Fisher-Eastwood to the zoo. As he's pushing her around on the way to see the hippopotamus he goes too fast, and she takes a spill. Diane Venora, the wife from whom he's estranged, has a fit when she sees the girl's bandaged face.

Dunsmuir House

2960 Peralta Oaks Drive, Oakland

Alexander Dunsmuir, son of wealthy Canadian coal baron Robert Dunsmuir, came to the Bay Area in 1878. He purchased the 50-acre estate in the rolling East Bay foothills, and built the elegant mansion as a wedding gift for his beloved Josephine in December 1899. The 37-room house, designed by San Francisco architect J. Eugene Freeman, is an example of Neoclassical Revival architecture and features a Tiffany-style dome, wood-paneled public rooms, 10 fireplaces, and inlaid parquet floors within its 16,224 square feet. Servants' quarters in the house are designed to accommodate 12 live-in staff. Tragically, Alexander became ill and died while in New York on his honeymoon; Josephine returned alone to her new home where she resided until her death in 1901. Between 1906 and the late 1950s the property was owned by the Hellman family.

Courtesy Dennis DeSilva/Studio Seven

The City of Oakland purchased the estate in the early 1960s with the intent of using the grounds and mansion as a conference center, which did not prove feasible, and it is now overseen by a nonprofit group to be used as an educational, historical, cultural, and horticultural resource. The Dunsmuir House mansion has been designated a National Historic Site, and both the mansion and the carriage house have been designated Historic Landmarks by the City of Oakland.

In 1976's *Burnt Offerings*, Oliver Reed and Karen Black, their son, and Aunt Bette Davis rent the mansion for a summer vacation from Burgess Meredith and Eileen Heckart. The family soon discovers that all is not as it should be: dead plants come back to life and the swimming pool kills bathers, while the house seems to get younger with each death.

In *Phantasm* (1979), Michael Baldwin is a 13-year-old boy living in a small northern California town. His parents have recently died, leaving him to live with his older brother Bill Thornbury. While watching a funeral in Morningside Cemetery from a distance, Mike sees some peculiar goings-on, motivating him to investigate the cemetery and its menacing mortician, Angus Scrimm. Dunsmuir House was used as the exterior of the mausoleum. The impressive stone-looking interior of the mausoleum was actually constructed of plywood and marble-colored plastic contact paper. Most of the rest of the film was shot in Southern California.

In *A View to a Kill* (1985), Tanya Roberts lives here while trying to recover control of her father's Sutton Industries. In this James Bond film, Roger Moore fights off the villains bent on harming the beautiful lady of the house.

At the end of *So I Married an Axe Murderer* (1993), San Francisco poet Mike Myers and his new bride, Nancy Travis, come to the Dunsmuir house on their honeymoon. Interiors and exteriors were used for filming the finale, including the rooftops where Myers fights with his wife's sister, Amanda Plummer, but an extra tower and mountain ranges were added using special effects.

In *True Crime* (1999), the mansion is the home of Governor Henry Lowenstein (Anthony Zerbe), to which Clint Eastwood races against the clock to have Hattie Winston, the grandmother of the real murderer, tell him the truth, so he can stop the impending execution of the man about to be lethally injected in San Quentin. Although a chase by police ensues through the Oakland area, note that one of the police cars chasing Eastwood has "LAPD" stenciled on the trunk over the left taillight.

Niles

One April afternoon in 1912, a troupe of thespians invaded this small agricultural community midway between Oakland and San Jose along the southern shores of the San Francisco Bay. The area had been previously scouted by film director and producer Gilbert M. Anderson. George Spoor, the "S" to Anderson's "A" in the Chicago-based Essanay Film Manufacturing Company, also hoped that the mild weather, sunshine, and scenery of Niles Canyon would provide the right backdrop for films. By June 1913 a new and fully equipped Essanay studio was ready for operation, eventually producing over 300 westerns, many of them starring Anderson as Bronco Billy. Wallace Berry, Chester Conklin, and Ben Turpin also appeared in many of the prolific company's films. Charlie

Niles was the site of many early silent films, including Charlie Chaplin's *The Tramp* (1915). *Courtesy of Pacific Film Archive, University of California, Berkeley*

Chaplin made some of his classic films here, including his masterpiece, *The Tramp,* which brought in a staggering $1 million dollars for the studio in 1915. But Essanay faced competition from independent upstart producers and studios such as Metro, Universal, and Paramount, and on February 16, 1916, the Niles Essanay studio closed down permanently.

Next to nothing remains of the heyday of filmmaking in Niles, which was later incorporated into the city of Fremont. The small town, cherishing its brief but brilliant past in the history of movie making, recently opened the Niles Essanay Silent Film Museum (you can visit them at http://nilesfilmmuseum.org) and proudly hosts the annual Bronco Billy Silent Film Festival.

Bridges Restaurant
44 Church Street, Danville

Mrs. Doubtfire (1993) is Chris Columbus's extremely popular comedy based on the novel *Alias Madame Doubtfire* by Anne Fine. The film's use of locations and its Oscar-winning make-up job transforming Robin Williams into a dowdy British housekeeper helped to reestablish San Francisco as a major movie set in the 1990s. In the famous scene at the fancy restaurant Robin Williams continually interrupts Pierce Brosnan trying to dine with Sally Field, dashing back and forth as Mrs. Doubtfire and Mr. Hillard.

Antioch Speedway
Contra Costa County Fairgrounds

Steelyard Blues, the 1973 comedy about a band of misfits who become involved in rejuvenating abandoned airplanes, starred Jane Fonda, Donald Sutherland, and Peter Boyle. Filmed entirely in the Bay Area, this was one of the first location shoots in Contra Costa County. The stars sat among the crowds watching the demolition derby at the County Fair's dirt track. Donald Sutherland lost his wedding ring here during filming.

Caldecott Tunnel
Between Oakland and Orinda

In George Lucas's *THX 1138* (1971), the final chase scenes of escaping Robert Duvall were filmed in "every tunnel in the area," including this one. Because shooting was done at night, neighbors often called the cops to complain, and a couple of times shooting was shut down.

Cowriter Walter Murch has said in interviews that George Lucas never explained the origins of the character names THX and LUH to him, but he believes that they are deliberate homonyms for sex and love—the two factors that set them apart from society. Filming began September 23, 1969, and ended seven weeks later, on November 12. Postproduction was done in the tiny attic of Lucas's Mill Valley house where Lucas cut the images by day, Walter Murch the sound by night, and they met over meals in between.

San Mateo, Santa Cruz, and Monterey Counties

In *Heaven Can Wait* (1978), Warren Beatty and Julie Christie fall in love at the Filoli Estate in Woodside. *Courtesy of Pacific Film Archive, University of California, Berkeley*

South of San Francisco through the counties of San Mateo, Santa Cruz, and particularly Monterey are a wealth of unexpected movie locations. This driving tour heads down the peninsula from San Francisco, crossing over to the coastal route, Highway 1, and ending up 100 miles south. It can be accomplished as a (very long) day trip or can be appreciated on the way to southern California, center of the motion picture industry.

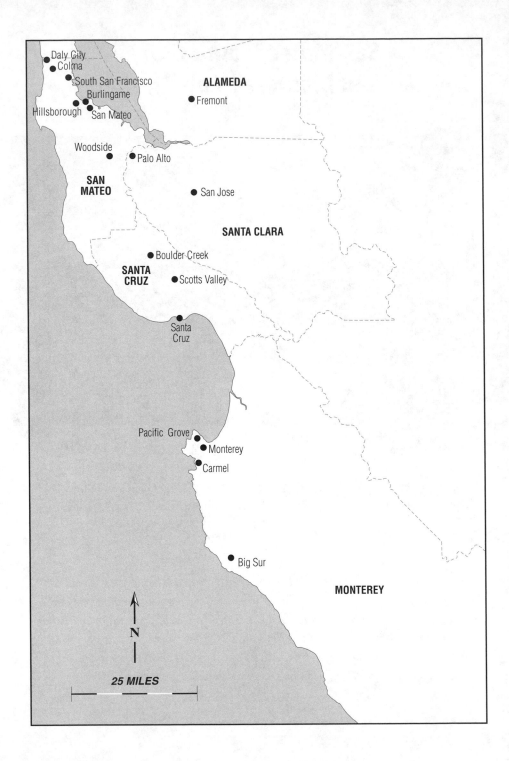

Daly City
Colma
South San Francisco
Burlingame
Hillsborough   San Mateo

ALAMEDA
Fremont

Woodside
Palo Alto

SAN
MATEO

San Jose

SANTA CLARA

Boulder Creek

SANTA
CRUZ
Scotts Valley

Santa
Cruz

Pacific Grove
Monterey
Carmel

Big Sur

MONTEREY

N

25 MILES

San Mateo County

Holy Cross Cemetery
1500 Mission Road, Colma

Colma is known as the City of the Dead, because of 16 cemeteries that dot its hillsides. It is quipped that Colma has more dead inhabitants than live ones. Holy Cross is the cemetery where Bud Cort and Ruth Gordon as *Harold and Maude* first encounter one another in Hal Ashby's 1971 offbeat comedy. The script by Colin Higgins follows a suicidal young man and a free-spirited older woman who find each other through their mutual interest in strangers' funerals and fall in love. Nearby at Oyster Point Boulevard and Eccles Avenue in South San Francisco is the site where Gordon lives in a charmingly eccentric antique railroad car, where she eventually seduces Cort. Or vice versa.

San Francisco International Airport
South San Francisco

Since it opened in spring 1927, San Francisco International Airport (SFO) has grown from a small administration building on 150 acres of unpaved cow pasture to 4.4 million square feet on 2,383 acres of developed land. It is located approximately 13 miles south of San Francisco, on Highway 101.

During the opening credits of *Guess Who's Coming to Dinner?* (1967) the song "The Glory of Love" is heard while Sidney Poitier and Katharine Houghton exit United gate 24, get their baggage, and hop into a taxi. In the classic Stanley Kramer film, her parents, played by Spencer Tracy and Katharine Hepburn, are less broad-minded about the "problem" of her doctor boyfriend being "Negro" than anticipated. Later in the film, Poitier's parents arrive at the airport and are equally surprised to learn their son's girlfriend is white.

The 1968 film *Bullitt* follows San Francisco police detective Frank Bullitt, assigned to guard an important witness in an upcoming trial. When the man is killed by assassins, Bullitt conceals the death and goes after the killers himself. The scenes in which Steve McQueen as Bullitt chases down the mysterious suspect on SFO runway #5 were shot by director Peter Yates in the middle of the night.

San Francisco Airport, 1968. *Courtesy San Francisco History Center, San Francisco Public Library*

In *Play It Again, Sam* (1972) Woody Allen plays a neurotic film buff who seeks female companionship after being abandoned by his wife. He is aided and abetted by his best friends, a married couple played by Diane Keaton and Tony Roberts, as well as the ghost of Humphrey Bogart. It was a very windy night at SFO, according to director Herbert Ross, as they restaged the final scene of *Casablanca* (1942) with Allen, Keaton, and Roberts in the Humphrey Bogart, Ingrid Bergman, and Paul Henreid roles.

Three years after lovable pets Chance, Sassy, and Shadow's trek through the woods and over the mountains in *Homeward Bound: The Incredible Journey* (1993), the Seaver family, who live in Marin, are about to leave for a vacation in Canada. At the beginning of *Homeward Bound II: Lost in San Francisco* (1996), when the animals are herded into the pet carriers at the check-in counter, they freak out and escape onto the runway before being placed in the plane. Now their family is in Canada while the pets are all alone in San Francisco.

Burlingame High School
1 Mangini Way, Burlingame

LouAnne Johnnson's nonfiction book *My Posse Don't Do Homework, Teacher* recounts her experience as an ex-marine accepting a full-time job at an East Palo Alto high school without realizing that the students in her class are highly intelligent, but have social problems. She either must give up or learn how to get the students' attention and help them learn. Michelle Pfeiffer portrays Johnson in John N. Smith's 1995 film version, *Dangerous Minds*, costarring George Dzundza, Courtney B. Vance, Robin Bartlett, and Beatrice Winde. The exterior of Burlingame High School was used for Parkmont High School.

Rose Court Mansion (formerly the George T. Cameron Estate)
815 Eucalyptus at Reddington, Hillsborough

Built in 1913 by Lewis Parsons Hobart, who was famous as the architect of Grace Episcopal Church and various country estates in Hillsborough. Hal Ashby shot his dark comedy *Harold and Maude* throughout the Bay Area in 1971, including this property about 10 miles south of Colma. Bud Cort lives here with his hilariously domineering mother Vivian Pickles, who arranges a series of girls for Cort to date. The scenes of Cort's various stagings of faux suicides were set in this mansion, including the music room and the library. Henry Dieckoff, who appears in the film as the butler, was the actual butler of the house. The original script reportedly called for *him* to drop the lemonade tray after "Sunshine" does her Juliet imitation, but Dieckoff thought it unbutler-like, so Vivian Pickles did the bit of business.

Filoli
86 Cañada Road, Woodside

Located 30 miles south of San Francisco on the eastern slope of the Coast Range, the 654-acre Filoli estate contains a historic house and 16 acres of formal garden. The Historical Marker here reads: "This

Filoli Mansion. *Courtesy of Barbara Braun*

country estate was begun in 1915 for Mr. and Mrs. William B. Bourn, II. Architect Willis J. Polk designed a modified Georgian style country house; subsequently the carriage house and garden pavilion were executed by Arthur Brown. The formal gardens were created by Bruce Porter. In 1937 the estate was acquired by Mr. and Mrs. William P. Roth."

Mr. Bourn owned the Empire Mine, a hard-rock gold mine in Grass Valley, as well as the Spring Valley Water Company. He arrived at the unusual name Filoli by combining the first two letters from the key words of his credo: "Fight for a just cause; Love your fellow man; Live a good life." The Bourns moved into the house in 1917, living there until they both died in 1936. Mrs. William P. Roth made this her home until 1975 when she donated 125 acres, including the house and formal garden, to the National Trust for Historic Preservation.

Heaven Can Wait, the 1978 remake of *Here Comes Mr. Jordan* (1941), has football player Warren Beatty prematurely called to heaven and sent back to earth in the body of corporate giant Leo Farnsworth. Dyan Cannon, as the murderous Mrs. Farnsworth, heads the cast, joined by Julie Christie, James Mason, and Jack Warden. Changing the original boxer to a football player, Beatty codirected with Buck Henry a script by Harry Segall, Elaine May, and an uncredited Robert Towne. Filoli's ballroom served as Beatty's workout room, and other memorable location scenes include a game of hide-and-seek on the grand staircase, as well as in the expansive gardens.

Brief shots of Filoli's red brick Georgian Revival house established the fictional Blake Carrington's home in ABC television's evening soap opera *Dynasty*, which ran from 1981 to 1989. The famous fight between Joan Collins as Alexis and Lynda Evans as Crystal ended in the lily pond here.

Filoli was used for three separate sequences in *The Joy Luck Club*, Wayne Wang's 1993 adaptation of Amy Tan's bestselling novel. San Franciscan Tan also wrote the screenplay and appears briefly at the beginning of the opening party scene. Eight interwoven stories tell the saga of four women, who form the Joy Luck Club. Each was born in China and survived tremendous hardships before eventually coming to America. The book and film are also about their assimilated American daughters. The death of one of the mothers ignites the retelling of their stories over mah-jongg, providing new understanding for the sometimes strained mother-daughter relationships. The largely Asian cast includes Kieu Chinh, Tsai Chin, France Nuyen, Lisa Lu, Ming-Na Wen, Tamlyn Tomita, Lauren Tom, and Rosalind Chao. Filoli was used to re-create three separate locations: a 1920s Shanghai ballroom; the Jordan family mansion (where Mrs. Jordan awkwardly tries to dissuade Rose from marrying her son Ted); and the scenes where the second wife offers An-Mei a pearl necklace, and later steals and kills the fourth wife's newborn son.

Interiors and exteriors of Filoli were used for the Stanhope Mansion where Leslie Mann's parents live in Sam Weisman's live-action film based on Jay Ward's classic cartoon, *George of the Jungle* (1997). It appears as if the estate is supposed to be in San Francisco, instead of many miles down the peninsula, when George is seen running down Lombard Street and instantly arriving at Stanhope Mansion. Then–San Francisco mayor

Willie Brown has a cameo with Holland Taylor in a wedding party scene, too. The 2003 sequel used only stock footage of the Golden Gate and Bay Bridges and leftover footage from Filoli. Another fancy wedding, in the 2001 romantic comedy *The Wedding Planner*, was filmed on the grounds, where the mansion's location is identified as "Napa."

Rupert Wainwrith's *Stigmata* (1999) follows Father Andrew Kiernan (Gabriel Byrne), a researcher of miracles on behalf of the Vatican, as he seeks the truth behind hairdresser Frankie Paige (Patricia Arquette), who exhibits the stigmata, the physical wounds Christ received from his crucifixion. His investigation is riddled with questions as he is torn between helping Frankie and revealing the discovery of a long-lost Gospel that would spell disaster for the future of the Catholic Church. Cardinal Houseman (Jonathan Pryce) battles Kiernan in an attempt to silence Frankie's message. Interiors and exteriors were shot here, standing in for the various Italian locations, including the place where the Vatican agents lock up Frankie at the end of the film. The misty morning ending in the garden was accomplished through the use of six big fog machines, and the statue in the background is of St. Francis of Assisi, the first person to bear the marks of the stigmata. The birds are flying into Patricia Arquette's palms because she is feeding them.

In David Fincher's 1997 thriller *The Game*, Michael Douglas's home, supposedly 2210 Broadway in San Francisco, is actually Filoli. In the contemporary scenes, the plain gravel forecourt of the mansion was made to look more like a wraparound driveway by the addition of the fountain, which was constructed of plastic foam. The flashback home movies show more of the pool and gardens. The interior shots of the kitchen were made in the original timeworn kitchen, which partially accounts for the very dim lighting used. The scenes in which the walls were defaced with graffiti were done by tacking up lightweight graffiti-painted foam core boards over the wood paneling. All of the scenes at the mansion were completed in one day.

Green Gables
329 Albion Avenue, Woodside

In Chris Columbus's *Bicentennial Man* (1999), Robin Williams plays Andrew, an android purchased by the Martins as a household robot, programmed to perform menial tasks. The family quickly realizes that he is no ordinary droid as Andrew begins to experience emotions and creative thoughts. The family home of Sam Neil and Wendy Crewsom, the parents of Hallie Kate and Lindze Letherman, is Green Gables, the Woodside estate of the Mortimer Fleishhacker family. With its 70-year-old house and formal gardens, it is the largest and most ambitious project of noted California architect Charles Greene. Down a stately flagstone staircase stands a Roman pool reminiscent of Hadrian's Villa near Rome. This Greene & Greene mansion is on the National Register of Historic Places.

Palo Alto Stock Farm Horse Barn
Fremont Street, Palo Alto

Eadweard Muybridge was born Edward Muggeridge near London in 1830. After working as a bookseller in New York and San Francisco he reinvented himself as a photographer specializing in Western landscapes. He was sought out by railroad magnate, former governor, and horseman Leland Stanford, who wanted to resolve the question of whether all four legs of a horse come off the ground at any point in a trot or gallop. Legend has it that this was to win a wager, but no evidence confirms this, and it eventually took five years and $50,000 to achieve the experiment. On June 15, 1878, one of Stanford's prize trotters pulling a two-wheeled cart sped down the track triggering 12 wires, each connected to a different camera. As the cartwheel rolled over each wire, it tripped the shutter of the attached camera, and all 12 exposures were made in less than half a second. Muybridge quickly developed the plates and the evidence was in: the horse did have all four feet off the ground in one frame.

Muybridge was hailed as a photographic wizard, and Stanford as his visionary patron. Within a year Muybridge had produced the first sequential photos of rapid motion, and also the first machine to project moving photographic images. Muybridge's new machine, the zoopraxiscope, was an adaption of the popular children's toy, the zoetrope, and used a large glass disk with the figures running around the edge. Although technically the zoopraxiscope didn't project Muybridge's photos, film historians consider it the forerunner to the movie projector. After a public showing of his invention in San Francisco in spring 1890, Muybridge embarked on a lecture tour of Europe. A serious rift with Stanford ensued, followed by the development of motion pictures in the early 1890s, eclipsing his reputation. Muybridge died in England in 1904.

Big Basin Redwoods State Park
21600 Big Basin Way, Boulder Creek

California's oldest state park, about 65 miles south of San Francisco, was established in 1902, consists of more than 18,000 acres, and is home to the largest continuous stand of Ancient Coast Redwoods south of San Francisco. This is the sylvan location, usually presumed to be Muir Woods in Marin County, where Kim Novak as Madeleine uses the redwood trunk to tell Jimmy Stewart as Scottie about her death, in Hitchcock's *Vertigo* (1958). It was the only time Scotts Valley resident Hitchcock ever filmed in this area. Big Basin was also the set for several Walt Disney productions, including a 1960 nature short and portions of the 1965 fantasy feature *The Gnomemobile* with Walter Brennan.

Bill Condon returned to the same spot 45 years after Hitchcock made *Vertigo* to film the final scene of *Kinsey* (2004), in which Alfred Kinsey (Liam Neeson) and his wife (Laura Linney) stop to seek solace in the redwoods on their way from an unsuccessful fundraising attempt in San Francisco. The exact location is not specified in the film, but it is assumed to be Muir Woods. When the location in Big Basin was scouted it was on a perfectly beautiful, clean sunny day, but on the day of filming the sky was dark and drizzling. Small lights were used instead of the previously planned large ones, and the filmmakers were pleased with the atmospheric results.

Cornwall Ranch
At the end of Canham Road, off Glenwood Drive, Scotts Valley

In September 1940, Alfred and Alma Hitchock bought a 200-acre tract of land known as "Heart of the Mountains" 67 miles south of San Francisco, between Santa Cruz and Los Gatos. The ranch included a main house, a tennis court, and a farmhouse with animals. There was a vineyard (they sold the Riesling grapes to Cresta Blanca Winery) and five acres of gardens landscaped by Roy Rydell. The Hitchcocks considered the estate a family haven and hosted famous Hollywood guests for gourmet meals, until they moved out in 1970. The property was sold a few years later.

Santa Cruz County

Santa Cruz has had a colorful history as a film location, boasting an estimated 75 silent films, or parts of them, and about 25 talkies. The Southern Pacific railroad shot the earliest films in 1915 to help drum up tourism. In 1916 when the infant film industry was beginning to migrate west from its East Coast birthplace, a movie studio was built in De Laveaga Park. Complete with stages, dressing rooms, and equipment, it was to be rented to visiting production companies, but the operation folded within a year. By then producers of the popular nickelodeon two-reelers had discovered, in places like Felton and Boulder Creek, the kind of lush forest locations they couldn't duplicate in Southern California. Between 1916 and 1920, the area was used in countless bucolic romances and westerns, among them a Cecil B. DeMille adventure called *A Romance of the Redwoods* (1917) starring Mary Pickford.

During filming of popular cowboy star William S. Hart's 1920 western *Testing Block* around Big Trees and in Capitola, the crew developed a special light allowing them to shoot at night when the days were too foggy. In 1923 while filming *The Eyes of the Forest* in Felton, Tom Mix and his famous horse, Tony, were slightly injured on a ridge pass by a special effects "explosion" set off too soon. Mix reportedly remained up on the pass for two hours until he managed to coax the frightened Tony back down. Around 1927 or '28, Wharton Film Classics, Inc. advertised temporary offices at 12½ Pacific Avenue in Santa Cruz.

Many of the films shot in the area in the 1920s were "programmers," quickly and cheaply made adventures, romances, or melodramas that would become the second half of a double-feature package. High-spirited Madge Bellamy, costumed in Tarzan-like animal skins, costarred with an elephant named Anna Mae in *Soul of the Beast*, a 1922 potboiler filmed in Boulder Creek.

Native daughter Zasu Pitts returned to Santa Cruz in 1925 to shoot part of *Thunder Mountain*, her only local film. Pitts, born in Kansas, moved to Santa Cruz as a child where she grew up in the family home at 208 Lincoln Street. Her unusual name was the result of her mother's desire to please both her sisters, Eliza and Susan; by taking one syllable from each name, she came up with the distinctive compromise of "Zasu." Pitts's talent for acting was recognized and encouraged from the time she was performing in school plays at Santa Cruz High. In 1914 she staged a benefit performance at the local Opera House to finance her trip to Hollywood, and set off to join hundreds of other young hopefuls, with promoter Fred Swanton as her agent. After her first film credit in 1916, she was "discovered" in 1917 by Mary Pickford. Director Erich von Stroheim recognized Pitts's potential for more serious roles, and in 1923 he cast her in the lead female role as the miserly Tina in his legendary epic, *Greed*. This was undoubtedly the high point of Pitts's career, who afterward was permanently typecast as a comedienne.

In 1925, ingenue Janet Gaynor arrived in Soquel to make *The Johnstown Flood*, which employed many locals as extras. Scenes for *Roadhouse*, featuring Lionel Barrymore, were shot in downtown Santa Cruz in 1928, the same year footage for Michael Curtiz's ambitious part-sound film *Noah's Ark* was shot in Big Basin. Big Basin also appeared as "the forest primeval" in the 1929 version of *Evangeline*.

In 1930, a talkie remake of the silent classic *Tol'able David* was shot in Felton, the only major feature filmed entirely in the Santa Cruz area. When Fred MacMurray starred with Claudette Colbert in *Maid of Salem* (1936), the Puritan-era village of Salem was reconstructed along Empire Grade. During the shoot, the crew stayed at the Hotel San Carlos in Monterey.

In 1940, Cary Grant arrived up on Graham Hill Road to film portions of Frank Lloyd's historical extravaganza *The Howards of Virginia*. During one scene, which called for him to sweep his young bride up the steps of their new home, the debonair Grant reportedly tripped over a gopher hole and dropped costar Martha Scott in an undignified heap. On the Graham Hill Road set of *The Romance of Rosy Ridge*, an updated bucolic romance made in 1946, Janet Leigh made her film debut opposite Van Johnson.

In 1966, Bruce Brown filmed at Steamer Lane off Lighthouse Point for the surfing documentary *The Endless Summer*. In the made-for-television movie version of *East of Eden* (1981), starring Jane Seymour, Santa Cruz portrayed Steinbeck's Salinas, as Mendocino had done almost 30 years earlier. Several scenes were shot in July 1981 at the Calvary Episcopal Church on Lincoln Street, the Hitchcock house on Ocean View Terrace, and the Capitola pier.

In 1976 the movie *Tilt* with Brooke Shields spent several weeks shooting principal footage in Capitola. Portions of the 1980 science fiction comedy *Heartbeeps,* with Andy Kaufman and Bernadette Peters, were shot in the meadows of the University of California at Santa Cruz, and scenes for the television series *The Gangster Chronicles* (1981) came from the Capitola wharf.

The Santa Cruz boardwalk has been featured in several major motion pictures. In Colin Higgins's 1971 *Harold and Maude,* Bud Cort is a 20-year-old obsessed with death who falls in love with 80-year-old free spirit Ruth Gordon. When Cort gives Gordon a souvenir bought among the arcades on the boardwalk here, she promptly tosses it into the waves. "So I'll always know exactly where it is," she smiles.

In *Sudden Impact* (1983), the fourth of the *Dirty Harry* series, a serial killer is on the loose in San Francisco and the police trace a link to a small town further down the coast. Harry Callahan upsets the press and the mayor and is shipped south to "San Paulo" to investigate. In Santa Cruz, portraying the fictional "San Paulo," Sondra Locke as Jennifer Spencer goes to an amusement park to restore the carousel. Scenes shot at the boardwalk also include the midway and the Giant Dipper.

In 1987 Frankie Avalon and Annette Funicello filmed *Back to the Beach* on the boardwalk. As a result of fatigue from long hours shooting the film, Funicello noticed an increase in the frequency and severity of minor multiple sclerosis symptoms that she had experienced off and on for several years, but requested that her husband tell no one on the set. After filming was completed, she was diagnosed with MS.

The 1976 made-for-television film *The Entertainer,* starring Jack Lemmon, was filmed extensively at the Boardwalk. Michelle Pfeiffer gets in trouble for taking the students here in *Dangerous Minds* (1995). In *The Lost Boys* (1987) Kiefer Sutherland plays a creepy vampire teen here.

Monterey County

The Monterey Peninsula has attracted cinematographers since 1897 when a cameraman working for Thomas Edison filmed the pounding Monterey surf and carriages arriving at the luxurious Hotel Del Monte. Relatively easy to reach by train (or private railroad car) and plane from Los Angeles, Monterey County's scenery has often stood in for far-off or historical locations. It has appeared as part of

In *Basic Instinct* (1992), the shoreline of Carmel stands in for that of Stinson Beach, where Sharon Stone's character Catherine has a home. *Courtesy of Pacific Film Archive, University of California, Berkeley*

Sherwood Forest in *The Adventures of Robin Hood* (1938), the coast of Cornwall in Alfred Hitchcock's *Rebecca* (1940), the island of Elba in *Desiree* (1954), Russia in *Anna Karenina* (1935), coastal Maine in *A Summer Place* (1959), the beaches of Normandy in *Breakthrough* (1950), and a Norwegian fishing village in *Edge of Darkness* (1942). More recently it has doubled as Louisiana swampland in *The Muppet Movie* (1979), Sausalito in *Star Trek IV* (1986), and Stinson Beach in *Basic Instinct* (1992). The area's white sand beaches, crashing waves, and gnarled cypress still attract filmmakers who sometimes use scenic spots to appear undisguised as themselves. (Many of these beautiful locations, used in nearly 200 films, can be viewed from bus tours offered by Monterey Movie tours [www.montereymovie tours.com].)

Possibly the first feature film shot in the area was *Rose of the Rancho* (1914). Filming was done in September 1914, using the city's historic buildings and scenic beauty as a backdrop. For *The Isle of Life* in 1916, Burton George directed scenes at the J. A. Murphy house in Monterey, old Hotel Del Monte and its polo grounds and bridal paths, along a street flanked by old adobes, and at Monterey harbor filled with fishing boats. The following year fishing scenes for *Gladsome* (1917) were filmed at McAbee Beach on Cannery Row. While a few scenes in *Cannery Row* were filmed along the Cannery waterfront in 1982, most of the Cannery Row street scenes were done in a sound studio in Culver City. Part of *Captain January* was shot at Fisherman's Wharf in 1936, and the following year scenes for *Captains Courageous* (1937) were filmed on Monterey Bay involving two schooners, which tied up at Wharf Number 2 in Monterey. Raoul Walsh shot scenes for *They Drive by Night* (1940), starring Ida Lupino, Ann Sheridan, and George Raft, at Wharf No. 2 as well. Fritz Lang directed Barbara Stanwyck, Paul Douglas, Robert Ryan, and Marilyn Monroe in *Clash by Night*. Clifford Odet's play is set in a small fishing town, shot on Monterey's Cannery Row in 1952.

Colton Hall was built in 1849 to serve as a public school and town meeting hall. It appears in *Dust Be My Destiny* (1939), *Four Daughters* (1938), and *California* (1947), starring Barbara Stanwyck and Ray Milland. Monterey stood in for the San Diego waterfront in *I Cover the Waterfront*, where the story is set. James Cruze's film crew was in Monterey for two months in 1933; in one filming sequence Sal Colletto, Beau Brummel of Fisherman's Wharf, was photographed at the wheel of his purse seiner, the *Dante Alighieri*, about a mile off Fisherman's Wharf. In 1958 Ted Balestreri, a freshman at Monterey Peninsula College who became co-owner of the Sardine Factory, had a speaking role in three scenes in *In Love and War* (1958), filmed at Fisherman's Wharf.

Psychopathic Louis Jordan threatens the safety of his wife Doris Day in *Julie* (1956) against scenes shot at Pebble Beach Lodge, Monterey Peninsula Airport, 17-Mile Drive, and Colton Hall. Monty Hellam, a former police judge, had a bit part at Colton Hall when Day went to the Carmel Police Station to report an attempt on her life. While on location, Day repeatedly complained to her husband Martin Melcher, producing his first film, that she felt ill and needed a rest. He insisted that she adhere to her Christian Science beliefs, and the film's shooting schedule, and "have faith" that whatever was ailing her would pass. Once shooting was completed, Day consulted her doctor in Beverly Hills, and discovered a large ovarian tumor, which required her to have a hysterectomy.

For *The Little Giant* (1933), a scene was shot in a polo field at the old Hotel Del Monte and was used for a comical scene in which Robinson and his fellow gangster characters try to play polo. Scenes in *Mutiny on the Bounty* (1935) were filmed in the Monterey Harbor aboard the ships *Pandora* and *Bounty*. *The Parent Trap* (1961) used the baggage counter at the Monterey Peninsula Airport, The Lodge at Pebble Beach, and Carmel Valley.

Scenes in *Shadows* (1922) were filmed at Fisherman's Wharf and in the 500 block of Larkin Street. The Larkin Street shots were night scenes, and people in the neighborhood sat on the bank of a vacant lot across the street and watched for several evenings; huge klieg lights in front windows of nearby homes were set up to illuminate the street. Members of the Monterey Civic Club were extras in a scene filmed at the waterfront, which showed the arrival of a minister.

In *Susan Slade* (1961) scenes were filmed at the old Monterey train station (with some locals reporting the train is heading in the wrong direction), Cypress Point, the airport, and the Pebble Beach Equestrian Center. Del Monte Beach stood in for the Palestinian shore in *Sword in the Desert* (1949). The *Ghost and Mrs. Muir* (1947) used a beach near Stillwater Cove in Pebble Beach. The Pebble Beach Golf Course appears in *National Velvet* (1944) with Elizabeth Taylor and the Cypress Point Golf Course in *Intermezzo* (1939). Fan Shell Beach appeared in *The Caddy* (1953) starring Jerry Lewis and Dean Martin.

Troopers Three (1930) was filmed at the Presidio of Monterey and the old polo grounds, now part of the Monterey Peninsula Airport and Naval Postgraduate School golf course. The horsemanship of the 11th Cavalry, stationed at the Presidio, was featured. Scenes filmed at the old Hotel Del Monte, now the Naval Postgraduate School, include *The Turning Point* (1920), *White Shoulders* (1922), *Sporting Youth* (1924), and *Tin Gods* (1926). Other Monterey movies include: *Samurai* (1944), *Sergeant Murphy* (1938), *Tiger Shark* (1932), *The Big Bounce* (1969), *Braveheart* (1926), *The Candidate* (1972), and *Gentleman's Agreement* (1947).

Monterey Bay Aquarium
886 Cannery Row, Monterey

When Leonard Nimoy directed *Star Trek IV: The Voyage Home* in 1986, he used this aquarium as the location (and logo) of the Cetacean Institute in Sausalito, where the humpback whales are being studied before being released into the bay. Many of the shots of the whales were in fact four-foot-long animatronics models shot in the swimming pool at the College of Marin. Four models were created, and were so realistic that after release of the film, U.S. fishing authorities publicly criticized the filmmakers for getting too close to whales in the wild. The scenes involving these whales were shot in a high school swimming pool. The shot of the whales swimming past the Golden Gate Bridge, filmed on location, nearly ended in disaster when a cable got snagged on a nuclear submarine, and the whales were towed out to sea. In one scene Nimoy and William Shatner ride a San Francisco "MUNI" bus to the "Cetacean Institute" in Sausalito, but MUNI does not operate buses over the Golden Gate Bridge to Marin County. Dustin Hoffman and Sharon Stone visited the Monterey Bay Aquarium's Outer Bay Galleries for the filming of *Sphere* in 1998.

Alfred Hitchcock used various Monterey County locations in his films. In 1940 for his film adaptation of Daphne du Maurier's *Rebecca*, he shot background footage with doubles for Laurence Olivier and Joan Fontaine at Point Lobos State Reserve on Highway 1 just south of Carmel as stand-in locations for both Monte Carlo and the grounds of Manderley, including Weston Beach, where the heroine watercolors at "Monte Carlo." The stairs to the beach at Manderley were at Gibson Beach. An exhibit in the Whaling Cabin describes the history of filming in the park. The following year in *Suspicion* (1941), Hitchcock used a twisty stretch of Highway 101 to stand in for West Essex in the climactic scene where Joan Fontaine almost jumps out of the car driven by a crazed Cary Grant.

At Cypress Point along scenic 17-Mile Drive, waves crash behind Madeleine and Scottie as they kiss on the rocky shore in *Vertigo* (1958). Later, when they arrive in San Juan Bautista, the livery stable on the main plaza, where Scottie and Madeleine, and later Scottie and Judy, say good-bye, was filmed on location in the open air "museum" amid historic artifacts. The nearby church was used to establish the site where they meet their fate. Brief interior views of the church were also used, but the staircase and tower were created in Hollywood.

Pacific Grove

In Roger Spottiswoode's *Turner & Hooch* (1989), Tom Hanks as detective Turner, and Hooch the slobbery dog, who is the sole witness to a murder, set out to solve a murder case. The Pacific Grove bank stands in for a small-town city hall, and a real estate office was transformed into a church for a wedding scene. Other scenes were filmed on the coastline along Ocean View Boulevard, the historic Retreat, and downtown.

When Sandra Dee and her parents come to stay at an inn run by Troy Donohue's parents, sexual sparks fly in *A Summer Place* (1959). Supposedly located in Maine, the inn was actually the private La Porte mansion at the corner of Lighthouse Avenue and 17-Mile Drive. Other East Coast scenes were filmed at Colton Hall, outside All Saint's Episcopal Church in Carmel, at Point Lobos, Pebble Beach, and at the Monterey Peninsula Airport.

Other Pacific Grove locations can be sighted in *Captain January* (1936), *The Eye of the Night* (1916), *Johnny Belinda* (1948), *Married Alive* (1927), *Primrose Path* (1925), and *Junior* (1994).

Carmel-by-the-Sea

Carmel's most famous cinematic figure is its former mayor Clint Eastwood, who set his directorial debut, *Play Misty for Me* (1971), in the area and named his production company Malpaso Productions after a creek just south of town. Scenes in *Play Misty for Me* were filmed at Carmel Highlands, Carmel Beach, the Windjammer Restaurant (later the Sandbar & Grill on Monterey's Municipal Wharf #2), Monterey Fairgrounds, and the Sardine Factory restaurant on Cannery Row.

Hog's Breath Inn
San Carlos between 5th and 6th Avenues, Carmel

The Hog's Breath Inn, one of the oldest dining establishments in Carmel, was once owned by Clint Eastwood, and is now owned by restaurateur Kaiser Morcus. It was reportedly a featured location in *Play Misty for Me*, as well as *The Eiger Sanction* (1975).

Carmel locations are also included in *Basic Instinct* (1992), when Michael Douglas goes to visit Sharon Stone at her house in Stinson Beach. A house at 157 Spindrift, off Highway 1 in Carmel, stood in for "Seadrift 1402." While some establishing shots were actually filmed at the Marin Headlands and Stinson Beach, most of the scenes of the beach house were filmed here and in the surrounding area at Garrapata Beach, south of Carmel, Carmel Highlands, and Carmel Valley Village.

Insane Jessica Walter is ejected from the Windjammer Restaurant in Carmel by Clint Eastwood in a scene from *Play Misty for Me* (1971), his directorial debut. *Courtesy Art, Music and Recreation Center, San Francisco Public Library*

A scene filmed at Bixby Creek on Highway 1 south of Carmel depicts the driver of a large truck crossing the bridge and continuing south until he reaches a turn in the road, where he drives over a cliff high above the ocean. This scene constitutes 10 to 15 seconds of the 1983 feature *Brainstorm*. *Thumb Tripping* (1972) features scenes filmed inside the Mediterranean Market and Harrison Memorial Library, which was turned into a city jail. *The Graduate* (1967) includes scenes filmed in front of the Carmelite Monastery. Other films shot in and around Carmel are:

All Men Are Enemies (1934), *The Beauty Market* (1919), *Blind Date* (1987), *California* (1947), *Chandler* (1972), *Changes* (1969), *Desire Me* (1947), *Eve's Secret* (1925), *Isle of Life* (1916), *Kings Go Forth* (1958), *The Lady Says No* (1952), *A Man of Honor* (1919), *Married Alive* (1927), *Miss Hobbs* (1920), *The Rosary* (1922), *Sandy* (1926), *Seems Like Old Times* (1980), *Shadows* (1922), *The Sunshine Gathers* (1924), *The Valley of the Moon* (1914), and *The Wrong Mr. Right* (1927).

Point Lobos

The first movie to be filmed at Point Lobos was *Valley of the Moon* (1914), directed by Hobart Bosworth and starring Jack Conway and Myrtle Stedman. Thus began a long period of moviemaking in this dramatic coastal promontory.

In 1919 a Monte Carlo–style set was erected at Sea Lion Point, with interior scenes filmed at the James estate in the Carmel Highlands. The silent film by Universal Pictures, *Foolish Wives* (1922), was written and directed by Erich von Stroheim, who also starred in it. In 1926 scenes for *Paid to Love* were filmed at Cypress Point, where a Monte Carlo set was built. Three years later the movie *Evangeline* (1929), directed by Edwin Carewe of United Artists, and starring Roland Drew and Dolores del Rio, hired many Carmel residents as extras. During one scene the village set was burned down, as well as surrounding trees and brush. For years after, many in the local community were opposed to film companies using Point Lobos. The perpetual debate on how or whether to preserve the landscape against filmmakers was referred to as the "movie battle."

MGM studios wanted to put up a few buildings at the Point Lobos State Reserve for scenes in *Desire Me* (1947), directed by George Cukor, but withdrew the idea when the Point Lobos League, fearful of a repeat of the earlier filming episode at Point Lobos that damaged the fragile environment, tried to stop the filming altogether.

In February 1946 a compromise was reached when MGM was allowed to film Greer Garson walking through the cypress trees and along the rocks near the ocean, and filming in the area continued.

Point Lobos is reputed to be the inspiration for Robert Louis Stevenson's classic novel *Treasure Island,* from which the 1934 movie was made. Films set in what is one of California's most scenic state reserves include: *Beautiful Monterey* (1917), *The Big Bounce* (1969), *Captain Janu-*

ary (1936), *Changes* (1969), *Conquest* (1937), *Daddy Long Legs* (1931), *Edge of Darkness* (1942), *Eleventh Hour* (1923), *He Was Her Man* (1934), *The Iron Mask* (1929), *Japanese War Bride* (1952), *Lassie Come Home* (1943), *The Love Light* (1921), *Maid of Salem* (1937), *The Miracle Man* (1932), *The Mistress of Shemstone* (1921), *My Blood Runs Cold* (1965), *The Notorious Landlady* (1962), *Paddy the Next Best Thing* (1933), *Pidgin Island* (1916), *Ramona* (1916), *Rose of the Golden West* (1927), *See America First* (1915), *Shadows* (1922), *A Summer Place* (1959), *The Sunshine Gathers* (1924), *Tess of the Storm Country* (1922), *The Valley of the Moon* (1914), *Why Women Love* (1925), and *The Woman on Pier 13* (1950).

Big Sur

The dramatic coastline of this area has long attracted filmmakers. In 1925 scenes for *My Son* were filmed at Knotley Landing on the coast south of Carmel heading toward Big Sur. In 1933 Harry Lachman directed Janet Gaynor in *Paddy the Next Best Thing* in scenes filmed along the coast south of Carmel. The Big Sur Hills appear in the background of a scene of *A Woman Rebels* (1936). Background scenes for key elements in *Suspicion* (1941) were filmed along the coastline between Carmel and Big Sur, standing in for England. There's 1941 footage of Hitchcock motoring up and down the scenic coastline. *Salome, Where She Danced* (1945), starring Yvonne DeCarlo, includes shots south of Carmel on a dirt road at the entrance to Garrapata Canyon.

Deep Valley starring Ida Lupino was shot entirely on location in Big Sur and Big Bear by Jean Negulesco in 1947. The rugged portrayal of the landscape, including heavy rainstorms, was intended to show the stark drama of Big Sur life in those days, including shots of the building of Highway 1 along the rugged coast. That same year the old Coast Guard station near Big Sur stood in for a nunnery in 19th-century New Zealand, the setting of *Green Dolphin Street* (1947). Lana Turner and Donna Reed are sisters competing for the same man, Van Heflin.

The restaurant Nepenthe ("isle of no care" in Greek) is famous for its connections to Rita Hayworth and Orson Welles. Various versions of the story exist, but according to Erin Gafill, grandson of original owners Lolly and Bill Fassett, Hayworth and Welles had been in San Francisco selling war bonds. Heading back to L.A. on the newly built scenic route, Highway 1, and looking for a spot to picnic, they took a meandering dirt road up a hill to find a cabin with a view overlooking the south coast.

They decided to buy the cabin as a retreat from the stresses of the movie industry. "Rita measured the windows for curtains, and Orson talked about laying in pipe for gas in the kitchen. Scrounging for a down payment, they came up with a little over $167 between them." Apparently neither ever came back to the cabin on the hill, selling it to the Fassetts in 1947. To get the deed signed off by both of them took two years, "what with Rita being in Brazil to film one movie, and Mr. Welles traveling in Europe, and neither one of them much caring to help the other out at that point."

In 1963 another Hollywood couple, Elizabeth Taylor and Richard Burton, made a lasting impression while shooting *The Sandpiper* in Big Sur. When they filmed the folk dancing at Nepenthe, the Fassetts' son Kaffe provided the choreography.

Much of *Celebration at Big Sur* was filmed at the 1969 Big Sur Festival, featuring Joan Baez; Joni Mitchell; Crosby, Stills, Nash & Young; John Sebastian; and Mimi Farina. Additional scenes for the 1971 documentary were filmed at Esalen, just south of Big Sur.

A few scenes for the original 1967 *Doctor Dolittle* were filmed at the Doud Ranch over four days. *One-Eyed Jacks* (1961) includes scenes filmed at Pfeiffer Beach, and parts of *The Master Gunfighter* (1975) were filmed south of Carmel at the Little Sur River and Garrapata Beach. Scenes in *Poetic Justice* were filmed near Big Creek Bridge over a three-day period in June 1992. *Zandy's Bride* was filmed in 1974 at Andrew Molera State Park, where a set depicting Monterey in the 1870s was built.

Roger Corman's 1963 low-budget terror flick, *The Terror*, set on the Baltic coast in the 19th century and starring pre-famous Nicholson and on-the-skids Boris Karloff, was shot on Pfeiffer Beach. Two years later *The Sandpiper* (1965), Vincente Minnelli's soaper about minister Richard Burton, who ruins his life and dumps Eva Marie Saint for the bohemian painter Elizabeth Taylor, was shot on Doud Beach and Pfeiffer Beach. Scenes filmed at Garrapata Beach south of the Highlands stand in for Marin County's Stinson Beach in *Basic Instinct* (1992).

Other films with scenes shot in the Big Sur area include *Incubus* (1966), *The Cat from Outer Space* (1978), *Play Misty for Me* (1971), and *Escape to Witch Mountain* (1975).

Resources

A wide variety of source information was used to assemble this book including books, magazine and newspaper articles, brochures, and Web sites. Some of the most helpful references are listed here.

Allon, David. "On Location: Northern California." *Hollywood Reporter*, July 1, 1988: S-1–S-33.

Ashcroft, Lionel. *Movie Studios & Movie Theaters in Marin*. San Rafael: Marin County Historical Society, 1998.

Barth, Jack. *Roadside Hollywood: The Movie Lover's State-by-State Guide to Film Locations, Celebrity Hangouts, Celluloid Tourist Attractions, and More*. Chicago: Contemporary Books, 1991.

Bell, Geoffrey. *The Golden Gate and the Silver Screen: San Francisco in the History of Cinema*. New Jersey: Fairleigh Dickinson University Press, 1984.

Chan, Vera H-C. "Hollywood by the Bay." Special to MercuryNews.com, posted June 6, 2002.

Crimmins, Peter. "Hollywood, North." *Urbanview*, Vol. 13 No. 16 (September 12, 2001): 6.

Donat, Hank. "Our Cinematic City, Ready for Its Close-up." *San Francisco Independent*, October 5, 2004: 4A.

Eddy, Cheryl. "You Give Love a Bad Name." *San Francisco Bay Guardian*, February 11, 2001.

Freeman, Andrea. "Starring San Francisco." *San Francisco Downtown*, October 2002.

Gelbert, Doug. *Film and Television Locations: A State-by-State Guidebook to Movie-making Sites, Excluding Los Angeles.* Jefferson, NC: McFarland & Co., 2002.

Golden, Fran Wenograd. *TVacations: A Fun Guide to the Sites, the Stars, and the Inside Stories Behind Your Favorite TV Shows.* New York: Pocket Books, 1996.

Grimes, Bob. "The Definitive Encyclopedia to the Films of Frisco." *San Francisco Examiner,* March 1, 1987: 68–70.

Hanson, Gladys. *San Francisco Almanac.* San Francisco: Chronicle Books, 1994.

Hartlaub, Peter. "Kablooey! There Goes San Francisco—Again." *San Francisco Chronicle*, April 10, 2003: section O, p. 1.

Jensen, Lisa. "On Location in Santa Cruz." *Good Times*, July 1, 1981: 14–15.

Kaufmann, Preston J. *Fox—the Last Word.* Pasadena: Showcase Publications, 1979.

Kiefer, David. "S.F. to Hollywood: Pay Up." *San Francisco Examiner*, September 17–29, 2002: 5A.

Kiehn, David. *Bronco Billy and the Essanay Film Company.* Berkeley: Farwell Books, 2003.

Knowles, Eleanor. "A Late-Night Movie Buff's Guide to San Francisco." *Passages*, April, 1977.

Kraft, Jeff, and Aaron Leventhal. *Footsteps in the Fog: Alfred Hitchcock's San Francisco.* Santa Monica: Santa Monica Press, 2002.

Lawson, Kristan, and Anneli Rufus. *California Babylon: A Guide to Sites of Scandal, Mayhem, and Celluloid in the Golden State.* New York: St. Martin's Griffin, 2000.

Levene, Bruce, editor. *James Dean in Mendocino: The Filming of* East of Eden. Mendocino: Pacific Transcriptions, 1994.

————. *Mendocino & the Movies: Hollywood and Television Motion Pictures Filmed on the Mendocino Coast.* Mendocino: Pacific Transcriptions, 2001.

Martin, James A. "Golden Gate, Silver Screen." *New York Times*, January 7, 1990: 514.

Monks, Dave. *The San Francisco Movie Map*. San Francisco: Reel Map Company, 1996.

Myrick, David F. *Telegraph Hill*. Second enlarged edition. San Francisco: City Lights Books, 2001.

Powers, Anne. "Hollywood North." *San Francisco Examiner Image*, August 10, 1992.

Reeves, Tony. *The Worldwide Guide to Movie Locations*. Chicago: Chicago Review Press, 2001.

Stack, Peter. "Hollywood Discovers Treasure Island's Huge Unused Airplane Hangars in Demand as Sound Stages for Movies and TV." *San Francisco Chronicle*, June 15, 1996: E–1.

———. "Real to Reel in the City." *San Francisco Chronicle*, July 1, 1998: D–1.

Stein, Ellen. "I Got My Start in San Francisco." *American Film*, July/August 1984.

Stitch, Sidra. *art-SITES San Francisco: The Indispensable Guide to Contemporary Art-Architecture-Design*. San Francisco: art-SITES Press, 2003.

Warner, Gary A. "Shot in San Francisco." *Orange County Register*, September 12, 1999.

Weirde, Dr. *Dr. Weirde's Weirde [sic] Tours: A Guide to Mysterious San Francisco*. San Francisco: Barrett-James Books, 1994.

Williams, Linda, ed. *San Francisco & Northern California*. DK Eyewitness Travel Guides. London: Dorling Kindersley Limited, 1999.

Woodbridge, Sally B., and John M. Woodbridge. *Architecture San Francisco: The Guide*. New York: Charles Scribner's Sons, 1982.

Zito, Kelly, and Dan Levy, and Bill Burnett. "Reel Estate: San Francisco Locales, Homes Take a Leading Role in the Movies." *San Francisco Chronicle*, March 13, 2003.

Useful Web Sites

Hank Donat's Mister San Francisco, www.mistersf.com

Internet Movie Database, www.imdb.com

Monterey County Film Commission, www.filmmonterey.org

Scott Trimble's Northern California Movies, www.norcalmovies.com

Sonoma Film Commission, www.sonoma-county.org/film/index.htm

Index

Academy of Sciences, 192–193
Acker, Sharon, 254–255
Adams, Brooke, 16, 37, 119–120, 138, 187
Adams, Orny, 276
Adventures of Robin Hood, The (1938), 308
After the Thin Man (1936), 54, 141–142
Alameda, 285–286
Alameda County, 261–291
Alameda County Courthouse, 281
Alamo Square Victorians, 185
Alcatraz Island, 253–258
Alda, Alan, 16, 245
Alexander's Ragtime Band (1938), 79, 96, 156
All About Eve (1950), 52, 95
All Men Are Enemies (1934), 314
Allen, Woody
    Play It Again, Sam (1972), 113, 126, 164, 194, 197,
        215, 298
    Take the Money and Run (1969), 122, 150, 222
Alley, Kirstie, 224
Alta Linda, 100
Alta Plaza Park, 179
Ameche, Don, 96, 157
American Can Company, 37
American Graffiti (1972), 29, 164, 227–228
American Zoetrope Studios, xiv, 122–123
And the Band Played On (1993), 16, 202
Anderson, Gilbert M., xiv, 289–290
Anderson, Loni, 177, 178
Anderson, Warner, 13
Andrews, Julie, 119, 157, 208
Angel Island, 258
Anna Karenina (1935), 308
Antioch Speedway, 290
Apocalypse Now (1979), 242–243
Aquatic Park, 108
Arau, Alfonso, 241
Arbuckle, Fatty, xiv, 54
Arkin, Alan, 62
"Armistead Maupin's Tales of the City." *See* "Further
    Tales of the City" (2001); "More Tales of the
    City" (1998); "Tales of the City" (1993)
Arnold, Tom, 172
Aron, Paul, 18
Around the Fire (1998), 158, 221
Around the World in Eighty Days (1956), 79

Arquette, Patricia, 302
Ashby, Hal, 156, 297, 299
Asian Art Museum, 18
Assassination of Richard Nixon, The (2004), 124, 272
Astaire, Fred, 177, 236–237, 262
Astin, Mackenzie, 31, 166
Attack of the Killer Tomatoes (1978), 112
Avalon, Frankie, 307

Bacall, Lauren, 143
Bachelor, The (1999), 63, 67, 121, 129, 131, 173, 193
Back to the Beach (1987), 307
Bacon, Kevin, 256
Bailey, Raymond, 13
Baker Beach, 165–166
Balboa Theater, 161
Baldwin, Michael, 288
Bale Grist Mill, 239
Balestreri, Ted, 309
Ball, Lucille, 285
Bancroft, Anne, 267
Bandits (2001), 219, 223, 260
Bank of America (22nd Avenue at Noriega), 197
Bank of America (38th Avenue at Balboa), 161
Bank of America Building, 80–83
Bank of America (North Beach branch), 150
"Barbary Coast," 78
Barbary Coast (1935), xvii, 79
"Barbary Coast" (ABC, 1975–76), 79
Barbary Coast Bunny (1956), 78
Barbary Coast Gent (1944), 78
Barbeau, Adrienne, 223
Barrymore, John, 54
Barrymore, Lionel, 306
Basic Instinct (1992), xiv, 44, 124, 136, 138, 147, 176–
    177, 227, 276, 308, 312, 316
Basinger, Kim, 11, 214
Bassett, Angela, 59
Baxter, Anne, 52
Bay, Michael, 97
Bay Bridge, 261–265
Beach Blanket Babylon, 151
Beach Chalet, 159
Beatty, Warren, 299–300
Beautiful Monterey (1917), 314
Beauty Market, The (1919), 314

Bedazzled (1967), 67
Bedazzled (2000), 10, 68, 74, 115, 127, 264
Bee Season (2005), 278, 282, 284
Bel Geddes, Barbara, 29, 135, 138–140
Belgravia Apartments, 102
Bellamy, Madge, 305
Belli Building, 120
Belushi, Jim, 264
Benjamin, Richard, 246, 268
Bennett, Bruce, 102
Bergen, Candice, 45, 125, 145
Berkeley Art Museum, 269–270
Berkeley BART Station, 266–267
Bernal Heights, 45
Berry, Ken, 149
Bicentennial Man (1999), 8, 94, 168, 169–170, 185, 260,
    302–303
Big Basin Redwoods State Park, 304
Big Bounce, The (1969), 310, 314
Big Sur, 315–316
Biggs, Jason, 269
Bikini Planet (2002), 282
Binoche, Juliette, 278
Birdman of Alcatraz, The (1962), 146, 257
Birds, The (1963), 58, 228, 233–237
Bisset, Jacqueline, 22, 126, 174
Black, Karen, 181, 288
Blackman, Sean San Jose, 31
Blakely, Susan, 177
Blanchett, Cate, 219–220
Blind Date (1987), 314
Bodega, 236–237
Bodega Bay, 233–235
Bogart, Humphrey, 60, 143, 147
Bogdanovich, Peter, 51, 131
Boorman, John, 255
Bosley, Tom, 246
Bostock, Barbara, 114
Bostwick, Barry, 22
Bosworth, Hobart, 314
Bowen, Jenny, 20
Bowles Hopkins Gallery, 149
Boyle, Peter, 245, 290
Boys and Girls (2000), 44, 108, 173, 188, 213, 269
Bradshaw, Dorothy, 99
Brainstorm (1983), 313
Braveheart (1926), 310
Breakthrough (1950), 308
Breeding, Larry, 21
Brennan, Walter, 304
Bridges, Jeff, 29
    Fearless (1993), 32, 83, 131, 136
    Jagged Edge (1985), 10
    Tucker: The Man and His Dream (1988), 14–15, 229,
        274
Bridges, Lloyd, 279
Bridges Restaurant, Danville, 290
Broadway, 125–126, 180
Broadway Auto Row, Oakland, 281
Broadway Tunnel, 119

Brocklebank, 97–98
Bron, Eleanor, 67
Brooks, Albert, 97, 168, 216
Brooks, Mel, 73, 169, 196
Brosnan, Pierce, 271
Brown, Bruce, 306
Buena Vista Café, 111–112
Buena Vista Park, 201
Bug's Life, A (1998), 265
Bullitt (1968), 32, 33, 42, 91, 98, 100, 174, 177, 297
Bullock, Sandra, 68, 285
Bulshofer, Fred J., 243
Burglar (1987), 36, 129, 188, 193
Burlingame High School, 299
Burnt Offerings (1976), 288
Burr, Raymond, 42, 86
Burritt Alley, 60–61
Burstyn, Ellen, 245
Burton, Richard, 316
By Hook or By Crook (2001), 15, 31
Byrne, Gabriel, 302
Byrum, John, 118

Caan, James, 62, 245
Cable Car Signal Box, 100–101
Caddy, The (1953), 310
Café Cantata, 174
Cage, Nicholas
    Peggy Sue Got Married (1986), 227, 232
    Rock, The (1996), 90–91, 97, 173, 256
    Wings of Desire (1988), 18
Caine Mutiny, The (1954), 147, 258
Cala Foods, 103
Caldecott Tunnel, 290
California (1947), 309, 314
California Hall, 23
California Palace of the Legion of Honor, 160–161
California Street, 71
Callaway, Cheryl, 99
Camille of the Barbary Coast (1925), 79
Campbell, William, 119
Candidate, The (1972), 55, 274, 310
Candlestick Park, 45
Cannery, The, 110–111
Cannery Row (1982), 309
Cannon, Dyan, 301
Can't Stop the Music (1980), 36
Cantinflas, 79
Captain January (1936), 309, 312, 314
Captains Courageous (1937), 309
Carewe, Edwin, 314
Caridi, Carmine, 10
Carmel-by-the-Sea, 312
Carne, Judy, 114
Carpenter, John, 223, 224, 233
Carr, Darleen, 34
Carrey, Jim, 247
Carter, Lynda, 177
Carter, Nell, 22
Carter, Thomas, 103

Cartwright, Veronica, 17, 234

Caruso, David, 67, 130, 259

Casey, Innis, 22

Cassell, Seymour, 31

Castro neighborhood, 202–208

Castro Theatre, x, 203

Casualties of War (1989), 206

Cat from Outer Space, The (1978), 316

Cathedral Hill Hotel, 22–23

Caviezel, James, 57, 125, 285

Celebration at Big Sur (1969), 316

Chamberlain, Richard, 140, 177

Chambers, Justin, 10

Chambord Apartments, 92

Chan Is Missing (1982), 88–89

Chandler (1972), 314

Changes (1969), 314, 315

Chaplin, Charlie, xiv, 29, 289–290

Charles Krug Winery, 241

Chartered Bank of London, 84

Chase, Chevy, 9, 14, 102, 126

Cheadle, Don, 272

Cheaper by the Dozen (2004), 231–232

Chen, Joan, 201

Cherish (2002), 32

Cheung, Maggie, 215

Children's Hospital and Research Center, Oakland, 282

Chiles, Lois, 246

Chinatown, 84–90

Christie, Julie, 96, 103, 140

Chu Chu and the Philly Flash (1981), 260

Church, Thomas Haden, 84

Citicorp Center, 69

City of Angels (1998), 17

Civic Center, 5–7

Civic Center Plaza, 16

Claremont Resort and Spa, 270–271

Clark, Petula, 236–237

Clarkson, Patricia, 71, 110–111, 131

Clash by Night (1952), 309

Class Action (1990), 10

Claude Lane, 64

Cliff House, 156

Clooney, Rosemary, 237

Close, Glenn, 10, 18, 94, 186

Club Fugazi, 151

Cock-Eyed World, The (1929), 260

Coffee Dan's, 52

Coit Tower, 140–142

Colbert, Claudette, 306

Cole Street, 188

Coleman, Dabney, 59

College Avenue, Berkeley, 271

Colton Hall, 309

Columbus, Chris

    Bicentennial Man (1999), 8, 168

    Mrs. Doubtfire (1993), 170, 180, 290

    Nine Months (1995), 23, 131, 136, 170

    Rent (2005), 260

Columbus at Vallejo, 127–128

Comedian (2002), 276

Condon, Bill, 222, 304

Connery, Sean

    Marnie (1964), 38

    Presido, The (1988), 165

    Rock, The (1996), 90–91, 97, 173, 256–257

Conquest (1937), 315

Conservatory of Flowers, 196–197

Considine, Kevin, 239

Contra Costa County Fairgrounds, 290

Contra Costa Times, 277

Convention (2003), 280

Conversation, The (1974), 22, 55, 58, 77, 179

Cook, Peter, 68

Coppola, Francis Ford, 122, 128, 240, 242–243

    Apocalypse Now (1979), 242–243

    Conversation, The (1974), 22, 55, 77, 179

    Finian's Rainbow (1968), 236–237

    Peggy Sue Got Married (1986), 225, 232

    Tucker: The Man and His Dream (1988), 14, 15, 229, 274, 278–279

Copycat (1994), 259

Corman, Roger, 316

Cornwall Ranch, 304

Cort, Bud, 156, 265, 297, 299, 307

Cosmos Company, 164

Cotati, 225

Cotten, Joseph, 231

Cow Hollow/Marina, 172–174

Cow Palace, 46–47

Crackers (1984), 31

Crawford, Joan, 97–98

"Crazy Like a Fox" (CBS, 1984–86), 69

Crissy Field, 170–172

Crocker-Anglo National Bank, 68

Cromwell, James, 67, 173

Crosby, Bing, 237

Crosland, Alan, 52

Cross, Flora, 278

Cruz, Penelope, 173, 185

Cruze, James, 309

Cucinotta, Maria Grazia, 76

Cujo (1978), 246

Cukor, George, 314

Culkin, Macaulay, 18, 57, 71, 102, 196

Curran Theater, 52

Curtin, Valerie, 18

Curtis, Donald, 76

Curtiz, Michael, 306

Cusack, Joan, 71, 94

Cybelle's Pizza, 102–103

Cypress Point Golf Course, 310

Daddy Long Legs (1931), 315

Daily, Elizabeth, 21

Dalmita, Lily, 260

Daly, Tyne, 16, 39, 142, 256

d'Amico, Marcus, 98, 119

Dangerous Minds (1995), 299, 307

Danilo's Bakery, 128–129

Danson, Ted, 247
  Getting Even with Dad (1993), 12, 18, 57, 71, 102,
    196
  Made in America (1993), 268–269, 274, 281
Dante, Joe, 140, 228
Dante Building, 133–134
"Dark Mansions" (ABC, 1985), 246
Dark Passage (1937), 143
Daves, Delmer, 38
"Davidson's Pet Shop," 58
Davidtz, Embeth, 185
Davis, Bette, 52, 245, 288
Day, Doris, 122, 216, 309
De Bartolo, Tiffanie, 31
De Palma, Brian, 206
De Putti, Lya, 260
"Dead Famous" (2004), 257
Dead Pool, The (1988), 37, 71, 89, 110–111, 131
Dean, James, 244
Dean, Loren, 225
DeCarlo, Yvonne, 315
Dee, Sandra, 312
Deep Valley (1947), 315
del Toro, Benicio, 32
DeMille, Cecil B., 131, 305
DeNiro, Robert, 45
Department of Public Health, 15–16
Dern, Bruce, 96, 232
deSantis, Stanley, 160
Desire Me (1947), 314
Desiree (1954), 308
Destination Tokyo (1943), 261
Deuel, Peter, 114
Devane, William, 181
DeVito, Danny, 113, 186, 269
Diamond, Val, 103
Dietrich, Marlene, 79
Dillon, Matt, 201
Dim Sum: A Little Bit of Heart (1986), 88
Dirty Harry (1971), xiii, 9, 25, 42–43, 82–83, 87, 108,
    133, 189–190, 199, 221, 260
Dirty Harry movies. *See Dead Pool, The* (1988); *Dirty*
    Harry (1971); *Enforcer, The* (1976); *Magnum Force*
    (1973); *Sudden Impact* (1983)
Disneyland's Golden Dreams (2001), 261
Dmytryk, Edward, 258
D.O.A. (1950), 55, 92, 188
Doctor Dolittle (1967), 316
Doctor Dolittle (1998), 110, 142, 176
Doctor Dolittle 2 (2001), 172
Dodge, Harry (aka Harriet), 15–16, 31
Dolores Park, 205–206
Dolphin Club, 107
Domergue, Faith, 76
Donen, Stanley, 67
Donner, Richard, 223
Donohue, Troy, 312
Dopamine (2003), 44, 107, 170
"Doris Day Show, The" (CBS, 1968–73), 122, 216
Dornacker, Jane, 124

Douglas, Kirk, 79
Douglas, Michael
  Basic Instinct (1992), 124, 136, 137, 147, 276, 312
  Game, The (1997), 63, 67, 302
  "Streets of San Francisco, The" (ABC, 1972–77), 138
Douglas, Paul, 309
"Down Time" (2001), 257
Downey, Robert, Jr., 62
Dr. Dolittle (1998), 76
"Drayton Gallery," 52
Dream for an Insomniac (1998), 31, 165
Dreyfuss, Richard, 30
Dukakis, Olympia, 119, 185
Duke, Patty, 125
Dunne, Irene, 135
Dunsmuir House, Oakland, 287–289
Dunwich Horror, The (1969), 244
Dust Be My Destiny (1939), 309
Duvall, Robert, 77, 187
  Bullitt (1968), 98, 100
  THX 1138 (1971), 266, 285
Dying Young (1990), 246–247
"Dynasty" (ABC, 1981–89), 301
Dzundza, George, 147

East Harbor, 173
East of Eden (1954), 244
East of Eden (1981), 306
Eastwood, Clint, xiv, 25, 206
  Dead Pool, The (1988), 71, 89, 110–111, 131
  Dirty Harry (1972), 9, 82–83, 108, 173, 189–190,
    199, 217
  Enforcer, The (1976), 39, 142, 256
  Escape from Alcatraz (1979), 255, 258
  Magnum Force (1973), 149
  Play Misty for Me (1971), 312
  Sudden Impact (1983), 41, 76, 100, 159, 307
  True Crime (1999), 221–222, 277, 278, 281, 286, 288
Ebersole, Christine, 277
Edge of Darkness (1942), 308, 315
EDtv (1999), xviii, 128
Edwards, Blake, 45, 68, 149, 163, 200, 220
Eiger Sanction, The (1975), 312
18th Street, 35, 36
Elbo Room, 31
"Electric Dreams" (1984), 257
Eleventh Hour (1923), 315
Elfman, Jenna, 203–204
Elizondo, Hector, 176
Elliott, Ross, 60, 83
Embarcadero One, 77
Emeryville, 265
Empire Strikes Back, The (1980), 258
Emporium, 60
End of the World in Our Usual Bed in a Night Full of Rain,
    The (1978), 45, 125, 145
End Up, The, 43
Endless Summer, The (1966), 306
Enforcer, The (1976), 10, 16, 39, 142, 256
Entertainer, The (1976), 307

Epstein, Rob, 11
Ernie's Restaurant, 122
"Erskine's Photo Studio," 174
Escape from Alcatraz (1979), 255, 258
Escape to Witch Mountain (1975), 316
Essanay Film Manufacturing Company, xiv, 289–290
Eszterhas, Joe, xiv, 67
Evangeline (1929), 306, 314
Everhart, Angie, 130
Eve's Secret (1925), 314
Experiment in Terror (1962), xviii, 45, 68, 114, 126, 149, 163, 200, 220, 263
Explorers (1985), 228
Eye of the Night, The (1916), 312
Eyes of the Forest, The (1923), 305

Fair Oaks, 32
Fairfax, 220–221
Fairmont Hotel, 94–97
"Falcon Crest" (CBS, 1981–90), 241
Family Plot (1976), 96, 181
Fan, The (1996), 45
Fan Shell Beach, 310
Fantasy Records, 265
Farley's Café, 35
Farmer's Daughter, The (1947), 225
Fat Man and Little Boy (1989), 188
Faye, Alice, 79, 96, 156
Fearless (1993), 32, 83, 131
Feldon, Barbara, 232
Ferguson, Colin, 94, 173
Ferry Building, 74–76
Field, Sally, 128, 180, 271
Fifth Horseman, The (1970), 104
50 First Dates (2004), 260
Filbert Street, 115, 140
Fillmore Street, 185
Filoli Mansion, Woodside, 299–302
Final Analysis (1992), 11, 214
Financial District, 51
Fincher, David, 302
Finding Nemo (2003), 265
Fior d'Italia Restaurant, 130
Fiorentino, Linda, 67, 259
Fire Station #43, 208
First Bank, 83
First Baptist Church, Oakland, 276
Fisher, Frances, 281
Fisherman's Wharf, 147–149
Flame of Barbary Coast (1945), 78
Flatiron Building, 20, 69
Fleischer, Richard, 79
Flower Drum Song (1962), ix–xii, 85, 88
Flubber (1997), 258, 260
Fog, The (1980), 223, 233
Fog City Diner, 144–145
Follow the Fleet (1936), 262
Fonda, Henry, 285
Fonda, Jane, 59–60, 290
Fontaine, Joan, 244, 311

Foolish Wives (1922), 314
Foote, Cone & Belding, 79
Ford, Glenn, 69, 114, 163
Ford, Harrison, 30, 77
Ford, Phillip R., 184
Forest Hills MUNI Station, 199
Forever Young (1990), 247
Forlani, Claire, 44, 108, 173, 188, 213, 269
Forrest, Frederic, 23, 55
Forrest Gump (1994), 173
Fort Mason Center, 174
Fort Point, 168–170
40 Days and 40 Nights (2002), 127, 201
Foster, Gloria, 286
Foster, Norman, 83
Foul Play (1978), 9, 14, 18, 126, 188
Four Daughters (1938), 309
Fox, Michael J., 206
Fox Theater Site, San Francisco, 18–19
Francisco Street, 176
"Frank Beachum's house," 278
Franklin, Carl, 285
Fraser, Brendan
    Bedazzled (2000), 10, 74, 115
    George of the Jungle (1997), 58, 68, 84, 114, 264
Freebie and the Bean (1974), 62
Freeman, Morgan, 36, 285
Fremont Street Exit, 71
French, Leigh, 103
Frenchman's Creek (1944), 244
Fricker, Brenda, 191
Friedkin, William, 67, 130, 259
"Fugitive, The" (2001), 247
"Full House" (ABC, 1987–95), 185
Funicello, Annette, 307
"Further Tales of the City" (2001), 196

Gabbiano's Restaurant, 76
Gable, Clark, 64–65
Galleria, The, 36
Game, The (1997), 63, 67, 302
"Gangster Chronicles, The" (1981), 307
Garcia, Andy, 112
Garrick, Barbara, 98, 193, 197, 199
Garson, Greer, 314
Garver, Kathy, 119
Gattaca (1997), 218
Gaynor, Janet, xiv, 306, 315
Gellar, Sarah Michelle, 233
Gentleman Jim (1942), xvii, 79
Gentleman's Agreement (1947), 310
George, Burton, 309
George of the Jungle (1997), 58, 83–84, 114, 151, 264, 301
George Washington High School, 163
Gere, Richard, 11, 15, 16, 278
Get Money (2003), 260
Getting Even with Dad (1993), 12, 18, 57, 71, 102, 132, 196
Ghirardelli Square, 110

Ghost and Mrs. Muir (1947), 310

Giannini, Giancarlo, 45, 125, 145, 241

Giardino, Tony, 144

Gibson, Mel, 247

Gibson, Thomas, 98, 119

Gladsome (1917), 309

Glass, Ned, 21

Glasser, Isabel, 247

Glaudini, Lola, 265

Gnomemobile, The (1965), 304

Goldberg, Whoopi, xiv
    Burglar (1987), 36, 129, 188, 193
    Made in America (1993), 264, 268–269, 271, 274, 281
    Sister Act (1992), 131, 207

Golden Dragon Restaurant, 89

Golden Gate (1994), 201

Golden Gate Bridge, 166–168

Golden Gate Park, 191–197

Goldthwait, Bobcat, 189

Good Neighbor Sam (1964), 215–216

Gooding, Cuba, Jr., 119

Gordon, Robert, 76

Gordon, Ruth, 156, 186, 265, 297, 307

Grace Cathedral, 93–94

Graduate, The (1967), 264, 267, 313

Grant, Cary, 306, 311

Grant, Hugh, 23, 120, 131, 136, 144, 170

Grant Avenue, x, 134–135, 135

Greed (1925), xiv, 156, 183, 306

Green Dolphin Street (1947), 315

Green Gables, 302–303

Green Street, 176

Green Valley Restaurant, 129

Greenwich, 115

Griffith, Melanie, 34, 232

Grimes, Gary, 244

Grimes, Tammy, 36

Groove (2000), 37, 43, 174, 260, 264–265

Guess Who's Coming to Dinner? (1967), 52, 164, 297

Guiggui, Martin, 22

Guns n' Roses, 37

Hackman, Gene, 22, 55, 77, 179

Haight Street, 188

Haiku Tunnel (2001), 279–280

Hall of Justice, 86

Halloween (1978), 223

Hamill, Mark, 224

Hamilton, Lisa Gay, 278

Hamlin Hotel, 20

Hancock School, 150

Hanks, Tom, xiv, 173, 311–312

Hannah, Daryl, 102

Happily Even After (2003), 280

Harmon, Mark, 136, 165

Harold and Maude (1971), 156, 265, 297, 299, 307

Harris, Barbara, 96

Harris, Ed, 37, 97, 256

Harris, Julie, 244

Harrison, Greg, 37, 174, 264–265

Hart, William S., 305

Hartnett, Josh, 127

Hathaway, Anne, 157

"Hawaii Five-O" (CBS, 1968–80), 188

Hawke, Ethan, 218, 228

Hawks, Howard, 79

Hawn, Goldie, 9, 14, 18, 126, 246

Hayashi, Marc, 88

Hayden, Sterling, 59

Hayes, Helen, 149, 168

Hayes Street, 183–184

Hayward, Susan, 222

Hayworth, Rita, 142, 158, 182, 315–316

He Was Her Man (1934), 315

Headly, Glenne, 18, 57, 196

Heard, John, 118

Heart and Souls (1993), 62

Heartbeat (1980), 118, 124

Heartbeeps (1980), 307

Heaven Can Wait (1978), 299–300

Hedren, Tippi, 38, 58, 234, 236

Helmore, Tom, 37, 97

Henry, Buck, 301

Henry J. Kaiser Auditorium, Oakland, 282

Hepburn, Audrey, 11–12

Hepburn, Katharine, 52, 178

Herbie Rides Again (1974), 67, 149, 168

Heritage House, 245

Higgins, Colin, 9, 18, 59–60, 265, 307

High Anxiety (1978), 73, 169, 196

High Crimes (2002), xv, 17, 36, 57, 83, 125, 285

Hills Brothers Plaza, 42

Hilton Hotel, 51

Hitchcock, Alfred, 14, 304
    Birds, The (1963), 58, 228, 233–235
    Family Plot (1976), 181
    Marnie (1964), 38
    Rebecca (1940), 308, 311
    Shadow of a Doubt (1943), 230–231
    Suspicion (1941), 311, 315
    Vertigo (1958), 21, 64, 95–96, 122, 160, 169, 173, 202, 304, 311

Hoffman, Dustin, 264, 267–268, 311

Hog's Breath Inn, Carmel, 312–313

Holbrook, Hal, 224

Holden, William, 177

Holly, Lauren, 42, 71

Holy Cross Cemetery, Colma, 297

Homeward Bound II: Lost in San Francisco (1996), 145, 298–299

Hopkins, Miriam, 79

Hopkins, Paul, 119, 146

Hoskins, Bob, 275

Hotel (1967), 97

"Hotel" (ABC, 1983–88), 96–97, 188

Hotel Bijou, 59

Hotel Majestic, 183

Hotel Oakland, 280–281

Houghton, Katharine, 52, 297

House on Telegraph Hill, The (1951), xvi, 138, 143
How Stella Got Her Groove Back (1998), 59
Howard, Ron, 30, 128
Howard, Silas, 15, 31
Howards of Virginia, The (1940), 306
Hudson, Rock, 115
Hulk, The (2003), 80
Hunt, Bonnie, 231–232
Hunter, Tab, 177
Hunters Point, 45
Hurley, Elizabeth, 10, 68, 74, 127, 264
Hussey, Ruth, 243
Huston, John, 60, 75, 262–263
Huston, Patricia, 114
Hutton, Timothy, 76
Hyams, Peter, 136
Hyatt Regency, 72–73
Hyde Street, 113, 114
Hyde Street Cable Car, 112–113
Hyde Street Pier, 108–110

I Cover the Waterfront (1933), 309
I Know What You Did Last Summer (1997), 233
I Remember Mama (1948), 135
I Want to Live (1958), 222
In Control of All Things (2004), 260
In Love and War (1958), 309
In Search of a Hero (1925), 243
Incredibles, The (2004), 265
Incubus (1966), 316
Indiana Jones and the Last Crusade (1989), 260
Indiana Jones and the Raiders of the Lost Ark (1981), 260
Industrial Light & Magic, xiv, 218
Innerspace (1987), 140
Intermezzo (1939), 310
Interview with the Vampire (1994), 20
Invasion of the Body Snatchers (1956), 20
Invasion of the Body Snatchers (1978), 16, 17, 20, 37, 77, 119, 138, 187
Iron Mask, The (1929), 315
Irons, Jeremy, 225
"Ironside" (NBC, 1967–75), 42, 86
Iscove, Robert, 213
Island of the Blue Dolphins (1963), 244
Isle of Life, The (1916), 309, 314
It Came from Beneath the Sea (1955), 45, 76, 167, 170

Jack (1996), 260
Jack London Square, Oakland, 283–284
Jackson, Janet, 280
Jacobs, Alan, 76
Jacobsen, John, 221
Jade (1995), 67, 85, 130, 259
Jagged Edge (1985), 10
James and the Giant Peach (1996), 259
James Bond movies. *See View to a Kill, A* (1985)
Japanese Tea Garden, 194–195
Japanese War Bride (1952), 315
Jasper Place, 134
Jazz Singer, The (1927), 52

Jewison, Norman, 244
Jitney Elopement, A (1915), 29
Johnny Belinda (1948), 244, 312
Johnson, Don, 18, 259
Johnson, Van, 147, 306
Johnstown Flood, The (1925), 306
Jolson, Al, 52
Jordan, Louis, 309
Jordan, Neil, 20
Jouanou, Phil, 11
Joy Luck Club, The (1993), 45, 88, 301
Judd, Ashley
    High Crimes (2002), 17, 36, 57, 83, 125, 285
    Twisted (2004), 12, 40, 42, 125, 127, 135
Julie (1956), 309
Junior (1994), 113, 186, 269, 312

Kahn, Madeline, 51
Kamikaze Hearts (1986), 202
Karloff, Boris, 316
Kasdan, Lawrence, 225
Kaufman, Andy, 307
Kaufman, Philip
    Invasion of the Body Snatchers (1978), 16, 20, 77–78, 138, 187
    Right Stuff, The (1983), 37, 47, 70, 124
    Twisted (2004), 12, 40, 42, 125
Kaye, Danny, 237
Kazan, Elia, 244
Keaton, Diane, 113, 173, 194
Keaton, Micheal, 34
Keith, Ian, 76
Keith, Robert, 83, 99
Kellerman, Sally, 214, 245
Kennedy Hotel, 42
Kezar Stadium, xv, 189–190
Kiger, Robby, 69
Kings Go Forth (1958), 314
Kinnear, Greg, 42
Kinsey (2004), 222–223, 304
Kinski, Natassja, 242
Kobart, Ruth, 221
Korda, Michael, 103
Kornbluth, Josh, 174, 279–280
Kramer, Stanley, 52, 164, 168, 178, 297
Kurtiz, Michael, 237
Kurtz, Swoosie, 16
KwikWay Drive-In, Oakland, 282

La Bodega, 135
Lachman, Harry, 315
Lady from Shanghai, The (1948), 86, 158, 193
Lady Says No, The (1952), 314
Lai, Leon, 215
Lake Merritt, Oakland, 281–282
Lancaster, Burt, 146, 257
Landes, Michael, 31
Land's End, 159–160
Lane, Diane, 204
Lang, Fritz, 309

Lansbury, Angela, 246
Larch, John, 9
Larkin Street, 114
Larkspur, 217
Lasser, Louise, 245
Lassie Come Home (1943), 315
Last Night of the Barbary Coast (1915), 78
Latham Square Building, 276–277
Lau, Andrew, 215
Law, Jude, 218–219
Law of the Barbary Coast (1949), 78
Lawrence Berkeley Lab, 270
Le Mat, Paul, 29
Leachman, Cloris, 10, 174
Leavenworth, 115
LeBrock, Kelly, 98, 137
Lee, Ang, 80
Lefty O'Doul 3rd Street Bridge, 39
Leigh, Janet, 306
Lemmon, Jack, 215–216, 307
Lester, Richard, 96, 103, 169
Levinson, Barry, 219
Lewis, Juliette, 71, 131, 173
Lexington Club, 31
Li Po, 88
Lineup, The (1958), xiv, 13, 43, 86, 99–100, 146, 155
Linklater, Hamish, 264–265
Linney, Laura, 159
    "Further Tales of the City" (2001), 197, 199
    Kinsey (2004), 222, 304
    "More Tales of the City" (1998), 94, 146, 173
    "Tales of the City" (1993), 112, 115, 161, 193
Little, Rich, 114
Little Giant, The (1933), 310
Live Nude Girls Unite (2000), 125
Livingston, John, 44, 107, 170
Lloyd, Frank, 306
Lloyd, Sabrina, 44
Locke, Sondra, 149, 307
Lohan, Lindsay, 240
Lolita (1997), 225
Lombard Street, 113–114, 115–116
London, Jack, 283–284
Long, Nia, 264, 268, 274, 281
Lopez, Jennifer, 10, 92, 94, 161
Lorre, Peter, 79
Lost Boys, The (1987), 307
Lotta's Fountain, 64
"Love Among Thieves" (1987), 11
Love Bug, The (1968), 110
Love Light, The (1921), 315
"Love on a Rooftop" (ABC, 1966–71), 114
Lowe, Edmund, 260
Loy, Myrna, 54–55, 141–142
Lucas, George, xv, 122, 218, 229
    American Graffiti (1972), xv, 29, 164, 227–228
    THX 1138 (1971), 29, 219, 266–267, 270, 285, 290–291
Lyne, Adrian, 225
Lyon Street, 176

MacDonald, Jeannette, 64–65
MacKerricher Park, 246
MacMurray, Fred, 147, 306
Macondray Lane Steps, 118
Macy, Bill, 76, 169
Made in America (1993), 264, 268, 271, 272, 274, 281
"Magic of David Copperfield IX: Escape from Alcatraz" (1987), 258
Magnin, Cyril, 9
Magnum Force (1973), 9, 36, 37, 149
Maid of Salem (1936), 306, 315
Majestic, The (2001), 247
Malden, Karl, 34, 230
Malle, Louis, 31
Maltese Falcon, The (1941), 60–61, 75, 262–263
"Man Loh's Oriental Roof Garden," 83
Man of Honor, A (1919), 314
Man Who Knew Too Much, The (1956), 14
Mankiewicz, Joseph L, 52
Mann, Leslie, 58, 83, 114, 151
Mare Island, 260–261
Marin, Cheech, 18
Marin County, 208–224
Marin County Civic Center, 218–220
Marin Headlands, 213
Marin Town and Country Club, 220
Marina Green, 170–172, 173
Mark Hopkins Hotel, ix, 98–100
Market Street, 59–60
Marnie (1964), 38
Marquee Lofts, 23
Married Alive (1972), 312, 314
Marriott Hotel, 59
Mars, Kenneth, 51
Marsh, Loren, 29
Marshall, 223
Marshall, Garry, 119, 165, 176
Martin, Dean, 269
Martin, Ross, 45, 68–69, 114, 126, 163, 200
Martin, Steve, 231–232
Martin Luther King Way, Oakland, 283
Marvin, Lee, 170, 254–255
Mason, James, 79
Mason Street, 102
Master Gunfighter, The, 316
Mastrantonio, Mary Elizabeth, 10
Matarazzo, Heather, 176
Maté, Rudolph, 55, 92
Matrix Reloaded, The (2003), 276, 283, 285–286
Matrix Revolutions (2004), 276, 283, 285
Maxie (1985), 18, 94, 186
May, Wood, 88
McCarthy, Kevin, 20
McConaughey, Matthew
    EDtv (1999), 128, 203–204
    Wedding Planner, The (2001), 10, 92, 94, 108, 161, 195
McDowell, Malcolm, 72, 84, 90, 110, 176, 222
McGhee, Scott, 278
McGovern, Elizabeth, 246

McGuire, Dorothy, 38
McKesson Building, 67–68
McLaglen, Victor, 260
"McMillan and Wife" (NBC, 1971–76), 115
McOrnie, Maggie, 267
McQueen, Steve, 297
    Bullitt (1968), 33, 91, 100, 174, 177
    Towering Inferno, The (1974), xviii, 81, 94
Mecca Restaurant, 204
Mel's Drive-In, 29, 164
Memoirs of an Invisible Man (1992), 102
Mendocino County, 243–247
Mennett, Tina "Tigr," 202
Metro (1997), 103, 260
Metro Theater, 175–176
Meyer, Emile, 13
Meyer, Nicholas, 72, 84, 222
Micklis, Michael, 246
"Midnight Caller" (NBC, 1988–91), 51, 188
Midnight on the Barbary Coast (1929), 78
Milland, Ray, 243, 309
Mills, Hayley, 230, 239
Minghella, Max, 278
Minnelli, Vincent, 316
Miracle Man, The (1932), 315
Miss Hobbs (1920), 314
Mission, The (2000), xvi, 29
Mission District, 29–33
Mission Dolores, 204–205
Mission Rock (Pier 50), 38
Missouri Street, 36
Mistress of Shemstone, The (1921), 315
Mix, Tom, 305
Modine, Matthew, 16, 34
Moffat, Donald, 185
Mollie Stone's Supermarket, 217
"Monk" (USA, 2002–present), 134
Monroe, Marilyn, 309
Monsters, Inc. (2001), 265
Monte Rio, 237
Monterey Bay Aquarium, 310–311
Monterey County, 307–316
Montgomery Street, 137–138, 143–144
Moore, Dudley, 67
Moore, Julianne, 23, 131, 136, 144, 170
Moore, Roger, 11, 39, 149, 288
Moorehead, Agnes, 143
Morcom Amphitheater of Roses, 282–283
"More Tales of the City" (1998), 94, 98, 146, 173
Morrow, Vince, 104
Mother (1996), 97, 168, 216
Mount Davidson Park, 198–199
Mountain View Cemetery, 272
Mr. Riccio (1975), 269
Mrs. Doubtfire (1993), 128, 150, 271, 284, 290
Mueller, Niels, 124, 272
Muellerleile, Marianne, 42
Muir Woods, 222, 304
Mull, Martin, 76, 169, 214, 215
Mulligan, Robert, 244

Mumford (1999), 225
Muppet Movie, The (1979), 308
"Murder, She Wrote" (CBS, 1984–89), 246
Murder in the First (1995), 10, 256
Murphy, Eddie
    Doctor Dolittle (1998), 76, 110, 142, 176
    Metro (1997), 103, 260
Murray, Don, 227
Music Concourse, 194
Mutiny on the Bounty (1935), 310
Muybridge, Eadweard, xiii, 98–99, 117, 303–304
My Blood Runs Cold (1965), 315
My Son (1925), 315
Myers, Mike, 44, 124–125, 134–135, 144–145, 151,
    164, 190, 256, 288

Napa County, 238–239
"Nash Bridges" (CBS, 1996–2000), 18, 51, 259
National Velvet (1944), 310
Neeson, Liam, 37, 222, 304
Negulesco, Jean, 244, 315
Neiman Marcus, 58
Net, The (1995), 68, 285
Never Die Twice (2001), 188
New Asia Restaurant, 89
Newman, Paul, 81, 177
Nichols, Mike, 264
Nicholson, Jack, 316
Niebaum-Coppola Winery, 240, 242–243
Night Full of Rain, A (1978), 45, 125, 145
Niles, 289–291
Nimoy, Leonard, 310–311
Nina M. Designs, 67
Nina Takes a Lover (1994), 51, 76
Nine Months (1995), 23, 103, 120, 131, 136, 144, 170
Nine to Five (1980), 59–60
Niven, David, 79
Noah's Ark (1928), 306
Nob Hill, xvi
Nob Hill, 51, 90–104
Noland, Lloyd, 38
Nolte, Nick, 118, 124
Nora Prentiss (1947), 102
North Beach, 120–136
North Beach Video, 128
Nosecchi Dairy, 228
Nothing Sacred (1997), 260
Notorious Landlady, The (1962), 315
Novak, Kim
    Pal Joey (1957), 142, 182
    Vertigo (1958), 21, 64, 96, 97, 116, 122, 142, 160,
        169, 173, 202, 204–205, 304
Novato, 223

Oakland, 272–289
Oakland, Simon, 222
Oakland City Center Marriott Hotel, 278
Oakland City Hall, 278–279
Oakland Technical High School, 274
Oakland Tribune Tower, 277

Oakland Zoo, 286
O'Brien, Edmond, 55, 146, 188
Obstacles (2000), 261
O'Connor, Carroll, 170
O'Connor, Frances, 68, 115
O'Connor, Pat, 23
O'Donnell, Chris, 63–64, 67, 121, 129, 131, 173, 193
O'Keefe, Dennis, 83
Old St. Mary's Church, 89
On the Beach (1959), 168
O'Neal, Ryan, 51, 102, 131
One-Eyed Jacks (1961), 316
O'Neill, Jennifer, 244
Other Sister, The (1999), 71, 131, 173
Overboard (1987), 246

Pac Bell Park, 40
Pacific Grove, 311–312
Pacific Heights, 176–191
Pacific Heights (1990), xvi, 34
Pacific Stock Exchange, 69
Paddy the Next Best Thing (1933), 315
Paid for Love (1926), 314
Pal Joey (1957), 142, 182
Palace Hotel. *See* Sheraton Palace Hotel
Palace of Fine Arts, 172–173
Palminteri, Chazz, 67, 259
Palo Alto Stock Farm Horse Barn, 303
Paramount Theater, Oakland, 274–276
Parent Trap, The (1961), 310
Parent Trap, The (1998), 240, 260
"Partners in Crime" (NBC, 1984), 177, 178, 188
Parton, Dolly, 59–60
"Party of Five" (FOX, 1994–2000), 180
Patch Adams (1998), 259, 260
Patinkin, Mandy, 18, 186
Patty Hearst (1988), 161, 188, 197, 268
Pebble Beach Golf Course, 310
Peck, Gregory, 167–168
Peggy Sue Got Married (1986), 225, 232
Pendleton, Austin, 51
Penn, Sean, 31, 63, 67, 124, 246, 272
Penngrove, 225
Pennsylvania Street, 36
Perez, Rosie, 32, 131, 136
Perrineau, Harold, Jr., 185
Perry, John Bennett, 84
Persky, Bill, 76
Petaluma, 225–229
Petaluma Speedway, 229
Peters, Bernadette, 307
Peters, Thomas Kimmwood, 164
Petulia (1968), 96, 103, 140, 146, 195
Peyser, Penny, 69
Pfeiffer, Michelle, 299, 307
Phantasm (1979), 288
Phenomenon (1996), 260
Philo T. Farnsworth, xii
Philo T. Farnsworth Lab, 144

Phoenix, River, 228
"Phyllis" (CBS, 1975–77), 10, 174–175
Pickford, Mary, 305, 306
Pickles, Vivian, 299
Pidgin Island (1916), 315
Pier 50 (Mission Rock), 38
Piers, The, 145–149
Pitt, Brad, 20
Pitts, Zazu, 305–306
Pixar Animation Studios, xiv, 265
Place, Mary Kay, 197
Platt, Oliver, 170
Play It Again, Sam (1972), 113, 126, 164, 194, 197, 215, 298
Play Misty for Me (1971), 312, 316
Playing Mona Lisa (2000), 197
Playland at the Beach, 158
Pleasance, Donald, 267
Pleasant Street, 92
Pleasure of His Company (1961), 177
Pleshette, Suzanne, 236
Plummer, Amanda, 288
Poetic Justice (1993), 280, 316
Point Blank (1967), 170, 254–255
Point Lobos, 314
Point Reyes, 223
Poitier, Sidney, 42, 52, 297
Pollyana (1960), 230, 238–239, 240
Pontiac Moon (1994), 247
Port of Oakland, 284
Portsmouth Square, 87–88
Posey, Parker, 115
Posey Tube, Oakland, 285
Posey-Webster Tube, Oakland, 284–285
Potrero Hill, 33–36
Potter School House, 236–237
Powell, William, 54–55, 141–142
Power, Tyrone, 79, 96, 156
Powers, Stephanie, 69, 149, 163
Prentiss, Paula, 271
Presidio, The, 165
Presido, The (1988), xvi, 85, 136, 165
Pretty Woman (1990), 15
Primrose Path (1925), 312
Princess Diaries, The (2001), xv, 119, 157, 165, 176, 208
Prinze, Freddy, Jr.
    Boys and Girls (2000), 108, 173, 188, 213, 269
    I Know What You Did Last Summer (1997), 233
Promise, The (1916), 243
Provine, Dorothy, 216
Pryce, Jonathan, 302

Quaid, Dennis, 37, 140, 240

Racing with the Moon (1983), 246
Radio Flyer (1990), 223
Railroad Square, 231
Ramis, Harold, 68, 74, 264
Ramona (1916), 315
Rappe, Virginia, xiv, 54

Raycliff Terrace, 177
"Real World" (MTV, 1994), 115–116
Rebecca (1940), 308
Red Diaper Baby (2004), 174
Redford, Robert, 42, 55, 274
Reed, Oliver, 288
Reeve, Christopher, 168, 224
Reeves, Keanu
    Sweet November (2001), 23, 35, 36, 69, 80, 172, 206
    Walk in the Clouds, A (1995), 241
Regency Building, 22
Reindel, Carl, 32
Reitman, Ivan, 113, 269
Remick, Lee, 45, 68, 114, 125–126, 149, 163, 200,
    263–264
Renella, Pat, 32, 100
Rent (2005), 260
Rest of Daniel, The (1992), 247
Reynolds, Debbie, 97, 168, 177, 216–217
Ribisi, Giovanni, 71, 131, 173
Richardson, Natasha, 161, 197, 240
Right Stuff, The (1983), 9, 37, 47, 124
Riot in Cell Block 11 (1954), 255
Ritchie, Michael, 274
Ritchie Family, The, 36
"Road Rules" (MTV, 1994–present), 260
Roadhouse (1928), 306
Roberts, Julia, 15, 246
Roberts, Tanya, 11, 39, 288
Robinson, Andy, 133
Robinson, Edward G., 79
Robson, Mark, 125
Rocco's Corner, 151
"Rock, The" (1967), 258
Rock, The (1996), 80, 90–91, 173, 256
Rodgers & Hammerstein, 85
Rodriguez, Paul, 271
Rogers, Ginger, 262
Romance of Rosy Ridge, The (1946), 306
Romance of the Redwoods, A (1917), 305
Rosary, The (1922), 314
Rose Court Mansion, Hillsborough, 299
Rose of the Golden West (1927), 315
Rose of the Rancho (1914), 308–309
Ross, Herb, 126–127, 164, 215, 298
Ross, Johnny, 42
Ross, Katherine, xiv, 264, 267
Rossellini, Isabella, 32, 136
Rowlands, Gena, 245
Royan Hotel, 31
Rubenstein, Jack, 69
Rubinek, Saul, 12, 57, 132
Rush, Barbara, 36
Rush, Richard, 62
Russell, Kurt, 246
Russian Hill, 107–120
Russians Are Coming, The Russians Are Coming, The
    (1965), xvi, 244
Rutledge, Mary, 79
Ryan, Frank, 144–145

Ryan, Meg, 18, 112, 136, 140, 165
Ryan, Robert, 309

Saget, Bob, 185
Saint James, Susan, 115
Saints Peter and Paul Church, 131–133
Salome, Where She Danced (1945), 315
Salvador (1986), 264
Same Time, Next Year (1978), 245
Samuel P. Taylor State Park, 220–221
Samurai (1944), 310
San Francisco (1936), xvii, 64
San Francisco Art Institute, 117–118
San Francisco Chronicle Building, 44–45
San Francisco City Hall, 8–11
San Francisco General Hospital, 32
San Francisco International Airport, 297–299
San Francisco Maritime National Historic Park, 108
San Francisco Public Library, 17–18
San Francisco Studios, 43
San Francisco Zoo, 197–198
San Francisco–Oakland Bay Bridge, 261
San Mateo County, 297–304
San Quentin, 221–222
San Rafael, 218
Sandpiper, The (1963), 316
Sandy (1926), 314
Santa Cruz County, 305–307
Santa Rosa, 230–233
Santoni, Reni, 25
Sartain, Gailard, 12, 57, 132
Saul Zaentz Film Center, 265
Sausalito, 214–217
Sausalito (2000), 7, 214–215, 260
SBC Park, 40
Schmiechen, Richard, 11
Schneider, Romy, 216
Schrader, Paul, 161, 197, 268
Schumacher, Joel, 246
Schwarzenegger, Arnold, 113, 186, 269
Sciorra, Annabella, 119, 218, 273
Scott, Campbell, 246
Scott, George C., 96, 103, 140, 146, 169
Scott, Martha, 306
Scott, Randolph, 262
Scott, Tony, 45
Scott Street, 178
Scrimm, Angus, 288
See America First (1915), 315
Seems Like Old Times (1980), 314
Seinfeld, Jerry, 276
Sergeant Murphy (1938), 310
Sergei, Ivan, 197
Serial (1980), 76, 214, 215
7th Street, 44
SFO (1999), 76
Shadow of a Doubt (1943), 230–231
Shadows (1922), 310, 314, 315
Shakur, Tupac, 280
Shalhoub, Tony, 134

Shankman, Adam, 94
Shannon Kavanaugh House, 186
Sharkey, Ray, 118
Shatner, William, 311
Shawn, Wallace, 31
Shenar, Paul, 246
Shepard, Sam, 124
Sheraton Palace Hotel, 65–67
Sheridan, Ann, 60, 83, 101, 102
Sherman, Vincent, 102
Shields, Brooke, 193, 306
Shields, Robert, 55, 274
Shilts, Randy, 16, 202
Short, Martin, 140
Siegel, David, 278
Siegel, Don, 16, 120
    Dirty Harry (1972), 25, 108, 134, 199
    Escape from Alcatraz (1979), 255, 258
    Invasion of the Body Snatchers (1956), xvii, 20
    Lineup, The (1958), xvi, 13, 43, 99, 146
Siegel Film, A (1993), xiii, 255
Simmons House, 177
Sinatra, Frank, 79, 142, 182
Sinyor, Gary, 63, 67
Sister Act (1992), 131, 207
Sister Act II: Back in the Habit (1993), 131
Skerritt, Tom, 22, 173
Skye, Ione, 31, 166
Slater, Christian, 20, 256
"Slaughterhouse Rock" (1988), 258
Slither (1972), 245
"Slut Central," 184
Smile (1975), 232
Smile Like Yours, A (1997), 42, 71, 94, 260
Smith, John N., 299
Smith, Kent, 102
Smith, Will, 264, 274, 281
Sneakers (1992), 42
Snipes, Wesley, 45
So I Married an Axe Murderer (1993), xviii, 44, 124–125,
    134–135, 144–145, 151, 164, 190, 256, 288
Soul of the Beast (1922), 305
South End Rowing Club, 107
South Park, 44
Southern Pacific Hospital, 188
Spacek, Sissy, 118, 124
"Spade & Archer's Detective Agency," 61
Sphere (1998), 260, 311
Spirit Is Willing, The (1966), 244
Spoor, George, 289–290
Sporting Youth (1924), 310
Spottiswoode, Roger, 16, 311
Spreckels Mansion, 182
Spring Mountain Winery, 241
St. Elizabeth Apartment House, 102
St. Francis Hotel, xiv, 53–55
St. Germain Avenue, 200
St. Helena, 240–241
St. John's Presbyterian Church, 164
St. Joseph's Hospital, 202

St. Paul's Church, 207
Staglin Family Vineyard, 240
Stamos, John, 185
Stanton, Carl, 42
Stanwyck, Barbara, 309
Star Trek IV: The Voyage Home (1986), 121, 192, 308,
    310–311
Star Wars: Episode V--The Empire Strikes Back (1980),
    258
Star's Café, 23
Steelyard Blues (1973), 290
Steenburgen, Mary, 72, 84, 110, 176, 247
Steiner Street, 180, 187
Steinhart Aquarium, 192–193
Stevens, Connie, 38
Stevens, George, 135
Stewart, Jimmy, 21, 64, 97, 116, 122, 139, 142, 160,
    169, 173, 199, 202, 204–205
Stigmata (1999), 302
Stinson Beach, 223
Stockton Tunnel, 62–63
Stone, Oliver, 264
Stone, Sharon, 44, 136, 147, 176–177, 276, 311, 312
Strangers: The Story of a Mother and Daughter (1978),
    245
Street Music (1981), 20
"Streets of San Francisco, The" (ABC, 1972–77), 18, 34,
    43, 51, 138, 177, 188
Streisand, Barbra, 51, 102–103, 131
Sudden Fear (1952), 97–98
Sudden Impact (1983), 41, 76, 100, 149, 159, 307
Sullivan, Kevin Rodney, 59
Summer of '42 (1970), 244–245
Summer Place, A (1959), 308, 312, 315
Sunshine Gathers, The (1924), 314, 315
Superman (1978), 168
Surf Theater, 197
Susan Slade (1961), 38, 310
Suspicion (1941), 311, 315
Sutherland, Donald
    Crackers (1984), 31
    Invasion of the Body Snatchers (1978), 16, 17, 20, 37,
        77, 119–120, 138
    Steelyard Blues (1973), 290
Sutherland, Kiefer, 307
Sutro Baths, 155–156
Sutter-Stockton Garage, 63
Swedenborgian Church, 164
Sweet November (2001), 23, 35, 36, 69, 79, 172, 206,
    260
Swift, David, 216
Swing (2004), 22, 126
Sword in the Desert (1949), 310

Take the Money and Run (1969), 122, 150, 222
"Tales of the City" (1993), 98, 115, 118, 119, 151, 159,
    160, 166, 185. *See also* "Further Tales of the City"
    (2001); "More Tales of the City" (1998)
Tamalpais Building, 114–115
Tamita, Tamlyn, 45

Tandy, Jessica, 228, 234
Tate, Sharon, 125
Taylor, Elizabeth, 316
Taylor, Rod, 234
Taylor Street, 91, 149, 151
Telegraph Avenue, Oakland, 272
Telegraph Hill, 136–151
Telephone (1987), 43
Temescal Library, 272
Ten Commandments, The (1923), 131
Tenderloin, 20–25
Terror, The (1963), 316
Terror on Alcatraz (1986), 258
Tess of the Storm Country (1922), 315
Testing Block (1920), 305
Theron, Charlize, 23, 35, 36, 80, 206
They Drive by Night (1940), 309
Thibeau, Clarence, 255
Things to Come (1936), 72
3rd Street, 41
Thomas, Betty, 110
Thornbury, Bill, 288
Thornton, Billy Bob, 219–220
Thumb Tripping (1972), 313
Thunder Mountain (1925), 305
Thurman, Uma, 11, 218
THX 1138 (1971), 29, 219, 266, 270, 285, 290–291
Tiger Shark (1932), 310
Tilt (1976), 306
Time After Time (1979), 72, 84, 89–90, 110, 176, 193, 222
Times of Harvey Milk, The (1984), 11, 202
Tin Gods (1926), 310
Tobey, Kenneth, 76
Tol'able David (1930), 306
Tomlin, Lily, 16, 59–60
Tosca Café, 124
Towering Inferno, The (1974), 72, 80–81, 94, 177, 179
Toy Story (1995), 265
Toy Story 2 (1999), 265
Tracy, Spencer, 52, 164, 178
Tramp, The (1915), 289–290
Transamerica Building, 77–78
Transbay Terminal, 71
"Trapper John, M.D." (CBS, 1979–86), 188
Travis, Nancy, 134–135, 164, 190, 288
Treasure Island, 258–260
Treasure Island (1934), 314
Troopers Three (1930), 310
True Crime (1999), 221–222, 277, 278, 281, 286, 288
Tucker: The Man and His Dream (1988), 10, 14, 229, 261, 272, 274, 278–279, 280–281
Tunney, Robin, 32–33
Turner, Kathleen, 225, 227, 232
Turner & Hooch (1989), 311–312
Turning Point, The (1920), 310
20,000 Leagues Under the Sea (1954), 79
Twin Peaks, 199
Twisted (2004), 12, 40, 42, 125, 127, 135, 260

Under the Tuscan Sun (2003), 204
Underwood, Ron, 62
Uninvited, The (1943), 243
Union Square, 51, 55, 58
Union Street, 138–140
University of California at Berkeley, 267–269
Until the End of the World (1991), 124

Vaillancourt Fountain, 73–74
Vallejo Street, 80, 126–127, 136, 176–177
Vallejo Street Garage, 151
Valley of the Dolls (1967), 125
Valley of the Moon, The (1914), 314, 315
Van Dyke, W. S. (Woody), 55, 64
Van Fleet, Jo, 244
Varennes Alley, 136
Vaughn, Robert, 94, 100, 177
Vegas in Space (1991), 184
Venora, Diane, 286
Vera-Ellen, 237
Verhoeven, Paul, 124, 147, 227
Vernon, John, 9, 254–255
Vertigo (1958), 21, 29, 37, 64, 95–96, 116, 122, 138–140, 142, 160, 169, 173, 199, 202, 204–205, 304, 311
Vesuvio's, 124–125
Veterans' War Memorial Building, 11–12
View to a Kill, A (1985), 10–11, 39, 149, 288
Village of the Damned (1995), 224
von Stroheim, Eric, xiv, 156, 183–184, 306, 314

Wachowski, Andy and Larry, 286
Wainwrith, Rupert, 302
Walk in the Clouds, A (1995), 241
Walken, Christopher, 11
Walker, Nancy, 36, 115
Wallace, Dee, 246
Wallach, Eli, 99, 155–156
Walsh, Raoul, 79, 260, 309
Wang, Wayne, 45, 88, 301
War Memorial Opera House, 13–15
Ward, Fred, 37, 255
Ward, Vincent, 119
Warden, Jack, 31, 69
Warner, David, 72, 90, 176
Washington, Isaiah, 278, 281
Washington Square Park, 130–131
Waterfront South of Bay Bridge, The, 37–42
Watts, Naomi, 124, 272
We Sold Our Souls for Rock and Roll (2001), 258
Weaver, Signourney, 259
Weaving, Hugo, 286
Webster Tube, Oakland, 284–285
Wedding Planner, The (2001), 10, 92, 94, 108, 137, 147, 194, 195, 302
Weir, Peter, 32, 136
Weisman, Sam, 83, 114, 301
Welch, Raquel, 68
Weld, Tuesday, 214
Welles, Orson, 158, 193, 315–316

Wender, Wim, 18, 124

Wertmüller, Lina, 45, 125, 145

West, Paula, 8

What Dreams May Come (1998), 119, 218, 260, 273, 276, 282

What Price Glory? (1926), 260

What's Up, Doc? (1972), xv, 51, 85, 102–103, 113, 179

When a Man Loves a Woman (1994), 112

White Christmas (1954), 237

White Shoulders (1922), 310

Who Framed Roger Rabbit (1988), 275–276

Why Women Love (1925), 315

Wilder, Gene, 98, 137

Williams, Cindy, 23, 55, 179

Williams, Robin, xiv, 8
  Bicentennial Man (1999), 94, 169–170, 185, 302–303
  Flubber (1997), 258
  Mrs. Doubtfire (1993), 128, 170, 180, 271, 284, 290
  Patch Adams (1998), 259
  What Dreams May Come (1998), 119, 218, 273, 276

William's Films, 104

Willis, Bruce, 219–220

Wilson, Bridgette, 195

Wilson, Hugh, 188

Wings of Desire (1988), 18

Winston, Hattie, 288

Winters, Jonathan, 22

Wired (1989), 246

Wise, Robert, 143

Witt, Alicia, 197

Woman in Red, The (1984), 98, 137, 188

Woman on Pier 13, The (1950), 315

Woman on the Run (1950), 60, 83, 86, 100, 101

Woman on Top (1999), 173, 185

Woman Rebels, The (1936), 315

Wong, B. D., 16

Wong, Victor, 88

Wood, Natalie, xiv, 274

Woodard, Alfre, 225

Woods, James, 264, 281

Worne, Duke, 243

Wright, Robin, 173

Wright, Teresa, 231

Wrong Mr. Right, The (1927), 314

Wyman, Jane, 230, 241, 244

Wynn, Keenan, 149, 170, 255

Yamashita: The Tiger's Treasure (2002), 260

Yates, Peter, 100, 297

York, Michael, 246

York Hotel, 21

Young, Loretta, 225

Yours, Mine and Ours (1968), 285

Zaentz, Saul, 265

Zandy's Bride (1974), 316

Zellweger, Renee, 63–64, 67, 173

Zemeckis, Robert, 275

Zemrak, Derek, 283

Zerbe, Anthony, 288